New Communication in the Post-Pandemic Era: Media, Education, and Information

Hasan Kemal Suher, Tuna Tetik, Deniz Denizel (Eds.)

New Communication in the Post-Pandemic Era: Media, Education, and Information

PETER LANG

Bibliographic Information published by the Deutsche Nationalbibliothek
The Deutsche Nationalbibliothek lists this publication in the Deutsche Nationalbibliografie; detailed bibliographic data is available online at http://dnb.d-nb.de.

Library of Congress Cataloging-in-Publication Data
A CIP catalog record for this book has been applied for at the Library of Congress.

This publication is funded by Bahçeşehir University.

Book Cover by Dilay Özgüven

ISBN 978-3-631-85565-2 (Print)
E-ISBN 978-3-631-86177-6 (E-PDF)
E-ISBN 978-3-631-86279-7 (EPUB)
10.3726/b18868

Peter Lang – Berlin · Bern · Bruxelles · New York · Oxford · Warszawa · Wien

This publication has been peer reviewed.

www.peterlang.com

To all doctors, nurses, healthcare professionals, frontline workers, and support services all around the world...

Acknowledgements

Firstly, we are proud to present our gratitude to Prof. Haluk Gürgen for his comprehensive and seminal *Foreword.*

Haluk Gürgen, Ph.D.
Prof. at Bahçeşehir University

We would like to express our sincere thanks to the *Editorial Advisory Board* members for their invaluable contributions to our book, including mentoring, text selection, peer-reviewing, and the final evaluation.

İdil Karademirlidağ Suher, Ph.D.
Prof. at Bahçeşehir University

Nazlı Eda Noyan, Ph.D.
Prof. at Bahçeşehir University

Nilay Ulusoy, Ph.D.
Prof. at Bahçeşehir University

Yeşim Ulusu, Ph.D.
Prof. at Bahçeşehir University

Tirşe Erbaysal Filibeli, Ph.D.
Assoc. Prof. at Bahçeşehir University

Güven Çatak, Ph.D.
Assist. Prof. at Bahçeşehir University

İpek Torun, Ph.D.
Assist. Prof. at Bahçeşehir University

We would like to thank our authors for their comprehensive studies in their *Chapters.*

Afra Balcı Arslan, Ph.D.(c)
Doctoral Candidate at Bahçeşehir University

Burcu Eker Akgöz, Ph.D.
Assoc. Prof. at Bahçeşehir University

Cemal Barkın Engin, Ph.D.
Assist. Prof. at Bahçeşehir University

Çakır Aker, Ph.D.
Assist. Prof. at Bahçeşehir University

Çisil Sohodol, Ph.D.
Prof. at Bahçeşehir University

Deniz Denizel
Res. Assist. at Bahçeşehir University

Dilay Özgüven, Ph.D.(c)
Doctoral Candidate at Bahçeşehir University

Ece Arıhan, Ph.D.(c)
Doctoral Candidate at Bahçeşehir University

Elif Engin, Ph.D.
Assoc. Prof. at Bahçeşehir University

Görkem Bir, Ph.D.(c)
Res. Assist. at Bahçeşehir University

Hasan Kemal Suher, Ph.D.
Prof. at Bahçeşehir University

İdil Karademirlidağ Suher, Ph.D.
Prof. at Bahçeşehir University

Murat Çöpçü, Ph.D.
Inst. at Bahçeşehir University

Nazlı Eda Noyan, Ph.D.
Prof. at Bahçeşehir University

Nilay Ulusoy, Ph.D.
Prof. at Bahçeşehir University

Nilüfer Geysi, Ph.D.(c)
Res. Assist. at Bahçeşehir University

Nisa Yıldırım, Ph.D.
Assist Prof. at İstanbul Gelişim University

Ömer Vatanartıran, Ph.D.

Assist Prof. at Bahçeşehir University

Öykü Türkeli, Ph.D.(c)
Res. Assist. at Bahçeşehir University

Savaş Arslan, Ph.D.
Prof. at Dokuz Eylül University

Selcan Yeşilyurt, Ph.D.
Inst. at Bahçeşehir University

Sinan Aşçı, Ph.D.
Assist. Prof at Bahçeşehir University

Şafak Şahin, Ph.D.
Assist. Prof at Bahçeşehir University

Tolga Hepdinçler, Ph.D.
Assist. Prof at Bahçeşehir University

Tuna Tetik, Ph.D.
Assist. Prof. at Bahçeşehir University

Yahya Burak Tamer, Ph.D.
Assoc. Prof. at Bahçeşehir University

Yeşim Ulusu, Ph.D.
Prof. at Bahçeşehir University

We would specially thank Dilay Özgüven for her extraordinary work on our book's cover, and Deniz Eyüce Şansal for her invaluable contribution.

Hasan Kemal Suher
Tuna Tetik
Deniz Denizel

Editors,
New Communication in the Post Pandemic Era: Media, Education, and Information

Contents

Foreword

The present pandemic, due to which we are suffering the loss of many lives and struggling with economic hardship, has forced us to rethink and question our lives, jobs, consumption habits, and many more aspects. We have become more reflective of our social and moral values, which are among the main determinants of our choices and behavior. We have begun to look at life, people and work from different vantage points to reevaluate and gain new habits. As a result of our growing ability to dispense with what we used to believe to be indispensable, we become braver, and we adopt and embrace new perspectives and new behavior with more ease. In short, we are now in the process of a rapid change on all fronts.

Unfortunately, however, we have also observed many governments fail the ordeal of the pandemic. Critical errors have been committed on many issues. Countless hardships have been and continue to be endured due to delayed and inefficient decisions, faulty implementations and shortages that are still to be remedied. Economic hardships and losses have become unavoidable. Businesses have closed down; poverty and unemployment have increased. We have witnessed the governors of numerous countries, including those of developed countries such as the USA and UK, specifically eschew clear and transparent communication of timely and accurate information, hide the truth and even lie blatantly. Sadly, people lived and still struggle to live through this situation in great astonishment, anxiously thinking and not knowing how to preserve their lives, jobs and incomes, with a burning pain inside and paying a dire price. In short, the pandemic was not managed correctly. We failed to implement what we knew about how to manage a crisis. While the crisis had to be managed in a coordinated effort under the leadership of the central government, guided primarily by public and local authorities and the media and all other civil and private institutions, this could not be achieved in many countries. They failed to come together to join forces and act in solidarity.

The pandemic started and continues to unfold in the already ongoing era of post-truth. Citizens were unable to reach true and accurate information, notably due to this era's main premises. We have deviated from the principles of clarity and transparency. Truths have been veiled; lies have become ordinary. Official statements that are not founded on facts and objective truths deepened the crisis. As they failed to fulfill their promises to their fellow citizens, authorities did not shy away from resorting to lies. In this atmosphere, in which accountability was put on hold, everyone spoke as they saw fit; some believed some did not, words lost their critical value.

The post-truth era is defined as an age in which it does not matter much whether what is being said and explained is a lie as long as they match people's beliefs and sentiments. As a consequence of the intense flow of information and especially of the confusion created by disinformation and informational pollution that push their intellectual limits, people have given up on searching for facts, for the truth that would help them understand and explain what is happening around them. The dictionary definition for post-truth, which was chosen as the word of the year by Oxford Dictionaries in 2016, is "relating to or denoting circumstances in which objective facts are less influential in shaping public opinion than appeals to emotion and personal belief." The current literature on the subject observes that addressing emotions and personal opinions is more effective than objective truths in shaping public opinion and behavior. It emphasizes that compatibility between reality and our judgment of it in our minds is no longer the issue, that everyone has their truth and truth itself no longer matters. It is becoming increasingly common practice to twist and transform objective truths to one's own opinions and convictions, to accept lies as if they were true, rather than harmonize people's opinions and convictions with the truth. For example, research shows that voters support a political party and its leader based on their feelings, personal convictions, beliefs and judgment, and not whether the party's and its leader's discourse is founded on facts. The persistent and blind defense of fabricated or manipulated truths by the masses is the most tragic aspect of this post-truth era.

Generally, the post-truth era manifested itself very clearly, especially with the 2016 presidential elections in the USA and the Brexit referendum in the UK around the same time. Indeed, in both these cases, campaigning politicians distorted the truth to an extent incomparable to previous eras. Moreover, data proved that their political discourses were inconsistent and even full of false statements.

However, with the pandemic, we are also witnessing populist politics, which were on the rise until recently and avoided clarity, transparency, and accountability, lose part of their effect on the masses. Many people attribute Trump's election defeat, who had to leave the presidency to Biden, to his failure to recognize the gravity of the pandemic and manage the ensuing crisis, to his veiling of truth and his lies. Academic and political spheres discuss whether this situation in the USA could also affect other leaders who use populist politics. The opinion that, in the post-pandemic world, people will not be able to discard truth as quickly as they used to and that partisanships relying on strong emotional bonds will weaken is also constantly gaining supporters.

In fact, it seems highly unlikely that the post-truth era will come to an end and that populist leaders will lose their power until the hegemony of the neoliberal economy and populism that continues to mark the world of politics ever-increasingly since the eighties are ended. However, history shows us very clearly that all pandemics prompted some radical changes, be they positive or negative. So, perhaps, even if they do not disappear for good, as a consequence of this pandemic, neoliberalism and its handmaid populism will be exposed and lose power and help people lift the blinds over their eyes.

Numerous scientific researches, articles, and books on the changes and transformations brought on by this global pandemic have been and will be published. I believe that this book will hold a special place among these. This edited volume which consists of articles by academics of Bahçeşehir University's Faculty of Communication, discusses, from multiple perspectives and various areas of the field of communication, the pandemic's effects and the transformation that it sets in motion. Therefore I wanted to ask, in this brief foreword, whether the pandemic could help bury post-truth, populism, and their mastermind neoliberalism into the depths of history as a way to make up, partially, for the great suffering it caused.

I believe that in order to re-establish a more conscious, responsible, productive, and happy life that prioritizes the sustainability of nature and the human, we should continue our search for the truth that is nurtured by the knowledge of reality. Once the time comes for a calmer reflection on our present situation, this study and similar ones will, in my opinion, contribute to our analysis and understanding of the pandemic era and how it shaped our future. I want to congratulate and thank all my colleagues who contributed to this book.

Haluk Gürgen
Prof. at Bahçeşehir University,
Public Relations and Publicity Department.

Tolga Hepdinçler

Nostalgia for the Past or New Horizons for the Future: A Short Introduction to Information Practices of the Pandemic

At the time of writing this text, the number of cases worldwide was over 150 million, and the number of people who lost their lives since late 2019 was over 3 million. As stated in the title of the book, we were far from the period we can call Post. Therefore, the recommendation of this study can be seen as questioning a possible future. With an optimistic disposition, the experiences of the present can give insight into the projected Post. Although the process is incomplete and the damage is not fully calculated, each island of experience that occurs during the pandemic process provides a view for possible options for the future. Here, two major questions about the -post provide motivation to the academicians and intellectuals although they echo banal: "Will we go back to the beautiful days of past?" and "are we going to build a brand-new world order?" These questions, which are nostalgic at one end and futuristic at the other, both can be answered with experiences in the present. The nostalgic axis of this motivation reminds me, a Deleuzian term *repetition,* that he concerned on events connected to each other throughout cycles; similarities constitute equalities and laws (Deleuze, 2014, p. 1). This also is strictly connected to our habits that generalize our conception of the world. We can easily assume that our pleasure, joy, and passion were taken away by an unpredictable law. May be more devastating exercises like medieval plagues, Spanish Flu or more recent HIV, Ebola, SARS did the same thing to our planet. But we know how to deal with them, and we know how to conquer our lost pleasures. This creates a psychological motivation to protect ourselves from an ongoing trauma and optimism for turning back our habits, hoping that the sun will rise every day, the waterfall flows down as they were. On the other hand, this optimism reminds me of an unfinished painting titled *Dying Edith* (1918) by Egon Schiele Austrian painter who died because of the Spanish Flu. The painting sketches wife of Schiele, Edith, infected as like her husband, in her deathbed with her sick face, she died a few days later and Egon, also died three days after her. The picture, which gives the impression that they have silently accepted the disease they were caught, can take away the thought that we will return to good days. It causes us to remember the inevitability of falling into a pessimism that causes us to despair that every time we lose, every experience is difficult to replace. However, the same painter in his finished picture before just before their pass, *The Family* (1918) contrary depicts a hope for the future during the most devastating and worst traumatic disease in world history. It depicts both Egon and Edith with their unborn child in a hypothetical time, may be in the future, while the world in turmoil. This is a future that never happened before; it is a new order, a hope to the future during the most devastating and worst traumatic disease in world history. As the modern conception of time taught us, we move to a future with a progress that consists of experiences of the past as knowledge that are not spoiled by memories. The memories trapped with traumas cannot find a place in progress. Thus, forgetting is the precious diamond for us as like Marcel Proust, who tried to regain the time, he lost. In his seminal seven volumes novel on time *In Search of Lost Time* (1913–1927), he constructs a universe where all the past pains, sorrows, and despairs cured by the desire for an ultimate reality. Deleuze stated again, the search Proust had it is not a process or effort of a recall, exploration of memory is to be taken as "the search for the truth" (Deleuze, 2008, p. 3). Perhaps what the pandemic makes us think of will be the lessons to be learned to think about what the next new forms of truth will be and to establish the so-called new world order at the intellectual level by leaving the past behind. Our memories about the sorrowful past are there only they needed to cure the past for the future. Thus, while the pandemic is expanding, we may be forcing ourselves to forget what causes pain and hoping to cure it by designing a better future.

Under all this optimism, treating the COVID-19 pandemic as one of the events that shook human history can be presented to us as a meaningful (may be a pessimist) horizon. For example, the concept of *the black swan*, conceptualized by Nassim Nicholas Taleb in his inspiring work, may offer the possibility for us to analyze the current situation and its possible consequences. Taleb defines the concept of *The Black Swan: The Impact of the Highly Improbable*, which was published by Taleb in the distant past in 2007, in three stages. First, it is an *outlier*, as it lies outside the realm of regular expectations because nothing in the past can convincingly point to its possibility. Second, it carries an extreme impact. Third, in spite of its outlier status, human nature makes us concoct explanations for its occurrence *after* the fact, making it explainable and predictable (Taleb, 2007, p. xviii). While he widens his examples through the dawn of the WWI, the rise of Hitler and the succeeding war, the collapse of Soviets, and 9/11, he simply says black swan is a process of rarity, extreme impact, and retrospective predictability. Although Taleb stated that, while COVID-19 was limited to China at the beginning of the epidemic, it is not a Black Swan, but may be a portent of a more fragile global system (Avishai, 2020), It is possible to call it the black swan, the size of which it reaches today. The more recent experience of the Spanish Flu that claimed 50 million casualties worldwide has been over a century and other epidemics of the 20th and 21st century affected a limited population. This makes our pandemic experience predictable as a possibility but not predictable due to the extreme size of its impacts on the human population. The next step will be to find answers and explanations, then to understand how we cure, revised, or transform the global effects of the disease. Although we have no idea when the pandemic will end, all the treatments that were offered will create defensive anticipation. As Fishman stated, as like intellectual responses after the 1993 World Trade Centre bombing and the 9/11 attack, the epidemic started in Wuhan can be described as a new form of destruction of catastrophic proportions as a *transforming event.* Although he stated with a negative fashion as like;

> *Because of the scope of its devastation, the novel coronavirus pandemic may be considered a "transforming event" comparable to the 9/11 attack, although the damage wrought by this pandemic has been many times more severe in all respects. Further, the geopolitical rivalry looming in the background has been an added source of tension. This event may have been a type of accident, the consequences of which were mismanaged, or there may have been a clumsy cover-up, which raises many questions* (Fishman, 2020, p. 4).

The coronavirus eventually gives an opportunity to determine the scope of the damage to transform what went wrong in Wuhan and then at the global level. If we go back to our double-ended exit note above about the past and the future, our biggest gain is the experience of how we manage a process that we still do not know the end of today. Whether a nostalgic return or a new world order is aimed, our individual or global escape from the process will create a paradigm shift for the future that has not yet been theorized.

This book you are reading basically focuses on the media industries during the pandemic. It is waiting to be printed in late 2021. Thus, it only consists of a process of understanding what exactly is going on in the various communication practices (in a general term in the media) and predictions of the future of communication, creativity, and media-related industries. Every creative medium mentioned here has been affected and affected by the process in terms of their production processes, industrial structures, application, and consumption patterns. For example, the fact that the global cinema industry lost $7 billion in the first four months of the pandemic (March 2020) indicates how vulnerable and fragile the channels mentioned here (Stoll, 2021a). The closure of movie theatres, cancellation of screenings, and festivals cause this figure to grow exponentially. While some sectors are growing rapidly, the film industry appears to be the most fragile sector in every term. In the middle and long terms, while production processes can possibly find new channels of distribution such as streaming, the traditional channels of distribution fall apart if the pandemic restrictions appear to be a permeant practice. Also, the industries are lacking crisis management, and a quick response will fall apart as stated in the recent report of PWC (PricewaterhouseCooper), most companies already have business continuity plans, but those may not fully address the fast-moving and unknown variables of a pandemic like COVID-19. Typical contingency plans are intended to confirm operational effectiveness following events like natural disasters, cyber incidents, and power outages, among others. They do not generally take into account the widespread quarantines, extended school closures, and added travel restrictions that may occur in the case of a global health emergency (PricewaterhouseCoopers, 2021). Worse still, the labor force dependent on these industries reflects a growing concern on a massive unemployment and long-term structural changes (Comunian & England, 2020). Though there are possible exit routes for the industry when considered in the context of the industry, there are concerns about how structural changes will transform the workforce operating in the sector. The fact that media industries, which are going through a structural change, have to make or bring the change permanent will cause a process that will require a redefinition of existing areas of expertise.

But if we look at the current situation of COVID-19 media, it is not so disappointing in the short term measured. Such as, Video Gaming Industry has a significant growth compared to other media industries. It is possible to say that the processes of the closing home have a positive effect on sectors that produce products that are consumed in the home environment, as like video and online games. And more, pandemic proposes the emergence and rise of new media sectors such as online entertainment and online education. Thus, these industries can be seen as booming investment opportunities in this era (Tashanova et al., 2020). The rising popularity of online communication channels such as Zoom Video Communication, the rise of the subscription to online entertainment Netflix, Amazon Prime, HBO can easily be seen as the beneficial side of the Corona crises. We might ask how this future might offer a better future for the media industries. The digital media that the process showed us; they are getting more attention than ever before. During the time of home closure, it has become possible to observe with our own audience experiences that especially digital media platforms, online marketing industries, and SVODs such as Netflix, Amazon Prime, and online gaming platforms are on the rise. The fact that Netflix reached 16 million new members as of April 2020 and 20 million new members in the ongoing process (Richter, 2021) at the beginning of the lockdowns, and the huge increase in the duration of the pandemic (Tankovska, 2021) of YouTube can be easily given as examples to these observations. If we check the unpredictable facts as well, it is possible to see we have some benefits on the creation and distribution of the media content. An unpredictable fact comes from the rise of television broadcasts that have been losing momentum against online entertainment and streaming services. The facts below may define the corona momentum in the old sector:

- In the USA, TV audience of four major broadcast networks increased 28.4 % between Feb.-Mar. 2020 (Stoll, 2021b).
- The average daily television viewing time in Finland increased from 170 minutes in March 2019 to 212 minutes in March 2020. In the following month, the average viewing time grew even more, by roughly 29.5 percent, in comparison with 2019 (Niinimaki, 2021).
- In France, 55 % of the TV audiences stated that they are watching more TV shows than usual in May 2020 (Statista Research Department, 2020).

While these facts point to an unpredictable revival, the new contents emerged as a result of pandemic lockdowns. Especially integration of online communication channels such as Zoom and Facetime created a new format while this is also integrating public and private space. The film industry also argued and, in some cases, used similar practice as a new form and storytelling. American film director Natali Morales's *Language Lessons* (2021) premiered in Berlinalle, British film director Rob Savage's found-footage horror movie *Host* (2020), Turkish film director Reha Erdem's comedy *Hey There!* (2021) can be the examples in a dozen of films that practice the new way of pandemic communication. But it may be predictable that the future of those formats is controversial due to the fatigue caused by the use of online communication.

With a general evaluation, it is possible to say that the media industry has drawn a largely optimistic picture in the process. Although we have questions about when the epidemic that collapsed into the world like a nightmare will end and whether it will be permanent or not, the desire and ability to get rid of the destructive situations of human nature manifests itself in the examples evaluated above. Although the forms of truth that we can design for our new future do not bring back the time we lost, it is possible to say that practices that were not in our horizon of experience before, communication practices in this context also create new forms of perception in a highly determinist perspective. Therefore, this book is not only a prediction about the future of the industry but also shows how the adjective "new" permeates all our experiences.

References

Avishai, B. (2020, April 31). The pandemic isn't a Black Swan but a Portent of a more fragile global system. *The New Yorker*. [Accessed on May 1, 2021]. Retrieved from https://www.newyorker.com/news/daily-comment/the-pandemic-isnt-a-black-swan-but-a-portent-of-a-more-fragile-global-system.

Comunian, R., & England, L. (2020). Creative and cultural work without filters: Covid-19 and exposed precarity in the creative economy. *Cultural Trends, 29* (2): 112–128. https://doi.org/10.1080/09548963.2020.1770577

Deleuze, G. (2008). *Proust and signs*. (R. Howard, Trans.). Continuum Impacts. London, Oxford, New York, New Delhi, Sydney: Bloomsbury.

Deleuze, G. (2014). *Difference and repetition*. (P. Patton, Trans.). London, Oxford, New York, New Delhi, Sydney: Bloomsbury.

Fishman, J. (2020). "This is different" – The Coronavirus Pandemic as a "transforming event." *Israel Journal of Foreign Affairs, 14* (1): 3–7. https://doi.org/10.1080/23739770.2020.1763028.

Niinimaki, E. (2021). Average daily time spent on watching TV during the COVID-19 pandemic in Finland 2020. *Statista*. [Accessed on May 1, 2021].

PricewaterhouseCoopers. (2021). COVID-19 and the media industry. *PwC*. [Accessed on May 1, 2021]. Retrieved from https://www.pwc.com/us/en/library/covid-19/coronavirus-impacts-media.html.

Richter, F. (2021). Netflix subscriber growth slows after pandemic boost. *Statista*. [Accessed on May 1, 2021].

Statista Research Department. (2021). Impact of the lockdown caused by coronavirus on TV show consumption in France 2020. *Statista*. [Accessed on May 1, 2021].

Stoll, J. (2021a). Global film industry revenue losses due to the coronavirus 2020. *Statista*. [Accessed on May 1, 2021].

Stoll, J. (2021b). Coronavirus TV viewing: Broadcast network audience growth U.S. 2020, by daypart. *Statista*. [Accessed on May 1, 2021].

Taleb, N. N. (2007). *The black swan: The impact of the highly improbable*. New York: Random House.

Tashanova, D., Sekerbay, A., Chen, D., Luo, Y., Zhao, S., & Zhang, Q. (2020). Investment opportunities and strategies in an era of Coronavirus Pandemic. *SSRN Electronic Journal*. http://dx.doi.org/10.2139/ssrn.3567445.

Yeşim Ulusu, Hasan Kemal Suher, Öykü Türkeli, and *Görkem Bir*

The Effect of E-Service Quality, E-Satisfaction, and E-Loyalty on Consumers' Online Repurchase Intentions during Pandemic in Turkey

Abstract: The internet is an essential medium for business. Recently, e-commerce uptake in Turkey has increased rapidly worldwide, primarily due to the Pandemic caused by the SARS-CoV2 virus (COVID-19). As a result, the service quality of online shopping platforms has become a distinct competitive advantage tool for online companies. The main questions to be addressed in this article are: "How e-service quality affects consumers' buying behavior?" and "which dimensions of e-service quality are more important drivers of their choices?" Accordingly, this research examines the effects of the dimensions of e-service quality, e-satisfaction, and e-loyalty on consumers' online repurchase intentions. This study also aims to determine the difference between the behaviors of customers before and during the Pandemic. One of the crucial outcomes of the analysis is the increase of online shopping during the pandemic cycle compared to previous years. Secondly, the study has shown that the most critical dimension of e-service quality is reliability. As the reliability level increases, repurchase intentions increase as well. When the e-satisfaction variable was added to the model with the hierarchical regression analysis, both reliability and e-satisfaction levels had a statistically significant effect on online repurchase intention. When e-loyalty was added to the model as a third variable, both e-satisfaction and e-loyalty significantly dominated the model. The third outcome shows that before the Pandemic, consumers mainly used online shopping platforms for the clothing product category, but online shoppers mostly preferred the food product category during the pandemic cycle. The last findings indicate that the most used online shopping platform before the Pandemic was Yemeksepeti.com, but this title switched to Trendyol.

Keywords: e-Service Quality, e-Satisfaction, e-Loyalty, Online Repurchase Intentions, COVID-19 Pandemic, Online Shopping, e-Commerce

Introduction

According to Grandon and Pearson (2004), "e-commerce is the process of buying and selling product or services using electronic data transmission via the internet and WWW" (Grandon & Pearson, pp. 197–216). E-commerce provides many benefits to both sellers and buyers, and due to the advantages of the online business model over the traditional one, expectations around e-commerce are increasing considerably. However, some firms have successfully achieved tangible improvements in e-service quality by integrating e-commerce into their activities. Studies emphasize the influence of the e-service quality factors such as reliability, responsiveness, online system quality, and security/privacy (Brynjolfsson & Kahin, 2000, p. 198).

The digital marketing world has been changing a lot since the start of the COVID-19 Pandemic. With this period, one of the key factors of succeeding in the digital era has become more critical than ever: E-service quality. As the popularity of online shopping grows during the Pandemic, this component has become more vital for online shopping sites. E-commerce sales are expected to account for 19,5 % of all retail sales in the world in 2021 (e-Marketer, n.d.). This statistic shows that the online shopping trend is increasing despite the global economic uncertainty caused by the COVID-19 Pandemic. Another research revealed that 36,5 % of the individuals had engaged with online shopping activities during the pandemic period (Turkish Statistical Institute, 2020). The study conducted in collaboration with We Are Social and Hootsuite (2020) reveals that at least 90 % of the world population purchased a product online (with any device) during the pandemic year 2020 (Kemp). Turkey's situation is not different from the world itself. The same research also indicates that the top 20 most visited sites during 2020 included online retail stores such as sahibinden.com (5th rank), n11.com (8th rank), hepsiburada.com (12th rank), and finally trendyol.com (14th rank).

Past research confirmed that e-service quality, e-satisfaction, and e-loyalty strongly affect online customer repurchase intention. Literature review on e-service quality showed a few of the research conducted on the subject and its effects on consumer repurchase intentions during the COVID-19 pandemic period. Within the marketing field, there is a consensus that a good service quality enriches the perceived value, providing customer satisfaction that contributes to loyalty (Parasuraman & Grewal, 2000, p. 169). The purpose of this article then is to examine the relationship between e-service quality, e-satisfaction, and e-loyalty on online customers' repurchase intentions during the Pandemic.

Digitalization of the marketplace as a new marketing paradigm has changed many concepts about marketing operations. Therefore, with e-service quality being granted a new definition, customer satisfaction and loyalty had to be defined and updated for the digital world (ibidem). That is why at the theoretical background of this study, we provide a formal statement for the terms with every definition. The sampling method, limitations, and data analysis acquired from an online survey are also explained in the methodology part of the article.

Literature Review

e-Service Quality

To understand the broad concept of e-service quality, it is necessary to start from the beginning with the definition of quality pertinent to the marketing world. Quality, which has been a critical component of business life, means "the degree of excellence in something" (Lewis, 1989, p. 4). Quality was mistakenly defined as goodness or even luxury (Crosby, 1979, pp. 1–2). Crosby (2009) was one of the first authors who conceptualize this word as one of the most prominent indicators for a successful business. To him, "quality is free, but not having a quality is not free." Here, not having quality is used to mean "all the actions that involve not doing the job right in the first place" (ibidem). Measuring quality is as challenging as defining quality because it has varied meanings in different contexts of products, services, and industries (Wicks & Roethlein, p. 82).

During the 1980s, there was a search for a particular definition of quality. There emerged an academic curiosity around the term "service quality" (Parasuraman & Zeithaml, 1988; Lewis, 1989). The famous article "A Conceptual Model of Service Quality and Its Implications for Future Research" was one of the most important outcomes of this emerging academic curiosity by Parasuraman, Zeithaml and Berry in 1985. In the article, the authors define three characteristics of service: intangibility, heterogeneity, and inseparability (Parasuraman et al., p. 42). They agree that understanding the term service quality is related to products being perceived more quickly than service quality. To measure the real service quality, companies have to compare consumer expectations with service performance (ibidem). Parasurman et al. (1985) finally add that service quality also includes the process of delivery and not just the outcome of the service (ibidem).

Parasuraman, Zeithaml, and Berry (1985) are the first to conceptualize service quality. Following in-depth interviews and focus groups conducted with executives and consumers, they specified ten service quality dimensions. These ten dimensions include reliability, responsiveness, competence, access, courtesy, communication, credibility, security, understanding/knowing the customer, and tangibles. They also note that the relative importance given to these dimensions varies among customers due to their different characteristics (ibidem).

Lehtinen and Lehtinen (1982) assume that service quality is established during the communication between the customer and the service provider. They state that service quality consists of three quality dimensions: physical quality (equipment, facilities, etc.), corporate quality (image of the service provider), and interactive quality (the quality of interactions between the contact person and customers and also between customers). It can be said that the first conceptualization of the term mainly explains it as the fitting of service level to consumer expectations (Lehtinen & Lehtinen, p. 12). Grönroos' (1984) definition of service quality is one of the proofs of this understanding. He defines the term as "the outcome of an evaluation process where the consumer compares his expectations with the service he perceives he has received" (Grönroos, p. 37).

Due to technological changes such as the internet, digitalization has become the most popular word globally. As a result, the whole marketing world, from marketing channels to services, has to keep up with this new digital era. E-service quality is one of these digitized marketing components (Durmuş, Ulusu & Erdem, 2013, p. 420). Rust and Lemon (2001) underline that with rising utilization of the internet, three main changes have occurred in people's daily life: true interactivity became a central part of the service, brands started to act in a customer-specific point of view and focused more on the situational personalization (Rust & Lemon, p. 85). Although the letter "e" gives a new meaning to service quality, there were several things that have stayed the same such as consumers' evaluations established from experience-based norms (Van Riel, Lilijander & Jurriens, 2001, pp. 360–362).

According to Bressolles and Nantel (2008), one of the most apparent differences between traditional and electronic service quality is interpersonal interaction. E-service quality refers to the changing from interpersonal interaction to human-machine interaction (Bresolles & Nantel, pp. 1–2). New consumers of these new channels also expect at least the same service quality as offline consumers (Santos, 2003, p. 235; Van Riel et al., 2001, p .360).

Bressolles, Durrieu, and Giraud (2008) updates the service quality scale for the new world, underlining that the new e-service quality scale includes five variables consist of 18 items: information (3 items), ease-of-use (5 items), site design (3 items), reliability (4 items) and security (3 items) (Bressolles, 2006, p. 44).

Santos (2003) agrees that e-service quality can increase the brand's attractiveness, provide a positive word of mouth, and help the brand benefit from maximized competitive advantages (Santos, 2003, pp. 233–236). He defines the term as "providing consumers with a superior experience concerning the interactive flow of information" (Santos, pp. 233–236). E-service quality also helps customers' involvement in the product development process and because it allows companies to get faster feedback and helps brands form better relationships with customers (Van Riel et al., 2001, p. 260).

During the Pandemic, e-service quality has not lost value as a marketing component. On the contrary, it became more critical. We witness that although economic uncertainty increases each day, e-retailing stays unaffected. That is why online services and their quality is a distinctive value contributing to companies' competitive advantage each day.

e-Satisfaction

Customer satisfaction is defined as the perception of pleasantness and fulfillment for a brand's service (Shankara, Smith & Rangaswamy, 2003, p. 153). Another definition is that customer satisfaction is the "interpretation of the exchange relationships" in the marketplace. Dwyer et al., (1987) underlines that customers' perception of the effectiveness of this exchange is a critical mobility barrier and a potential competitive advantage for the brand, which detaches them from the price competition (Dwyer et al., p. 7).

According to Anderson and Srinivasan (2003), electronic satisfaction is "the contentment of the customer concerning his or her prior purchasing experience" (Anderson & Srinivasan, p. 125). Kotler (2003) defines customer satisfaction as a "forward-looking metric," and if customer satisfaction decrease, market share decreases as well (Kotler, p. 41).

A traditional marketing understanding has proven that it is almost impossible to gain their loyalty (Anderson & Srinivasan, 2003, p. 123; Bowen & Chen, 2001, p. 213). For example, Bearden and Teel (1983) found that customer satisfaction positively affects loyalty, which leads customers to repeat their buying behavior (Bearden & Teel, p. 27). Although the new digital era has changed a lot in the marketing world, customer satisfaction and loyalty are still bonded (Anderson & Srinivasan, 2003, pp. 123–124). Despite that, some researchers also show that e-satisfaction and e-loyalty are not substitutes for each other (Bloemer & Kasper, 1995; Oliver, 1999). A customer can be loyal without being too satisfied; it is also very possible for a customer to be highly satisfied with service quality and not be loyal (Shankar et al., 2003, p. 154).

e-Loyalty

Whether the customers buy products of a particular brand randomly or are there a behavioral pattern to explain why the consumers repeat their purchase of a specific brand has always been discussed in the marketing literature. Through the years, most of the research focused on the reasons for a consumers' repurchase behavior, and loyalty found out powerful effect on consumers' repurchase intentions (Brown, 1952, pp. 251–253).

Kotler (2003) suggests that companies need to be aware of the distinction between their profitable and unprofitable customers and pay more attention to profitable ones to maintain customer loyalty. He argues that the customers who most likely to benefit from the company's offers are the ones that will stay more loyal to the company. He also underlines that loyal customers ensure that the company benefits from this situation in "long-term cash flow and generating a stream of referrals." He adds that it would be illogical to think that the loyal customer would not go to another company that offers the customer what they have now and more (Kotler, pp. 98–99).

Reicheld and Sasser (1990) argue that loyal customers make more purchases than non-loyal and new customers. They tend to provide more profit to the company than the new customers (Reicheld & Sasser, p. 106). Compared to an offline shopping environment, online shopping offers more opportunities in terms of interaction and personalization. Consequently, these offers influence e-satisfaction and e-loyalty as much as they do in offline shopping environments (Shankar et al., 2003, p. 153; Wind & Rangaswamy, 2001, p. 14). In addition to the definition of e-satisfaction offered above, e-loyalty is defined as "the intention to revisit a website or to purchase from it in the future" (Cyr, Bonanni & Ilsever, 2005, p. 25). Anderson and Srinivasan (2003) define e-loyalty as the customer's favorable attitude toward an electronic business resulting in repeat buying behavior (Anderson & Srinivasan, p. 100).

Online Repurchase Intention

There is much research about satisfaction, loyalty, and their effects on customers' repurchase intentions. Numerous factors have been found influential such as trust and adjusted expectations (Lin & Lekhawipat, 2014, p. 597). There are many definitions of repurchase intention. For example, Copeland (1923) defines repurchase intention "as the intention to repeatedly purchase a particular product" (p. 283). Kuo, Hu, and Yang (2013) define repurchase intention as a degree that shows how much a customer wants to purchase the same product and service. They further add that repurchase intention also a simple, objective, and observable predictor of the customers' future buying behavior (Kuo et al., p. 170).

In the context of online shopping, repurchase intentions are described as "the re-usage of the online channel to buy from a particular retailer" (Khalifa

& Liu, 2007). Traditional marketing view believes that repurchase intention only come into existence if customers believe in the brand and also becomes loyal to the brand; nowadays, the emerging research about online repurchase behavior shows that customers can have online repurchase intention even if they do not have any positive feelings for the brand (Han, Back & Barrett, 2009, s. 563).

Methodology

The primary purpose of this research is to examine the effects of the dimensions of e-service quality, online customer satisfaction, and e-loyalty on consumers' online repurchase intention. The research model, sampling plan and setting, instrumentation, data collection procedures, and data analysis methods are described and discussed below.

Research Instrument

Data was collected through an online questionnaire survey. In this study, a quantitative, non-experimental, explanatory research design was used to test hypotheses and answer research questions about customers' online shopping behaviors. To test the effects of E-service quality, online customer satisfaction, and online customer loyalty on online repurchase intention during the COVID-19 Pandemic, hierarchical regression analysis was used. The questionnaire consisted of six parts and included filter questions. All filter questions required "yes" responses. The purpose of filter questions was to ensure that the respondents were eligible to take the survey. Individuals using online shopping platforms during the COVID-19 Pandemic, daytime undergraduate, postgraduate, and Ph.D. students of the Communication Faculty of Bahçeşehir University were considered eligible.

Following measures which have already proposed in the relevant literature are employed in this study: Scale for e-service quality developed by Bressolles (2006) consisting of five variables incorporating 18 items; information (3 items, with a=.93), ease of use (5 items, with a=.95), site design (3 items, with a=.90), reliability (4 items, with a=.88) and security (3 items, with a =.86); scale for e-satisfaction consisting six items with a=.89 (Anderson & Srinivasan, 2003); scale developed by Anderson and Srinivasan (2003) for e-loyalty (2003) comprising 7 items with a =.91 and finally, the scale for online repurchase intention developed by Holloway et al. (2005).

Sampling and Data Collection

The target population is all Bahçeşehir University students, including undergraduate, postgraduate, and Ph.D. students. Convenience sampling, which is one of the non-probability sampling methods, was used as a sampling method. The sample consists of 200 daytime undergraduate, postgraduate, and Ph.D. students studying in the Communication Faculty of Bahçeşehir University in İstanbul who speaks English.

The sample size requirement for multiple regression is based on the formula n>50+8m, where n is the sample size and m is the number of predictor variables (Tabachnick & Fidell, 2013). In this study, there are 7 independent variables in total. This means that our sample size, which consists of 200 participants, is valid to use.

Descriptive statistics and multiple hierarchical regression analysis were employed to test the hypothesis and answer the research question using IBM SPSS 15.

Research Question and Hypothesis

The research question is formulated to explore the consumers' preferences for and frequency of online buying behavior before and during the COVID-19 pandemic period. Descriptive statistics are employed to measure the socio-demographic characteristics of participants and their shopping experiences. Based on both the theoretical and the empirical review conducted for this study, the research question and the hypothesis are formulated as follows:

- **RQ**: What are consumers' intentions to engage in online buying behavior before and during the COVID-19 pandemic period?
- Based on the literature review of theoretical studies, the hypothesis is proposed as follows:
- **H**: There is a significant relationship between e-service quality (information, ease of use, reliability, site design, and security), e-satisfaction, e-loyalty, and online repurchase intention.

The research model is shown below:

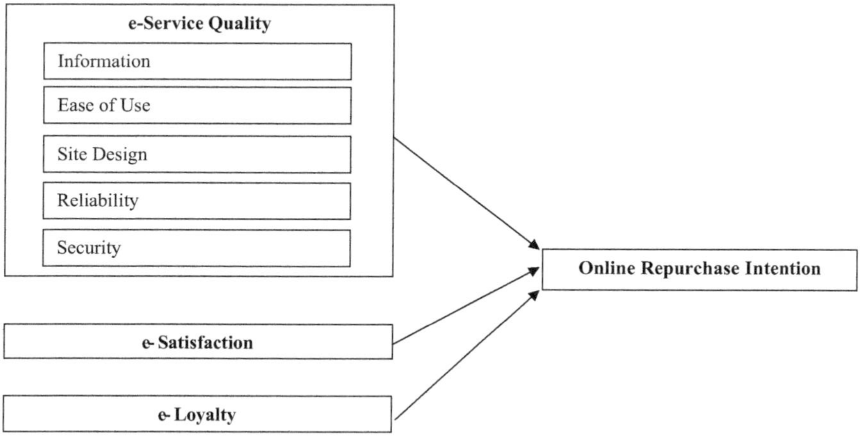

Fig. 1.1: The Research Model of the Study.

Findings

Before testing the central hypothesis, this section provides participants' socio-demographic profile (their gender, level of education, marital status, employment status during the COVID-19 Pandemic) as well as descriptive statistics regarding participants' online shopping behavior in terms of their preferred shopping platforms and the product category they buy on these platforms before and during the COVID-19 pandemic period. Following that, means and standard deviations related to measurement scales are reported along with Cronbach's Alpha levels. In this study, reliability was assessed with Cronbach's Alpha coefficient. Ideally, Cronbach's Alpha of a scale must be above .7 (DeVellis, 2003, p. 29).

Tab. 1.1: Gender of the Participants.

	f	%
Male	65	32,50
Female	135	67,50
Total	200	100

Tab. 1.2: Marital Status of the Participants.

	f	%
Single	167	83,5
Married	30	15
Divorced	3	1,5
Total	200	100

Participants consist of 200 individuals. To obtain their social demographics, 5 questions in total were directed. Results show that 32,55 % of the participants are males and 67,50 % are females. While 83,5 % of the participants are single, %15 are married, and finally, 1,50 % are divorced.

Tab. 1.3: Level of Education of the Participants.

	f	%
Bachelor's Degree	149	74,50
Master's Degree	38	19,00
Ph.D. Degree	13	6,50
Total	200	100

In total, 74,50 % of the participants have a bachelor's degree, while the percentages of the participants with master's degree and Ph.D. degree are 19 % and 6,50 %, respectively.

Tab. 1.4: Employment Status.

	f	%
Employed for wages	50	25,00
Self-employed	9	4,50
Out of work and looking for work	4	2,00
Out of work but not currently looking for work	2	1,00
Homemaker	2	1,00
Student	133	66,50
Total	**200**	**100**

When they were asked for their employment status, it was found that 25 % of them were employed for wages, 4,50 % were self-employed, 2 % were out of work and looking for a job, 1 % were out of work but not looking for a job, 1 % was a homemaker, and finally 66,50 % of the participants were students.

Tab. 1.5: Weekly Usage of Online Shopping Platforms before COVID-19 Pandemic.

	f	%
Never	26	13,00
Once a week	133	66,50
2–3 times a week	35	17,50
Every day of the week	6	3,00
Total	200	100,00

Among the participants, 13 % had never used online shopping platforms before the COVID-19 Pandemic. Conversely, as also described in **Tab. 1.6**, none of the participants claimed they had never used online shopping platforms during the COVID-19 Pandemic. Besides, 39 % of them claimed that they had been shopping from the online platforms once a week during the Pandemic, and 51 % of the participants had been shopping from the online platforms 2 or 3 times a week during the COVID-19 Pandemic. Finally, the remaining 10 % indicated that they had been using shopping platforms every day during the Pandemic. As it can be seen in **Tab. 1.6**, the majority of the participants (%51) had used online shopping platforms 2 or 3 times a week during the COVID-19 Pandemic, and fewer individuals (17,50 %) indicated that they had been shopping from online platforms 2–3 times a week before the Pandemic. Finally, 3 % of the participants claimed that they had been using online shopping platforms every day before the COVID-19 Pandemic. As can also be seen in **Tab. 1.5**, most participants had used online shopping platforms once a week before the COVID-19 Pandemic.

Tab. 1.6: Weekly Usage of Online Shopping Platforms during COVID-19 Pandemic.

	f	%
Never	0	0
Once a week	78	39
2–3 times a week	102	51
Every day of the week	20	10
Total	200	100

As shown in **Tab. 1.7**, it was found that before the Pandemic, Yemeksepeti was the most used online shopping platform. Following the Pandemic, Yemeksepeti had become the third most used online platform. Moreover, while before the Pandemic, Trendyol was the second most used online shopping, during the Pandemic, Trendyol had become the most used online shopping platform. The third most used online shopping platform before the Pandemic was online markets such as Getir, Migros, Bana Bi', Carrefour, etc. However, they had become the second most used online shopping platform during the Pandemic. As reported in **Tab. 1.7**, all of these changes were found to be statistically significant.

Tab. 1.7: Frequencies and Percentages of the Participants' Choices of Online Shopping Platforms before and during the COVID-19 Pandemic.

	Before Pandemic Period			**During Pandemic Period**		
	Responses			**Responses**		
	N	**%**	**Rank**	**N**	**%**	**Rank**
Trendyol	142	20,60 %	2	175	21,00 %	1
Online Markets (Getir, Migros, Bana Bi, Carrefour)	99	14,40 %	3	167	20,00 %	2
Yemeksepeti	155	22,50 %	1	166	19,90 %	3
Hepsiburada	84	12,20 %	4	103	12,30 %	4
ÇiçekSepeti	65	9,40 %	5	74	8,90 %	5
n11.com	50	7,30 %	6	52	6,20 %	6
GittiGidiyor	43	6,30 %	7	46	5,50 %	7
Morhipo	25	3,60 %	8	27	3,20 %	8
Sahibinden.com	25	3,60 %	8	25	3,00 %	9
Total	668[a]	100 %		835[a]	100 %	
[a] More Than One Answer						
Chi-Square=1037.311, df=81, p<0.00						

Before the Pandemic, clothing was the most bought product category from the online shopping sites, and the same type was found to be the second most purchased platform during the Pandemic. While accessory was the third most bought product category before the Pandemic, it was the least bought one during the Pandemic. Finally, being the fourth most-bought category during the Pandemic period, personal care products and cosmetics had become the third most purchased category during the Pandemic. As also illustrated in the table below, all of these changes were found to be statistically significant.

Tab. 1.8: Frequencies and Percentages of the Participants Choices of Product Category They Bought from Online Platforms before and during the COVID-19 Pandemic.

	Before Pandemic Period			**During Pandemic Period**		
	Responses			**Responses**		
	N	**%**	**Rank**	**N**	**%**	**Rank**
Food Products	134	20,30 %	2	171	18,00 %	1
Clothing	149	22,60 %	1	161	16,90 %	2
Personal Care Products and Cosmetics	98	14,90 %	4	140	14,70 %	3
Cleaning Supplies	56	8,50 %	6	127	13,30 %	4
Medical Supplies (Masks, Cologne, Sanitizer)	24	3,60 %	7	126	13,20 %	5
Electronic Products	96	14,60 %	5	120	12,60 %	6
Accessory (Shoes, Jewelry, Glows, Eyewear, Hats)	102	15,50 %	3	107	11,20 %	7
Total	659[a]	100 %		952[a]	100 %	
[a] More Than One Answer						
Chi-Square=319.183, df=49, p<0.00						

Reliabilities and the means and standard deviations on the measurement scales used in this study are represented in the tables below. Most of the e-service quality scale items' means are above 4. Cronbach's Alpha for the scale was found as information: .83, ease-of-use=.87, site design=.84, reliability=.80 and security =.91. Therefore, the reliabilities of the e-service quality scale are above the acceptable alpha level of internal consistency. All of the dimensions' Cronbach's Alpha levels are above the accepted level for each dimension of the e-service quality scale.

Tab. 1.9: Mean, Standard Deviation, and Reliability of the e-Service Quality Scale.

e-Service Quality	Mean	Std. Dev.	Dimensions	Mean	Std. Dev.	Cronbach's Alpha
This site provides relevant information	4,29	0,624	e-Service Quality "Information"	4,22	0,569	0,839
This site provides accurate information	4,20	0,636				
This site provides in-depth information about the product(s) of service(s) proposed	4,16	0,698				
This site is easy to use	4,50	0,665	e-Service Quality "Ease of Use"	4,40	0,532	0,873
It is easy to search for information	4,38	0,607				
This is easy to navigate	4,41	0,674				
The organization and layout of this site facilitate the search for information	4,31	0,631				
The layout of this site is clear and simple	4,39	0,686				
This site if colorful	4,20	0,839	e-Service Quality "Site Design"	4,02	0,827	0,841
This site is creative	3,88	1,030				
This site has an attractive appearance	3,97	0,969				
The product or service is delivered by the time promised by the company	4,21	0,782	e-Service Quality "Reliability"	4,12	0,700	0,801
You get what you ordered from this site	4,23	0,796				
You get your merchandise quickly when you order	4,13	0,876				
After-sale support on this site is excellent	3,91	1,054				
I'm confident in the security on this site	4,16	0,867	e-Service Quality "Security"	4,03	0,903	0,919
I feel like my privacy protected on this site	3,97	1,027				
I trust the web administration will not misuse personal information	3,95	1,018				
1 Strongly Disagree- 5 Strongly Agree						

Tab. 1.10: Means, Standard Deviations, and Reliability of the e-Satisfaction Scale.

Online Customer Satisfaction	**Mean**	**Std. Dev.**	**Cronbach's Alpha**
I am satisfied with my decision to purchase from this Website	4,18	0,737	0,855
If I had to purchase again, I would feel differently about buying from this Website.	4,17	0,978	
My choice to purchase from this Website was a wise one	4,17	0,762	
I feel badly regarding my decision to buy from this Website	4,31	0,888	
I think I did the right thing by buying from this Website	4,24	0,738	
I am unhappy that I purchased from this website	4,38	0,900	
Total	4,24	0,638	

*Reverse Coded
1: Strongly Disagree
5: Strongly Agree

All of the means for the items in the e-satisfaction scale are above 4. The Cronbach's Alpha of the e-satisfaction scale was found as .85. Therefore, the reliability of the e-satisfaction scale is above the acceptable .7 alpha level.

Tab. 1.11: Means, Standard Deviations, and Reliability of the e-Loyalty Scale.

e-Loyalty	**Mean**	**Std. Dev.**	**Cronbach's Alpha**
I seldom consider switching to another Website	2,03	1,111	0,741
As long as the present service continues, I doubt that I would switch websites.	3,89	0,859	
I try to use this Website whenever I need to make a purchase	4,10	0,799	
When I need to make a purchase, this Website is my first choice.	4,17	0,771	
I like using this Website	4,17	0,698	
To me, this site is the best retail Website to do business with	4,02	0,786	
I believe that this is my favorite retail website	4,09	0,801	
Total	3,78	0,527	
1 Strongly Disagree-5 Strongly Agree			

Most of the means of the items in the e-loyalty scale are above 4. Cronbach's Alpha of the e-loyalty scale was found .74. Therefore, the reliability of this scale is above the acceptable alpha level of internal consistency.

Tab. 1.12: Means, Standard Deviations, and Reliability of the Online Repurchase Intention Scale.

Online Repurchase Intention	**Mean**	**Std. Dev.**	**Cronbach's Alpha**
The next time I purchase this product online, I will buy from the same online retailer	4,18	0,712	0,907
I would be willing to purchase from this company again.	4,20	0,702	
I would purchase from this online retailer again in the future.	4,23	0,742	
I would be very likely to increase my shopping activity with this online retailer	4,05	0,870	
Total	4,16	0,671	
1.Strongly Disagree-5 Strongly Agree			

Means accounted for all of the items in the online repurchase intention scale are above 4. Cronbach's Alpha for the scale was found .90. Therefore, it can be concluded that the reliability of the scale is above the acceptable level of internal consistency. All construct reliabilities were well above the acceptable alpha level of .70 (Nunnally, 1978).

For testing the central hypothesis, a hierarchical multiple regression is used to examine the effects of e-service quality, e-satisfaction, and e-loyalty on online customer repurchase intention. A total of 7 independent variables grouped in 3 separate blocks are included in the analysis (**Tab. 1.13**). Hierarchical multiple regression is used to determine how much variance in the criterion, dependent or outcome variable is explained by predictors (independent variables) when they are entered in analysis in a particular sequence. Potentially, the more variance that a predictor explains, the more critical that variable would be. Variables may be entered in analysis in a particular sequence on practical or theoretical grounds (Howitt & Cramer, 2011, p. 341). From a realistic view, it would be logical to observe how much e-service quality dimensions explain customers' repurchase intention in total. Then, we examine the effect of the e-satisfaction variable on repurchase intention. Finally, we report the impact of the e-loyalty variable on repurchase intention in total.

Entering these variables into analysis in a predetermined order like this enables us to see how much each group or block of variable contributes to how well customers' repurchase intention can be predicted (Pallant, 2016). Thus, in the first stage of the regression analysis, e-service quality, namely information, ease of use, site design, reliability, and security, were entered as a block. In the second stage, e-satisfaction and the third stage, e-loyalty, were entered as independent variables, as seen in **Tab. 1.13**.

Preliminary analyses were conducted to ensure there is no violation of the assumptions of normality, multicollinearity, and homoscedasticity. In the first step, e-service quality dimensions, as the only predictors, explained 43.9 % of the statistically significant variance ($F(5,194) = 30.38$, $p < .001$). In the second step, e-satisfaction was added and explained an additional 7,2 % of the variance in online repurchase intention. This was also a statistically significant contribution ($R^2 = 0.072$, $F(1,193) = 28.55$, $p < .001$). In the third step, the e-loyalty variable was added into the equation and explained another 10,5 % of the variance in online repurchase intention. The result was again, statistically significant ($R^2 = 0{,}105$, $F(1,192) = 52.70$, $p < .001$).

Tab. 1.13: Hierarchical Regression Analysis Predicting Online Repurchase Intention with e-Service Quality variables, e-Satisfaction, and e-Loyalty.

Hierarchical Step	Predictor Variables		Total R	Incremental R
1	e-Service Quality Variables	Information	0.439*	0,439*
		Ease of Use		
		Site Design		
		Reliability		
		Security		
2	e-Satisfaction	Satisfaction	0.511*	0,072*
3	e-Loyalty	Loyalty	0.603*	0.105*

The hierarchical regressions estimate both incremental and total variances of dependent variable groups for each step, and final coefficients are reported in **Tab. 1.14**. Absolute beta coefficients are determined following the third step, and their respective significance values can be seen in **Tab. 1.14**.

Tab. 1.14: Final Beta Coefficients Table of the Hierarchical Regression Analysis Predicting Total Repurchase Intentions with e-Service Quality variables, e-Satisfaction, and e-Loyalty.

	Final Beta	**R^2**	**Sig.**
e-Service Quality "Information"	0,090		0,162
e-Service Quality "Ease of Use"	0,137		0,059
e-Service Quality "Site Design"	-0,017		0,767
e-Service Quality "Reliability"	0.180*		0,006
e-Service Quality "Security"	-0,066		0,252
R^2		**0,439**	
e-Satisfaction	0.186*		0,002
R^2 change		**0,072**	
R^2 after step 2		**0,511**	
e-Loyalty	0.433**		0,000
R^2 change		**0,105**	
R^2 after step 3		**0,617**	

*$p < 0.05$ **$p < 0,001$

To determine how well each of the variables contributes to the final equation, we need to examine the coefficients in **Tab. 1.14**. When all the variables entered in the equation, besides the "reliability" dimension of e-service quality, e-loyalty (beta=.43), and also e-satisfaction (beta=.18) made a unique, statistically significant contribution. None of the e-service quality dimensions other than "reliability" made a notable contribution.

Conclusion

The primary purpose of this research was to examine the effects of the dimensions of e-service quality, online customer satisfaction, and e-loyalty on consumers' online repurchase intentions. Results of the hierarchical regression analysis partially support the central hypothesis. In contrast to what is indicated by the main hypothesis, dimensions of the e-service quality, namely information, ease of use, site design, and security, had no significant effect on online repurchase intention; only reliability has a considerable impact. However, in agreement with the hypothesis, e-satisfaction and e-loyalty significantly affected online repurchase intention.

One of the essential outcomes of this research is the rise of online shopping during the pandemic period compared to previous years. Online shopping trend during the pandemic period has been increased in Turkey and parallel with the world. It can be suggested that as the business world has been completely transformed to adapt to the new online world today, all industries have to integrate e-commerce and e-service strategies in their strategic business and marketing planning processes as soon as possible if they want to compete in the game.

Another outcome of this research is that the reliability dimension has a significant effect on online repurchase intention. Within this research, it was measured using the scale developed by Bressolles (2006) consisting of four items as follows: "The product or service is delivered by the time promised by the company," "You get what you ordered from this site," "You get your merchandise quickly when you order," "After-sale support on this site is excellent." Results show that, as the reliability level increases, the repurchase intentions of online customers increase as well. This can be interpreted as consumers' online shopping preferences primarily shaped by on-time delivery and after-sale support services quality. Therefore, it can be inferred that as long as a shopping platform considers these aspects of the "reliability" dimension, the possibility of intentions to repurchase from the same platform increases. Furthermore, when the e-satisfaction variable was added to the model with hierarchical regression analysis, both reliability and e-satisfaction levels had a statistically significant effect on online repurchase intentions. Consequently, it can be argued that when the reliability (delivery on time and after-sale support services) increases, e-satisfaction (satisfaction from purchase decision, intention to buy for the second time from the same site, and thinking about doing the right thing by buying from the online shopping platform) increases as well. When e-loyalty (to be the first choice, fond of using the website, believing that this is the favorite retail shop, and not considering switching to another website) as a third variable was added to the model; both e-satisfaction and e-loyalty dominated it. It can be inferred that when consumers are satisfied with the online shopping platform and form loyalty, their repurchase intentions increases.

The third outcome of this research indicates that before the Pandemic, consumers used online shopping platforms primarily for the clothing product category, but online shoppers mostly preferred the food product category during the Pandemic. As the findings suggest, Yemeksepeti.com, the most used online shopping platform before, was replaced by Trendyol during the Pandemic. While consumers were using online shopping platforms once a week earlier, this behavior has considerably changed in a way that caused them to start using these platforms 2–3 times a week.

In conclusion, as the online shopping platforms are growing in numbers with an increase in profit every day, the Online business world has to respond to consumers' needs and preferences about e-service quality to gain a competitive advantage. Also, the COVID-19 Pandemic has shown that to make a difference in online business; it is necessary to form loyalty and create satisfaction among consumers. Online retailers working hard to immunize online consumers against switching behavior with strategies should know that increasing website traffic and attracting new customers are great, but no longer enough. Loyal customers can be built with a greater understanding of them and more efficient website systems.

This study has several limitations concerning time and cost, which did not allow the collection of a larger and more rigorously selected sample. Future researchers should aim to improve upon this effort.

References

Anderson, R. E., & Srinivasan, S., S. (2003). E-satisfaction and e-loyalty: A contingency framework, *Psychology and Marketing*, *20* (2): 99–121.

Bearden, W., & Teel, J. E. (1983). Selected determinants of consumer satisfaction and complaint reports. *Journal of Marketing Research*, *20* (1): 21–28.

Bowen, J. T., & Chen, S. (2001). The relationship between customer loyalty and customer satisfaction. *International Journal of Contemporary Hospitality Management*, *13* (5): 213–217.

Bressolles, G., & Nantel, E. J. (2008). The measurement of electronic service quality. *International Journal of E-Business Research*, *4* (3): 1–19.

Bressolles, G. (2006). La qualité de service êlectronique: NetQu@l Proposition d'une échelle de mesure appliquée aux sites marchands et effets modérateurs. *Recherche et Applications en Marketing*, *21* (3): 19–45.

Brown, G. H. (1952). Brand loyalty-fact or fiction?. *Advertising Age*, *23* (9): 53–55.

Brynjolfsson, E., & Kahin, B. (2000). *Understanding the digital economy*. Boston: MA: MIT Press.

Copeland, M. T. (1923). Relation of consumer's buying habits to marketing methods. *Harvard Business Review*, *1* (3): 282–289.

Crosby, P. B. (1979). *Quality is free: The art of making quality certain*. New York: New American Library.

Cyr, D., Bonanni, C., Bowes, J., & Ilsever, J. (2005). Beyond trust: Website design preferences across cultures. *Journal of Global Information Management*, *73* (14): 24–52.

DeVellis, R. F. (2003). *Scale development: Theory and applications* (2nd ed.). London: Sage Publication.

Durmuş, B., Ulusu, Y., & Erdem, Ş. (2013). Which dimensions affect private shopping e-customer loyalty? In M. Özşahin (Ed.). In *The Proceedings of 9th International Strategic Management Conference*. Elsevier.

Dwyer, R. F., Schurr, P. H., & Oh, S. (1987). Developing buyer-seller relationships. *Journal of Marketing, 56* (4): 6–21.

E-Marketer. (n.d.). Graph illustration of e-commerce share of retail sales (2019–2024). Retrieved from https://www.oberlo.com/statistics/ecommerce-share-of-retail-sales.

Grandon, E., & Pearson, J, M. (2004). Electronic commerce adoption: an empirical study of small and medium US businesses. *Information and Management, 42* (1): 197–216.

Grönroos, C. (1984). A service quality model and its marketing implications. Eu*ropean Journal of Marketing, 18* (4): 36–44.

Han, H., Back, K. J., & Barrett, B. (2009). Influencing factors on restaurant customers' revisit intention: The roles of emotions and switching barriers. *International Journal of Hospitality Management, 28* (4): 563–572.

Holloway, B. B., Wang, S., & Parish, J. T. (2005). The role of cumulative online purchasing experience in service recovery management. *Journal of Interactive Marketing, 19* (3): 54–66.

Howitt, D., & Cramer, D. (2011). Intr*oduction to SPSS statistics in psychology for version 19 and earlier*. (5th ed.). London: Pearson Education.

Kemp, S. (2020). Digital 2020: Turkey. [Power point slides]. SlideShare. Retrieved from https://datareportal.com/reports/digital-2020-turkey.

Khalifa, M., & Liu, V. (2007). Online consumer retention: Contingent effects of online shopping habit and online shopping experience. *European Journal of Information Systems, 16* (6): 197–216.

Kotler, P. (2003). *Marketing insights from A to Z: 80 Concepts every manager needs to know*. New Jersey: John Wiley & Sons.

Kuo, Y.-F., Hu, T.-L., & Yang, S.-C., (2013). Effects of inertia and satisfaction in female online shoppers on repeat-purchase intention: The moderating roles of word-of-mouth and alternative attraction. *Journal of Service Theory and Practice, 23* (3): 168–187.

Lehtinen, U., & Lehtinen, J. R. (1982). *Service quality: A study of quality dimension*. [Unpublished working paper]. Helsinki: Service Management Institute, Finland OY.

Lewis, B. R. (1989). Quality in the service sector: A review. *International Journal of Bank Marketing, 7* (5): 4–12.

Lin, C., & Lekhawipat, W. (2014). Factors effecting online repurchase intentions. *Industrial Management & Data Systems, 114* (4): 597–611.

Türkiye İstatistik Kurumu. [Turkish Statistical Institute]. (2020). Hanehalkı bilişim teknolojileri (BT) kullanım araştırması. [Household information technologies (I.T.) research]. Retrieved from https://data.tuik.gov.tr/Bulten/Index?p=Hanehalki-Bilisim-Teknolojileri-(BT)-Kullanim-Arastirmasi-2020-TS33679.

Nunnally, J. C. (1978). *Psychometric theory* (2nd ed.). New York: McGraw Hill.

Pallant, J. (2016). *SPSS survival manual.* (6th ed.). New York: McGraw Hill.

Parasuraman, A., & Grewal, D. (2000). The impact of technology on the quality-value-loyalty chain: A research agenda, *Journal of Marketing, 28* (1): 168–174.

Parasuraman, A., & Zeithaml, V. A. (1988). SERVQUAL: A multiple-item scale for measuring consumer perceptions of service quality. *Journal of Retailing, 64* (1): 12–40.

Parasuraman, A., Zeihtaml, V. A., & Berry, L. L. (1985). A conceptual model of service quality and its implications for future research. *Journal of Marketing, 49* (4): 41–50.

Reichheld, F., & Sasser, W. E. (1990). Zero defections: quality comes to services. *Harvard Business Review, 68* (5): 105–111.

Rust, R. T., & Lemon, K. N. (2001). E-service and consumer. *International Journal of Electronic Commerce, 5* (3): 85–101.

Santos, J. (2003). E-service quality: A model of virtual service quality dimensions. *Managing Service Quality: An International Journal, 13* (3): 223–246.

Shankara, V., Smith, A. K., & Rangaswamy, A. (2003). Customer satisfaction and loyalty in online and offline environments. *International Journal of Research in Marketing, 20* (2): 153–175.

Tabachnick, B., & Fidell, L. S. (2013). *Using multivariate statistics* (6th ed.). New York: Pearson Education.

Takeuchi, H., & Quelch, J. A. (1983). Quality is more than making a good product. *Harvard Business Review, 61*: 139–145.

Van Riel, A., Lilijander, C. R., & Jurriens, P. (2001). Exploring consumer evaluations of e-services: A portal site. *International Journal of Service Industry Management, 12* (4): 359–377.

Wicks, A. M., & Roethlein, C. J. (2009). A satisfaction-based definition of quality. *Journal of Business & Economic Studies, 15* (1): 82–111.

Wind, J., & Rangaswamy, A. (2001). Customerization: The next revolution in mass customization. *Journal of Interactive Marketing, 15* (1): 13–32.

Şafak Şahin

How Advertising, the Most Powerful Tool of Marketing, Survived during and after COVID-19?

Abstract: All over the World, COVID-19 has affected several industries economically. Most affected areas are especially heavy industries, logistics, services like tourism, and food beverage. All these industries are directly related to marketing communication and advertising. In this study, it is examined that how the different fields of marketing communication, such as advertising, digital marketing, retail advertising, and creative executions are affected by the COVID-19. How social media marketing affected? Was it positive or negative? Or, when it is considered that in the period of pandemia, how audiences consume the traditional media? Understanding all these issues is so essential to evaluate the situation of marketing communication, advertising, and digital marketing after COVID-19. So, to consider well; statistics, opinions of high-level professionals, numbers, qualitative differences are the main units of this chapter and discussed by presenting the different approaches from different countries, including Turkey.

Keywords: COVID-19, Advertising, Marketing Communication, Digital Advertising, Content Creation

Marketing Issues in the Times of Crisis

It is a fact that pandemia is one of the examples of crisis for businesses. Alike industries, the companies of marketing have tried to survive during this pandemia because of cost-cutting reflexes of brands. Coronavirus, since the day it emerged, has affected the whole world. And continuing to affect the sectors where the virus is spreading, such as Turkey, India, Russia, Brazil, France, and the USA in April-May 2021 (worldometer.com, 2021; WHO, 2021). Besides the academic studies, there are several reports, statistics, and data to emphasize the effect of COVID on the marketing-advertising field, which is served by institutions such as Statista, E-marketer, Warc, Eurostat, AMA, iab, etc. In the study of Hoekstra and Leeflang (2020), the impact of COVID on the marketing field is especially on "assortment," "price and price promotions," and "communication." According to them, many companies have a limited vision of what efficiency means. Companies primarily focus on short-term cost reductions at the micro-level and devote little or no attention to the time, energy, and (ethical background of) production factors used in their operational processes. This limited approach has been taken to an excessive degree at some companies, resulting in large-scale outsourcing instead of in-house production, low stock levels, a high degree of dependence on foreign manufacturers (e.g., in China), and low prices (such as for groceries) (Hoekstra & Leeflang, 2020). Not only for global or big companies, but crises also have a huge impact on small businesses. The enormous effect of COVID-19 can be compared with the big global economic crises such as the one in 2008. In both crises, the demand of the consumers decreased dramatically. The report of Mc Kinsey represents this situation with a comparative graphic below (McKinsey, 2020).

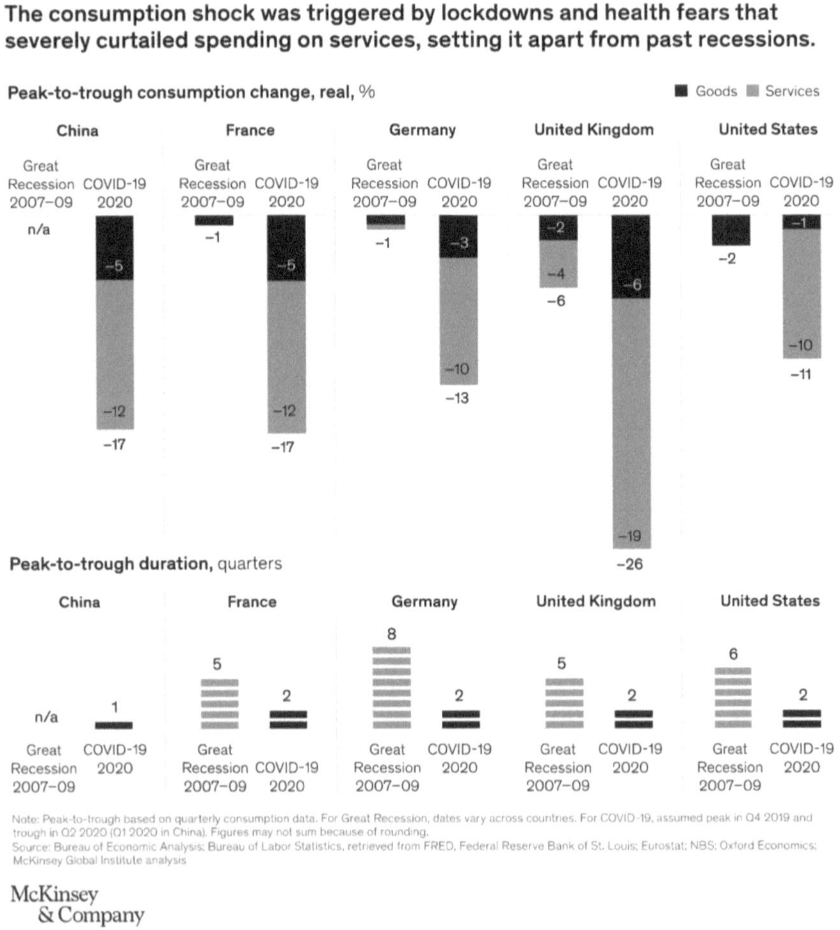

Fig. 2.1: Peak-to-trough Consumption Change, Real, %.

As it is seen in the graphic of McKinsey, the demand, and naturally, consumption of consumers decreases both for goods and services. It means that for all businesses, they have to take a range of actions not only for the short term but also for the long term. For these actions, Bourletidis and Triantafyllopoulos (2014) explain the situation by mentioning the related studies. According to them, there are no easy solutions and direct effective strategies to anticipate crisis effects. In the wake of the economic crisis, many firms were faced with severe threats that called for immediate action to ensure firm survival. When choosing the measures to cope with this crisis, responsible decision-makers were confronted with the challenge to manage the trade-off between the benefits and costs of short-term crisis reactions (Rhodes and Stelter, 2009). On the one hand, short-term action like massive cost-cutting, cash generation, shorter reporting cycles, increased employee monitoring, and tight budget control seemed necessary to cope with a decline in orders and revenues and to ensure an appropriate and well-coordinated response to changed environmental conditions. On the other hand, such short-term measures might damage the long-term growth potential and go at the expense of the long-term health of the firm as key stakeholder relations may be irreversibly harmed (Asel et al., 2010).

In the COVID-19 crisis, firms and brands tried to take action to absorb the negative effect of low consumption. One of these precautions is cutting the media investments. For a better understanding of the marketing communication side of the economic systems, it should be well analyzed the media investments of the brands.

Media Investments

In the field of marketing, to understand and evaluate the general situation of media, the reports of financial, advertising, audit, etc., companies can be very useful and beneficial. Two of these organizations in the world are Deloitte and Zenith Media. According to their report published in Turkey in cooperation with the Turkish Advertisers Association, the amount of all media investments in the world was announced (Deloitte Turkey, 2020).

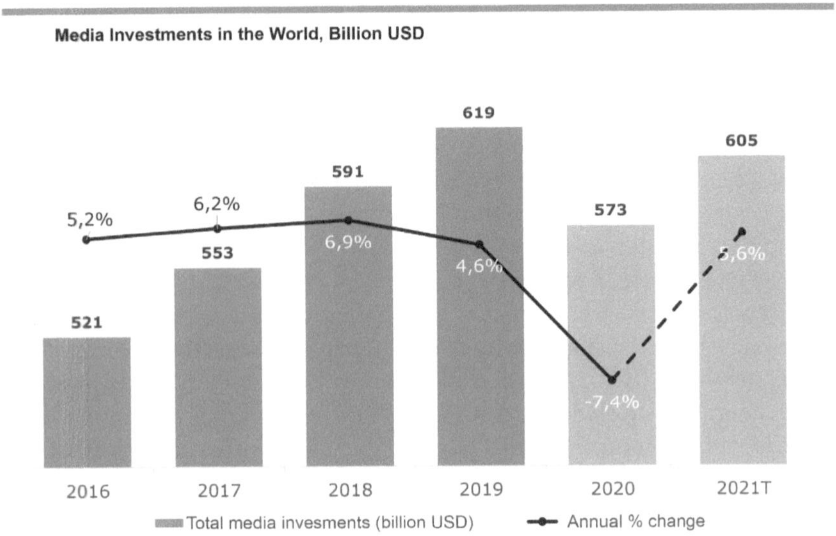

Fig. 2.2: Media Investments in the World, Billion USD. Source: Due to the data taken from Zenith, December 2020 by Deloitte Turkey and Turkish Advertisers Association. (Media & Advertising Investments Report, 2020).

Digital Media in the New Era

The share of digital media investments in total investments exceeds 50 %. Due to the report, while digital media investments continued to grow, the shares of other channels decreased. The impact of the pandemic is seen especially in the shrinkage in the total shares of the cinema and outdoor sectors. In 2020, 52 % of the total media investments, which are estimated to have shrunk by 7.4 % worldwide, are made to digital channels, while the digital growth share is predominantly from print media and TV.

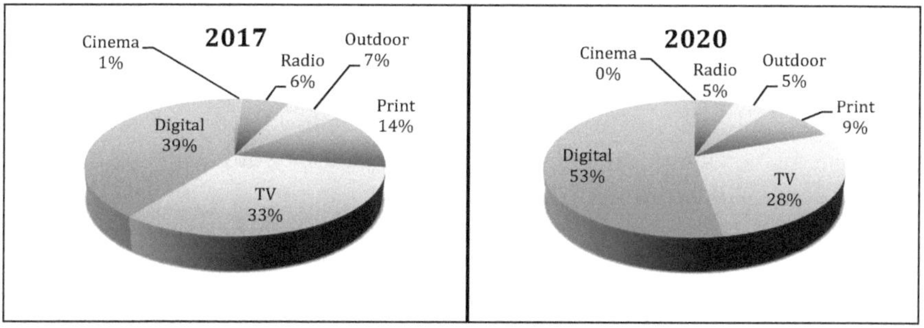

Fig. 2.3: Advertising Investments on Media in Turkey. Source: Due to the data taken from Zenith, December 2020 by Deloitte Turkey and Turkish Advertisers Association. (Media & Advertising Investments Report, 2020).

According to the report of Deloitte Turkey and Turkish Advertisers Association; in 38 countries that have over 1 billion US dollar media investment, the total investment volume is 559 billion dollars. And this amount represents %95 of all global media investments. The media investments in these 38 countries decreased nearly %7,2 (in local currency) by 2020. No doubt, COVID-19 has a significant effect on this result.

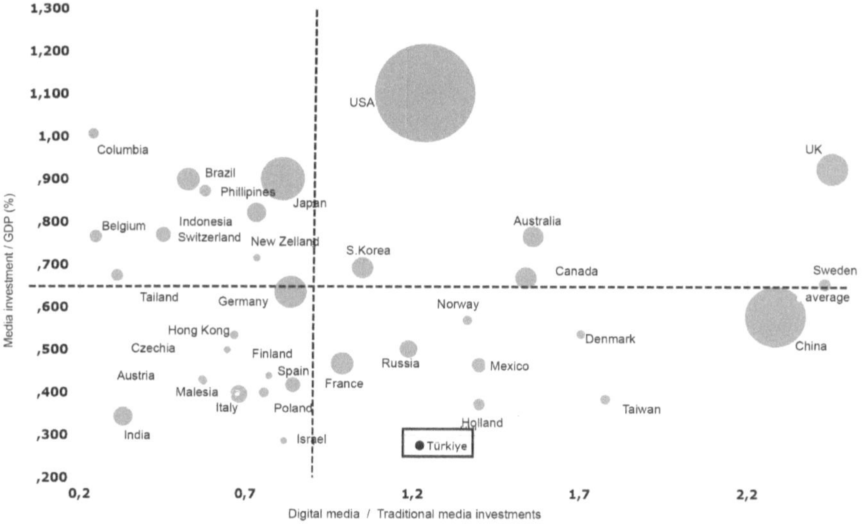

Fig. 2.4: Comparative Media Investments in the World. Source: Due to the data taken from Zenith, December 2020 by Deloitte Turkey and Turkish Advertisers Association. (Media & Advertising Investments Report, 2020).

This graphic above shows us that even in extreme conditions and a dramatic decrease in investments, digital media can find its solution by the interest of the consumers.

As an example, the rise of Spotify usage can be considered as an indicator of digital media consumption and also investments. Especially with the development of smartphones, in the COVID lockdowns, consumers preferred similar digital platforms for more secure self-entertainment opportunities like Spotify.

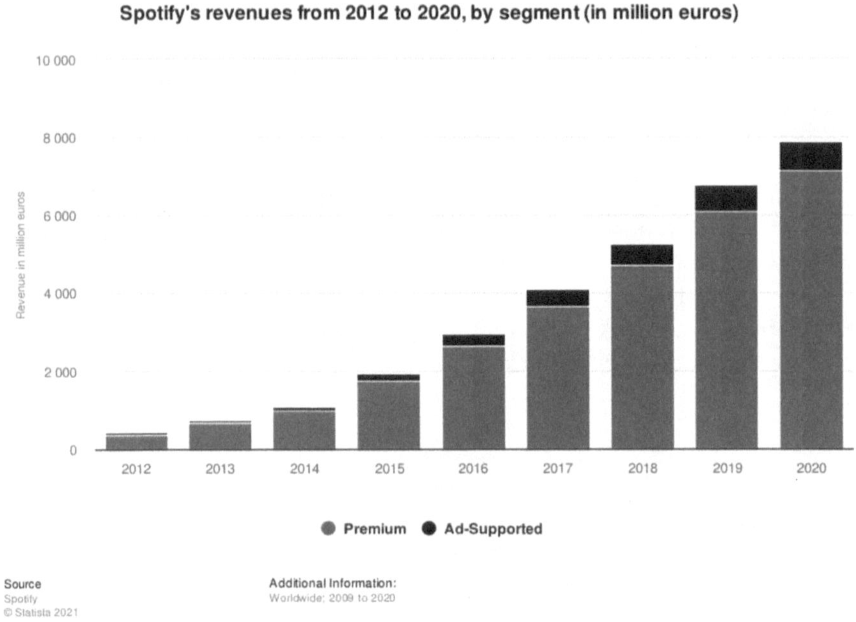

Fig. 2.5: Spotify's Revenues from 2012 to 2020, by Segment (in Million Euros).

This chart shows not only the rise in subscription revenues also represents the contribution of advertising investments on Spotify media (Statista, 2021). According to the Statista Research Department, Spotify generated about 7.1 billion euros in premium revenue and 745 million in ad-supported revenue. Both figures were the highest reported to date, with premium revenue having grown by more than two billion euros since 2017. Contributing to Spotify's success was its strong global subscriber base – as of the first quarter of 2019, the music streaming platform had 100 million subscribers worldwide. Spotify has proved popular in multiple markets across the world, namely the United States, where more than 25 percent of 18 to 34-year-olds reported using the service.

This explanation and information can be clearly understood as the changing media consumption of the consumers. According to a study by Gangadharbatla (2021), we also are witnessing changes in individuals' media consumption habits. COVID-19 has accelerated cord-cutting behaviors and individuals' move to streaming content in a big way. He gives an example from the study of Gruenwedel (2020); Roku added 2.9 million new incremental active users during the third quarter of the pandemic bringing their total user base to 46 million, and streaming hours increased by 200 million hours over the second quarter (Gruenwedel, 2020). He continues with the ad spends. Spendings have been slowly moving to streaming video platforms even before the pandemic. Now with COVID-19 and increased stay-at-home restrictions, people's subscription and consumption of streaming content has risen to record levels (Beech, 2020). Households in lockdown may be moving away from shared media consumption to individual consumption at the convenience of each family member (Sheth, 2020).

Importance of the Content Creation

In the light of this approach mentioned above, due to the tendency of high content consumption, brands have started to give importance to produce more effective content. According to a business journalist and content marketer Linda Pophel (e-Content, 2021); for content marketers, COVID-19 has meant a sudden shift away from blatantly overt promotion, and a pivot toward thoughtful, helpful, and safety-related messaging that resonates with consumers who are feeling the pinch (both financially and from a health-and-wellness standpoint).

It would not be wrong to say that traditional advertising could survive by finding ways to integrate with content creation implementations. In this way, advertising has become a part of e-commerce, especially on social media platforms. The owner and the CEO of Facebook, Mark Zuckerberg, mentioned this point. Meanwhile, Facebook continues to build out its e-commerce offerings on different fronts, including the enhanced ability for creators to make money and expanded digital-payment capabilities.

"Commerce has been growing in our services for a while, but it has become a lot more important as the pandemic has accelerated a broader shift towards businesses moving online," CEO Mark Zuckerberg stated (Campaign.co.uk, 2021).

The company says more than a billion monthly active users visit its Facebook Marketplace. In terms of digital payments, Facebook is working on both its Diem digital currency and Novi digital wallet to boost its internet commerce business.

Campaign.co.uk presents the speech of Zuckerberg: "Commerce across all these platforms is going to be very important, and certainly in a platform that we're building like this, we want to enable payments very easily to make it so the economics all work out for developers" (Campaign.co.uk, 2021).

It is stated in the web page with this graphic to emphasize the revenue growth of Facebook as a social media platform in different regions of the World.

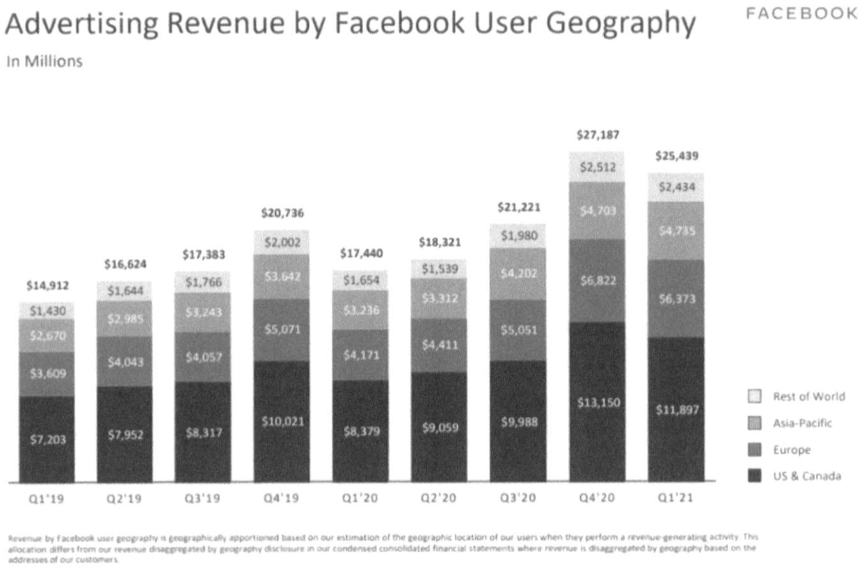

Fig. 2.6: Advertising Revenue by Facebook User Geography. Source: Campaign.co.uk.

This graphic gains ground with the article of Mark Beech, who is the former contributor of Forbes. According to him: "Increased consumption of digital content from mobile apps to free TV streaming and gaming has already been observed in China and Italy," says Maria Rua Aguete of Omdia, the tech research arm of Informa Tech: "Online streaming services provided by brands such as Netflix and now Disney+ are likely to see 12 % growth." She said the annual figures are revealing: "Ecommerce will be the other sector that will see a revenue boost as a result of the pandemic, adding $175 billion in revenue in 2020, which represents a 5 % increase." This week, the streaming service Disney+ became available in most countries in Europe, initially with reduced bandwidth. As a sign of growing demand, Facebook, Amazon, and YouTube have also lowered the quality of video streaming in Europe to ease the strain on the networks (Forbes, 2020).

Forecast of Marketing Communication

One of the biggest advertising agency groups in the World, Dentsu, released a report about the forecast of marketing communication in ten items. To understand under the light of their point of view, these items can be open minder for advertising professionals (Dentsu, Global Ad Spend Forecasts, January 2021):

1. Global advertising spend is forecast to recover to 5.8 % growth in 2021, reaching a total of US$579 billion, based on proprietary Dentsu data from across 59 markets.
2. This represents a significant recovery to advertising expenditure, but not enough to recoup the 8.8 % drop recorded over 2020.
3. A return to positive growth is predicted for all regions in 2021, driven by Western Europe (7.5 %), Asia-Pacific (5.9 %), and North America (4.0 %).
4. Following steep declines in 2020, the fastest-growing markets in 2021 are forecast to be India (10.8 %), the United Kingdom (10.4 %), and France (8.9 %).
5. By share of global ad spend, the top five markets in 2021 will be the United States, China, Japan, the United Kingdom, and Germany.
6. A Q2 recovery is expected, with ad spend increasing by 2 %, 13 %, 4 %, and 3 % across quarters versus 2020 on a like-for-like basis, reflecting the severe impact of lockdowns on ad spend in Q2 2020.
7. For the first time, digital will reach half of the total advertising expenditure in 2021, powering overall growth at a rate of 10.1 %.
8. Social (18.3 %), search (11.0 %), and video (10.8 %) are the leading sources of digital growth.
9. Traditional TV ad spend is forecast to grow by 1.7 % in 2021 to reach US $169 billion—a 30 % share of total ad spend. Sporting events, such as the UEFA European Football Championships and Tokyo Olympic & Paralympic Games, are expected to be key drivers of TV ad spend.
10. Growth in 2021 is expected to lay the foundation for a return to pre-pandemic spending levels in 2022, when we expect expenditure to reach US$619 billion (exceeding the US$600 billion recorded in 2019).

Conclusion

Although all the disruptive and negative effects of COVID-19 for all World economy, especially the advertising industry via the capability of doing cooperation with the related fields, managed to survive in some ways. These capabilities come from the power and experience of digital media and innovative, futuristic implementations such as social media, content platforms, video on demand, podcast, e-commerce, etc. Not only in developed economies but also in static and emerging markets, advertising reflexes could find a solution to reach its target audience. Due to several reports and forecasts, with the role of digital media platforms; brands, and companies can survive even such perilous disasters as COVID-19. Thus, advertising can continue to give lifeline support for weak economies.

References

Asel, J. A., Posch, A., & Speckbacher, G. (2010). *Squeezing or cuddling? The impact of economic crises on management control and stakeholder management*. Berlin: Springer – Verlag.

Beech, M. (2020). Covid-19 pushes up internet use 70% and streaming more than 12%, first figures reveal. *Forbes*. [Accessed on May 03, 2021]. Retrieved from https://www. forbes.com/sites/markbeech/2020/03/25/covid-19-pushes-up-internet-use-70-streaming-more-than-12-first-figures-reveal/?sh=7b3e8caf3104.

Bourletidis, K., & Triantafyllopoulos, Y. (2014). SMEs survival in time of crisis: Strategies, tactics and commercial success stories. *Procedia-Social and Behavioral Sciences*, 148: 639–644.

Campaign. (2021, April). Facebook ad revenue up 46% in Q1. [Accessed on May 1, 2021]. Retrieved from https://www.campaignlive.co.uk/article/facebook-ad-revenue-46-q1/1714344.

Deloitte. (2021, April). Türkiye'de tahmini medya ve reklam yatırımları. [Estimated media and advertising investments in Turkey]. (Report). [Accessed on Feb 26, 2021]. Retrieved from https://www2.deloitte.com/tr/tr/pages/technology-media-and-telecommunications/ articles/medya-yatirimlari-2020-raporu.html.

Dentsu. (2021, January). Global Ad spend forecast. [Accessed on Mar 17, 2021]. Retrieved from https://www.dentsu.com/reports/ad_spend_january_2021_asa.

Gangadharbatla, H. (2021). Covid-19 and advertising: The case for a paradigm shift. *Journal of Current Issues & Research in Advertising (Routledge), 1* (42): 1–18.

Gruenwedel, E. (2020). Roku swings to Q3 profit as subs, streaming hours increase. *MediaPlayNews*. [Accessed on Mar 27, 2021]. Retrieved from https://www. mediaplaynews.com/roku-swings-to-q3-profit-as-subs-streaming-hours-increase/

Hoekstra, J. C., & Leeflang, P. S. H. (2020). Marketing in the era of COVID-19. *Italian Journal of Marketing*, 249–260. https://doi.org/10.1007/s43039-020-00016-3.

McKinsey Global Institute. (2021, March). The consumer demand recovery and lasting effects of COVID-19. [Accessed on Apr 18, 2021]. Retrieved from https://www.mckinsey.com/ industries/consumer-packaged-goods/our-insights/the-consumer-demand-recovery-and-lasting-effects-of-covid-19.

Pophel, L. (2021). COVID-19's impact on 2021 content marketing strategy. *EContEnt*, Jan-Feb: 36–37. [Accessed on 5 May, 2021]. Retrieved from https://www.infotoday. com/it/jan21/Pophal--COVID-19s-Impact-on-2021-Content-Marketing-Strategy.shtml.

Rhodes, D., & Stelter, D. (2009). Seize advantage in a downturn. *Harvard Business Review*, 87: 50–58.

Sheth, J. (2020). Impact of Covid-19 on consumer behavior: Will the old habits return or die?. *Journal of Business Research*, 117: 280–283.

Statista. (2021). Spotify's revenues from 2012 to 2020, by segment. [Accessed on Apr 18, 2021]. Retrieved from https://www.statista.com/statistics/245125/revenue-distribution-of-spotify-by-segment/.

WHO. (2021). WHO Coronavirus (COVID-19) dashboard. [Accessed on May 04, 2021]. Retrieved from https://covid19.who.int/table.

Worldmeter. (2021). Countries where COVID-19 has spread. [Accessed on Mar 10, 2021]. Retrieved from https://www.worldometers.info/coronavirus/countries-where-coronavirus-has-spread/.

Nazlı Eda Noyan and *Murat Çöpçü*

Keep Calm and Animate

Abstract: The production never stopped for animation. Indeed, the medium has steamed ahead, and we will be seeing more and more animation thanks to the Pandemic. But for VFX teams, the production should resume. Unquestionably, what has been happening to the animation industry during the COVID-19 Pandemic will lay the foundation for the future of this industry, just like the rest of the sectors and life itself. It's more about thinking outside the box than anything else. Constructing a workflow at capacity, keeping the resilient teams together and in harmony, and adapting remote working tools is essential for developing virtual production technology. New creative processes, business, production, and exposure models will emerge from this digital and cultural transformation. And there will be new habits. So what will be these new models and habits? And what will be our, as the animation industry, responsibilities to the animation art and craft itself, to nature, to our audiences, colleagues, and students? What will be our new normal with new ethics, tools, dreams, and hopes? Focusing on the animation industry in Turkey, the article will try to answer these questions via interviews with animation industry professionals, artists, and educators. The article sections will include: During the Pandemic, Digital and Cultural Transformation, New Models and Tools, New Habits, The Future of Industry, Responsibilities Audiences, Colleagues, Students and to Nature.

Keywords: Turkish Animation Industry, New Normal, Pandemic

Introduction

While many prominent gastronomy writers were addressing the complicated situation of our food and beverage industry during the pandemic process and the strategies to overcome this situation, Vedat Milor's newspaper column titled "Why don't we have restaurants that may be awarded Michelin stars?" of Feb 7, 2021, allowed us to conceive of a relationship that we have not perceived before. As is well known, the Turkish Cuisine, despite its richness and uniqueness, is a treasure that has not been appraised to its rightful value in the world due to lack of recognition and reputation. While we were contemplating the reasons behind our animation industry's remaining an "infant" industry, which possesses the great legacy of storytelling based on Karagöz and Hacıvat of centuries, we found Milor's (2021) words very applicable to the animation industry as well:

> *A good palate and a family food culture are the beginning. But that is not enough. Knowledge of the ingredients is very important. Unpalatable food may result from good*

material, but producing succulent food from harmful ingredients is not possible. You have to understand this. But that's not enough either. You need to work, work hard, and even work like crazy... These are not conducive to your goal. You need to know whom to work with, what, and how to learn from whom. Intelligence and the ability to observe are essential, but if your ego is powerful, not much will ensue if you are an 'I know everything' type. You should be curious and open to learning new things. You would need patience too. If all these can be combined with a God-given talent, you will become an excellent chef, not a regular one. As a skill, I am sure that our country can cultivate this potential. But as long as the mindset does not change, if our attitudes remain the same, this potential will not emerge... What needs to change? First of all, the finances... Michelin star restaurants also have to be expensive. It has to because good and luxurious material is expensive.

All of these assertions are pretty valid for our animation industry, which has to recuperate from the state of developmental disorder and grow out of infancy. Fortunately, the Pandemic, which transformed "normal" into a kind of sweet nostalgia, did not decimate the animation industry as potently as it did the food and beverage industry on a global scale. On the contrary, as some traditional industry practices that debilitated collaboration began to disappear or transform, teams of artists and animators from all around the world discovered new opportunities to think, produce and share. In a time when stay-at-home orders have forced the overwhelming majority of live-action television and film production to stop, those working in animation have endured relatively little disruption (King, 2020). "Wunderman Thompson The Future 100 Report" claims it is predicted that the global animation market will climb from $ 272.1 million in 2020 to $ 473.7 million by 2026 with current exchange rates and that animation will be the future of visual media (2021). This is a prediction that commensurates with the appetite for cartoons, not only of children or young people, but also that of the adult audience, and that runs proportional to the expanding use of animation, not only in cartoons but also in visual effects. Putting aside the aspects of intellectual property, creative industry, cultural and economic value, animation exists to disrupt the routine of daily life by entering into a surreal and fantastic universe, to face the realities of the world in safe surroundings, to process them in our minds, to assimilate them, and to support our endurance. In other words, it is precisely a means of overcoming a crisis and healing in the emotional dimension!

During the Pandemic

During the Pandemic, while the live-action movies have come to a stand-still and the traditional cinema and TV production are being challenged, animation has experienced a kind of rebirth or "revival." This revival has emerged in response to the increasing demand for animated content. In some cases, with animation to support or "save" live shots and with pipelines and timing that provide fertile premises for the animation to develop and finally become visible and tangible. Undoubtedly, quarantine has forced managers and teams to think outside the box globally, and this has given impetus to the virtual production techniques and the development of the pipeline rather than technology, as Framestore's Fiona Walkinshaw points out (quoted in Kay, 2020). For example, season 7 of The Blacklist series ended with a live-action/cartoon hybrid episode with contributions from a team of 35 animators to complete the unfinished moments of the episode due to the coronavirus shutdown (Parisi, 2020). Although it did not receive positive reviews in technical analysis, this episode was an experimental and constructive attempt to introduce animation in response to a need. Also, productions such as CBS's Tooning out the News, Hulu's Solar Opposites, or Black-ish, One Day at a Time subsumed animated episodes. In addition to the myriad of animated children's content in America, successful, long-running projects for adults such as The Simpsons, South Park, new productions such as Big Mouth or BoJack Horseman, award-winning special projects such as Love, Death & Robots and Star Trek: Lower Decks, spin-off animated series of cult TV series such as Good Times and the X-Files underline the diversification and permanence of animation as a genre, according to Wunderman Thompson Intelligence Report on future trends and change, 2021. Suppose we add to this the unstoppable rise of a sister sector like the video games, advertising, and education sectors and new media such as visual novels and Webtoon, the never-receding popularity of comic books and illustrations. In that case, it becomes apparent that we are facing a growing giant.

Animator Glen Keane, who directed his first feature film this year with Netflix's Over the Moon, says, "The wonderful thing was that we had prepared for this, we just didn't know it" (quoted in Romano, 2020). Keane found the iPad "remarkably accurate" for finalizing the color and lighting for *Over the Moon*. This kind of work and the process for remote voiceover may be described as more straightforward to do remotely versus the earlier stages of developing a story and building out animations. It's becoming more common now to see animators, actors, teachers with their at-home setups, Studios, or educational institutions are driving to people's homes and hand over the equipment for remote working. Nevertheless, actors need specific setups, good acoustics, proper microphones, and as little noise as possible (Romano, 2020).

Rob Bredow, chief creative director of San Francisco-based ILM (Industrial Light & Magic), points out, "The earlier the production resumes, the better for everyone" (in Kay, 2020). Because the functioning of the teams that deal with visual effects are different from those, who work on full animation. Some animation or effects still rely on live-action filming to be completed. Christian Manz, the special effects supervisor on J. K. Rowling's Fantastic Beasts films, the latest of which has delayed filming at Warner Brother's Leavesden studios due to the virus, says there are limits replacing actors. "The big question is what can you get away without physically filming," he says. "To digitally build a location, you still need to capture [the real thing] somehow. If you are making a crowd of digital characters, you will still need references such as costumes and the film's [real] characters, all of that. It will be about how to shift some of the film work to computer generation" (in Sweney, 2020).

Kemp Powers, who straddles both animation and live-action between co-directing *Soul* for Pixar and writing for *Star Trek: Discovery*, thinks that it could be 'a rude awakening' for studios. According to Powers, "they think animation is just easy and it's not. It's some of the hardest work to do in Hollywood and I don't think it's necessarily respected as much as it should be" (in Romano, 2020). Some people see animation as 'a quick fix', but some ideas simply do not translate to animation well from live-action; nevertheless, the lockdown presented an incredible opportunity to get access to ideas that usually would not be immediately considered for an animation (Edwards, 2020). TVC's head of creative content solutions, Alex Black talks about the pitfalls to look out for in animation by emphasizing, "animations can be complex and take a lot more time to complete than many live-action projects, there are a *lot* of steps involved. Also, most decisions and changes have to be made during the storyboarding and design phases, so a lot more planning and forethought are needed. Any changes at the end of the project are very cumbersome and expensive" (in Black, 2020).

In live shootings, many things depend on a single player. However, production does not stop when the animated characters fall sick. That is because of the agile collaboration between dozens of different animators who focus on solving animation problems. Fortunately, some modifications and industry trends preceded the Pandemic; many studios were already trained to work remotely with their equipment. Teams around the world were executing their tasks in virtual production studios using workstations without borders. Visionary filmmakers such as George Lucas, James Cameron, and Peter Jackson had started a revolution by using virtual production in big-budget movies.

Transformation and New Models, Tools, Habits

According to Edwards (2020), COVID aside, the most significant change in the animation industry creatively or technologically has been the blending of mediums: More mixed media, Into the Spiderverse-style CG and 2D, with hand-drawn traditional 2D FX. Ahead of the Japanese Olympics, there has been a massive increase in the hand-drawn anime-inspired work, with so much referencing the incredible Studio Ghibli. Due to the Pandemic, we have noticed that virtual production techniques and real-time technologies have developed rapidly in filmmaking. This paradigm shift will have a considerable impact on the entire film industry. Virtual production consists of many departments and processes such as "pitchvis," "previs," "postvis," "performance capture," and real-time animation. We refer to a transformation in which post-producers are involved in the pre-production and shooting process as consultants and directly interact with the director, cinematographer, art department, and actors. Edwards (2020) believes "this as an area of growth, with cross-medium collaborations becoming more common, from illustrators, fine artists, digital artists, and developers. It's a challenge, as the animation production pipeline has more layers, so it ends up being inherently more complicated but ultimately has an amazing overall aesthetic. Maybe the events of 2020 will accelerate the growth of this technology" (ibidem).

Children's movies and especially animations, which have become the front line of the war of bypassing cinema distribution, have entered a new phase with Trolls: World Tour, which evolved into digital during the Pandemic and enjoyed the success of becoming the most-watched home movie (Alexander, 2020). Pixar and Disney decided to move *Soul* out of its planned November theatrical release and send it exclusively to the Disney+ streaming platform (Coggan, 2020). We will see if this move will become "a permanent situation" or not. The prevailing opinion is that even if people return to the movies after the Pandemic, this genie will not return to the bottle (Collins, 2020). While cinemas embody the most popular and affordable entertainment outside the home, new strategies are bound to be devised according to the economic impact this business creates. Warner Bros is building a studio set dedicated to making mid-range budget movies. They can move to animations, mid-budget and TV film series, shortened movie screenings, or direct digital distribution. Personalized content services such as Netflix, Disney+, and Amazon Prime, which provide plenty of quality and reliable content for the entire household, are likely to remain viable. The NFL's partnership with Nickelodeon is an initiative in this direction. The combination of quantity with quality has become a measure of brand trust and loyalty for family content, and it seems that animation will probably turn into one of the most prominent players here.

Transparency and comprehensiveness will transform the industry. Thanks to technologies, it has become increasingly easier to create short films.

The transformation has modified the industry to allow anyone to present projects, watch, learn, trade, and earn money, and if you happened to have a good command of technology and international communication, the environment has become democratized in that sense. Hair Love, which started as a Kickstarter campaign and won an Oscar for Best Short Animation in 2020, is a good example. Today, women are employed at all levels, from scriptwriters to studio managers. Studios have created new channels for public presentation and IP creation, and it appears that they will continue to do so. Listening to great studio producers and directors in online and open project presentations and evaluation meetings, getting feedback from them, and reaching them from many different geographies will lead to the telling of more diverse stories and new IPs democratization. All you have to do is to be present in business networks and channels where you can be aware of them. Here, of course, knowing foreign languages such as English will become more critical to become a world citizen. This demographic transformation has carried our industry forward creatively and conceptually and has become more reflective of the audience. You can produce a movie and let audiences thirsty for individual voices and sensitive to comprehensive personal stories taste it. Viewers will continue to demand short films, shows, and features that emphasize diversity and incomprehensiveness and reinforce underrepresented voices. In the past years, we have seen more and more projects highlighting this diversity globally. Unfortunately, their numbers are not yet high in our country. We should encourage them.

Creative partnerships thrive and expand with a high level of interaction and the environment and technology that make them viable. Animators can now use the most advanced software efficiently by accessing computers from their homes or outside their homes. You can even run an entire animation studio from a laptop and support programs remotely via a remote server and processing. 2D has grown into a new, preferred technique again, basically for this reason. With working from home prevailing, much 2D software runs smoothly even on laptops, which points out a smaller technology gap that needs to be bridged for 2D workers. According to Matt Maloney, Associate Chair of the SCAD animation degree program, today's producers, artists, parents grew up with many of the 2D classics of Disney and Ghibli (in Cartoon Brew Connect, 2020). Rather than the cold closeness of 3D to reality, 2D or even stop-motion's sincere closeness to childhood and fantasy is preferred – nostalgic or not. When you combine technology, accessibility, and portability with familiar aesthetics, the 2D genre seems to continue its growth and diversification.

The Future of the Industry and Our Responsibilities

Over the past year, we have experimented with and discovered new techniques to improve education without any loss, be it face-to-face or online. We have passed through a process whereby students conduct virtual internships and take special talent exams online. We have increasingly turned to pertinent technologies such as Teams, Zoom, Discord, Slack, and Adobe Connect. Students and creative teams are now accustomed to working, producing, and presenting remotely without face-to-face. However, there are also concerns about this negatively affecting the creative process and synergy. We will continue to use the screen sharing feature, which provides a real-time, interactive learning environment while teaching complex programs and techniques and during feedback sessions. This is because screen sharing, which allows for expressing constructive criticisms both verbally and visually, intensified the interaction between monitor control and messaging positively. With the chat functionality, students can now interact simultaneously, increasing the quality and quantity of dialogues. We have also witnessed the great benefit of recording and archiving all lectures. Unexpected names became guests in our lessons, and so long as differences in local times were taken into consideration, the dilemma of geographical distances was resolved. We could participate in festivals, conferences, virtual exhibitions, screenings, events simultaneously and globally. Before virtualization, we could not even imagine such levels of participation and possibilities.

In animation, you can learn the basic art, movement, modeling, texture, or lighting, but most of what we do pertains to teamwork and storytelling. The new generation that will shape the future of animation needs to develop are features such as human skills and mindsets and the knowledge and skills of animation. The formula for success is now the same for all animation and creative industry representatives, large and small, student and professional: being able to be part of a team even in a virtual environment, to be able to connect, to prepare a thoughtful, intelligent, attractive presentation and to deliver it with dynamic presentation skills, online or face-to-face, to be able to tell virtual or actual stories. And of course, especially with the pandemic doctrine comes further attributes such as adapting quickly, practicality, self-motivation, curiosity, enthusiasm, being without prejudice and being open-minded, being prepared, and having self-confidence, empathy, and global citizenship.

To better appreciate how the animation sector endured the Pandemic, a sector with only a meager market share and support, with a reputation nowhere near to what it deserves, with a limited competent and educated workforce, in February of 2021, almost a year later than the Pandemic's start, we asked the animation representatives in our country such as publishers, producers, directors, animators, visual effects designers, academicians, scriptwriters, content producers, and voice actors[1]:

1. (a) *What was your biggest challenge during the Pandemic?* **(b)** *How did you overcome this challenge?*	"My teammates' psychology got worse day by day, worrying about their health and losing their jobs. As a solution, I tried to support them by showing empathy as much as possible." *Anonymous* "Employee adaptation to the task and productivity declines were the most significant challenge we faced. I think we overcame this obstacle with more permissive job prospects and business management. After all, none of the owners or managers, or workforce of the business had experienced this before." *Kenan Aktaşın* "Getting used to conferencing online was the most challenging thing. We've never been subjected to delays, disconnections, and awkward silences to this extent. This difficulty was overcome by holding numerous meetings. Maybe we developed a new skill, and I'm not sure." *Cenk Köksal* "The difference between being on the monitor and communicating face-to-face with the person being contacted is profound for me." *Can Pekin* "The biggest challenge was communication difficulties with students in a virtual environment. I tried to draw them into the subject by finding as many different examples as possible." *M. Korkut Akaçık* "Team dynamics. We tried to overcome it as much as possible with weekly Zoom meetings." *Yeşim Aktaş*

	"Not being able to work one-on-one with students. Increasing feedback by eliminating excess projects and working hours." *Anonymous* "It was challenging to work from home while bringing up a child. The solution I came up with was working at night while the child slept." *Anonymous* "I did not endure a tremendous professional difficulty. I had already set up my studio and run it quite some time ago. During the epidemic, I welcomed the opportunity of acting more comfortably in dealing with the project in my studio." *Harun Can* "Lack of animators due to the high number of transitions to gaming companies. We tried to overcome it by training." *Haki Bal* "As we mainly collaborate with companies abroad, the digitalization of everything and the online fairs we attended made our work easier." *Evren Yiğit* "To secure enough projects to cover the cost of an in-house team of 90 people." *Mehmet Kurtuluş* "In the way of working, we immediately evolved to digital and lived no difficulties. Only our film could not be released because the cinemas were closed. But our solution for this issue was making TV movies." *Varol Yaşaroğlu* "Finance, support from banks." *Murat Kaya*

	"Budgets that were lowered or not increased on the pretext of the Pandemic. I cannot say that I overcame it." *Ayşe Ünal* "We converted our studio cloud-based end-to-end. We have been producing independently of the office for the past ten months. During this time, we made nearly 3 hours of 3D CGI animation." *Ahmet Erdal* "Under normal circumstances, we work via a network system; it was difficult to access the files while working from home during the pandemic process, and this was taking a long time. We tried to minimize these problems with some programs." *Merve Erik* "At the beginning of the Pandemic, I worried about how to find projects and continue earning money. But when I figured that this process would be a 'stagnation' process for everyone, I started to have very productive days when I started bringing to life the projects I envisioned for a long time. The material I produced for myself secured commercial interest." *Anonymous* "The most challenging problem was the slowdown in content production. We are trying to overcome it with new time scheduling." *Bora Durmuşoğlu* "Uncertainty and team management. I put more projects on the table and guided the team around them. I endorsed the principle of turning crisis into opportunity." *Murat Akbulut*

	"In working remotely, transferring and retrieving information succinctly was difficult. We could not overcome this, and we had to be satisfied with whatever's produced." *Anonymous* "In the advertising agency and post-production sector, there has been severe slowdown incoordination due to the transfer of the processes that need to be managed one-to-one in the office environment to online and the increase in the freelance workload of freelance designers, especially from abroad. Although online interviews and pre-ppm, ppm meetings could be held easily in the Zoom environment, production times during the post-production process increased due to coordination weaknesses." *Emre Şan*
2. (a) *When you compare the first few months of the Pandemic with the present?* **(b)** *What have you learned or perceived professionally?*	"I have always argued that an artist must be knowledgeable about the technical part of the work. The epidemic process vindicated me in this regard. An artist must possess sufficient knowledge of other fields related to his work." *Harun Can* "We quickly realized the possibility of working remotely in the early days. However, since we are doing artistic work, we have concluded that interaction and face-to-face meetings are indispensable for a healthier process in advancing the process." *Anonymous* "Contrary to what we think, the teams doing their job at the computer work from their homes and their performance has increased." *Mehmet Kurtuluş* "We created a more efficient and fast working system." *Varol Yaşaroğlu*

	"Digitalization and making product comparisons and contrasts. Being flexible while producing." *Murat Kaya* "That we do not need an office." *Ahmet Erdal* "Although our way of doing business seems to have changed a bit, we recognized that animation production processes are amenable for remote work, and in this way, viable results can be obtained, and also it is essential to reinterpret the concept of overtime as long as employees manage to maintain their work discipline." *Kenan Aktaşın* "You seize the opportunity to gauge better your team's strengths and weaknesses, equipment, and work techniques under extraordinary conditions. You also devise ways to access some knowledge and skills in a shorter time than usual, which may take much longer to acquire under normal conditions." *Arman Şernaz* "It is possible to work remotely. It was relatively much easier, especially in our profession. At first, I wasn't sure if the technology has developed to such an extent, but I soon realized it was." *Cenk Köksal* "We realized that many things that seemed impossible initially are actually possible and that digital transformation is vital." *İsmail Fidan* "I have experienced that taking a break from the daily routine occasionally to improve oneself and tackle innovations produce better performance in the long run." *Anonymous*

	"I am more patient and more cautious. My perception of time slackened." *Kerim Dündar* "Evaluating your question in terms of education and interaction, I think that the sharing surface reduced to the webcam frame does not meet the volumetric integrity of a classroom or workshop. I see that both sides have severe problems with concentration and focus." *Burak Şahin* "Although our profession can be executed remotely, the importance of synergy and team dynamics within the same ambiance should not be underestimated." *Yeşim Aktaş* "The difficulties we faced in the first few months have been replaced with new normal in professional terms. The students' examining each other's work on the same screen increased the competition and the quality." *Anonymous* "I realized again that this work could only be implemented in direct contact and with face-to-face communication." *Anonymous* "I think the dynamics of socialization and the effects of the human factor are beginning to fade. Although working from home seems to be a part of the process in the industry, the process involved in the customer-artist relationship has, unfortunately, become less stable during this period. Although the staff has somewhat overcome their initial reservations about not working in-house compared to the beginning of the pandemic period, it will not be possible to resume production with the earlier intensity for 1–2 years." *Emre Şan*

3. *Have you discovered anything about yourself or about animation that surprised you professionally?*	"Actually, we discovered that we could do with less." *Mehmet Kurtuluş* "In particular, the incredible technological development of animation programs has always surprised me." *Varol Yaşaroğlu* "What I am absolutely amazed by from day one is the reactions of our children." *Murat Kaya* "I think many of us went through a process in which our ability to adapt to these new conditions was tested. In this process, we witnessed that some companies and staff focused more on their salvation by acting self-centered; some took a more protective attitude by taking risks if necessary and tried to grow out of this process by implementing superior teamwork. In this sense, we can say that the pandemic process served as a litmus test of what companies and individuals care for. Although the demand for animation production decreased due to the panic that ensued at the beginning of the Pandemic, it was a surprising and pleasing development that quickly recovered and reached its previous level." *Arman Şernaz* "Nothing surprised me more than recognizing that I can work in real-time by connecting to a computer elsewhere from my own. Also, with people online, I discovered that everyone, anyone, is accessible." *Cenk Köksal*

	"At the beginning of the Pandemic, I had started on Augmented Reality. My work provided me with the opportunity to collaborate with a large company well known in the world. It was a process at which I worked hard and was proud of myself. I was surprised that 2020 became one of my most productive years." *Anonymous* "Thanks to the social isolation that the process brought along, I was able to find time to examine the productions that I did not know nor had the opportunity to explore." *Can Pekin* "This global phenomenon, which our generation has encountered for the first time, has allowed us to observe many new human behaviors and reflexes and a new awareness of world balance and life. Since animation is designing a model – creating an illusion of life, I would say that the Pandemic paved the way to new perceptions in itself for an animation designer." *Kerim Dündar* "It was a pleasing development that animation film festivals, in particular, were shared online. I think it will be beneficial to preserve this sharing even at a condensed capacity." *Burak Şahin* "I have observed that isolation increases creative thinking processes and new project designs." *Yeşim Aktaş* "Observing each other's work on the same screen increased competition and quality." *Anonymous* "The rapid rise of real-time engines." *Murat Akbulut*

	"The Virtual Production technology that we are setting up has been a new adventure in itself. Thanks to this technology, which replaces the Greenbox techniques, production and animation technologies coalesce in a much more impressive and practical way." *Emre Şan*
4. *What has this process took away from you and brought to you?*	"It justified my vision of setting up a pipeline for more individualistic and personal production." *Harun Can* "We only endured being away from cinemas, and the fact that the stores were closed also negatively affected the sales of licensed products." *Varol Yaşaroğlu* "The postponement of the release of my first motion picture to an uncertain date due to the Pandemic was my dream taken away in this sense. The biggest gain in terms of return is that realizing the importance of my work's innovative level." *Murat Kaya* "Animation is a kind of work that has to be carried out on the monitor all the time. This process became more complex with bans during the pandemic process. Because there was no difference between work and home, physical and mental fatigue and weariness piled up even more." *Merve Erik* "As far as I am concerned, on the positive side, I think my managerial skills sharpened and my use of time improved. On the negative side, I can say that the isolation caused by the Pandemic slowed down my recruiting of new individuals to the sector." *Arman Şernaz*

	"Not being able to socialize was the most significant thing it took away. However, I like being at home; not being able to go out whenever I want to make me feel a little restricted. With the interactions established in a co-working environment, you are updated professionally as you socialize with your colleagues. This updating could not be experienced as intense as before." *Cenk Köksal* "This was a year when I realized what I wanted to do in the oncoming years and how I needed to develop myself further. On the one hand, although I enjoyed the work that I do, on the other hand, there was this creeping feeling of burnout as a result of 'non-stop' production." *Anonymous* "I think the most important feature that I have attained from this process was "to adapt / to keep in pace with changes." I had a very stressful time adjusting the teaching I conceived initially to a form more suitable for the system. Although I still think that the distance education model is not as efficient as the face-to-face one for practical sessions, I am trying to conduct the lessons as effectively as possible. Considering that human beings are social, I don't think I have any loss other than missing the old-fashioned communication that we carry out outside of technological devices. I can only say that I realized how valuable even the simplest things are." *Can Pekin*

	"Not being able to travel and not being nourished by different cultures, the constriction of social life to such an extent affect my creativity and motivation. But at the same time, the restriction of human transit in the world, the reduction of our ecological footprint as human species have also indicated how quickly the nature we destroyed can be renewed. I witnessed how fast the delicate balances that allow us to live in peace can be upset. This has had positive benefits in terms of drawing a lesson. A new awareness and consciousness developed towards the Earth, our home. We have finally begun to question our human-centered living and habits." *Kerim Dündar* "This process brought in more than it took. We understood that we could reach the masses more easily through online platforms." *M. Korkut Akaçık* "Due to the Pandemic and the economic crisis, the anticipated wage increases could not be realized for the teams, so most of the experienced teams went abroad, moved to the TV series industry, or switched to the game industry, which made it difficult to form a group in my line of work. I think it is also realized that flexible and self-directed working hours did not create a problem as feared. On the flip side to this, the concepts of weekend and overtime disappeared completely, and requests for presentations and meetings on a Sunday began to be received at 11.00 pm." *Ayşe Ünal*

	"I believe that every situation that we think "took something from us" actually improves us and carries us to new adaptation and thought levels. I believe that the isolation we experienced in this period increased our awareness in every sense; it was a means to revise ourselves that led us to discover new communication and working methods." *Yeşim Aktaş* "The moments of spiritual satisfaction and fun brought about by doing a project shoulder-to-shoulder eroded." *Anonymous* "We better appreciated the value of publishing and content creation; we experienced how we should respond during the most challenging times by re-evaluating our responsibilities in terms of our work. It can be regarded as a very significant achievement." *Bora Durmuşoğlu* "As it coincided with the period during which we were busy setting up our studio, I did not feel professionally impacted. Since all the lectures I hold at universities went online, I was able to teach at three faculties simultaneously, but this situation did not wear me out much at all." *Emre Şan*

5. *How has the Pandemic affected or changed your animation-related business and production?*	"A decrease in production brought a reduction in business volume. Scalability gained importance. Those who failed to scale according to sectoral conditions experienced severe problems. To be able to enforce the workflow in different directions became imperative." *Harun Can* "As production shifted more to homes, there were situations where we faced difficulty managing teams. The inability of people to demonstrate self-discipline or to manage time well sometimes affected us negatively." *Evren Yiğit* "We evolved the ability to do anything entirely digitally and online. We also tested the premise that anything can be done while working from home." *Varol Yaşaroğlu* "We have sent our employees home away from the crowd in production, and our production evolved around this method. However, I do not think this is sustainable. Just as Covid vaccines were approved for emergency use, we also allowed the use of emergency methods." *Murat Kaya* "We lost some projects during the transition from an office-based studio environment to a cloud-based one, but our working comfort and productivity increased afterward." *Ahmet Erdal*

	"More intensive and effective remote working methods have taken their place as a new option in our production model. There evolved an understanding that we don't necessarily have to do everything inside the studio. Nevertheless, I think that working one-on-one makes a positive contribution to production psychology and the resulting product." *Arman Şernaz* "It actually allowed me more time for myself and my projects. This affected my production positively." *Cenk Köksal* "Around 50 % decline in the first few months, but later we adapted to a large extent." *İsmail Fidan* "The Pandemic provided me with an opportunity to explore the minor and the significant areas of animation. It enabled me to convert my works from two-dimensions to three into life, using augmented reality, which instigated new ideas." *Anonymous*

	"The distance education method for applied courses was initially a complex process to adapt to. For example, since the Animation Design course progressed through live model studies, the transformation towards distance education was complex during the Pandemic. Likewise, in courses such as Character Design, Illustration, and Concept Design, we faced similar transformation inconveniences since theoretical knowledge was developed over the students' works. We proceeded with design courses by utilizing reference photographs and by viewing student works via camera and e-mail. Nevertheless, adapting to a pretty different model from face-to-face training in terms of feel and practicality was challenging for both students and me. Besides, students' difficulties in accessing the internet – or their inability to access the internet - conscientiously challenged me in terms of their participation in class and in terms of assessing their homework and examinations (whether students are justified in these complaints or whether they are exploiting the situation is also another issue). A similar situation applies to class attendance due to their freedom to keep their cameras off. To be honest, I am unsure whether I have overcome this difficulty. In terms of production, although the isolation we have been exposed to for a long time has adverse psychological effects, I try to balance the decrease I experienced in terms of quantity by maintaining the quality level." *Can Pekin*

	"Since the economic stability of the clients and firms is now uncertain, I tried not to accept projects whose payment structure may be shaky. I was working intensely at the computer before the Pandemic. For this reason, my working and production processes have not changed much. I am on the computer for long hours. I think this applies to all those who work in the digital design sector." *Kerim Dündar* "In my opinion, postponing or canceling events such as conferences and film festivals has an adverse effect." *Burak Şahin* "In some of our projects, we experienced stagnation or a slowdown at the beginning of the pandemic process. However, at the same time, this process allowed us to generate new ideas. Our communication with many international companies was also reinforced as the online meeting environment has almost become the only meeting option." *Yeşim Aktaş* "The concept of working hours has folded. I am working day and night now." *Anonymous* "During the animation phase, those who were challenged most were the dubbing artists. Entering a tiny studio and recording audio was risky. But now many artists can record from home." *Anonymous* "The atmosphere of uncertainty and despair increased. It has become more challenging to consolidate teams. The development of the content industry gave hope again." *Murat Akbulut*

	"It affected adversely, working face-to-face is a must." *Anonymous* "Tiring and time-consuming processes such as physically going to another venue and physically attending meetings have disappeared. In a sense, I have saved time, but to accentuate again, I do not think that physical interactions can or will permanently replace them." *Emre Şan*
6. (a) *Have your projects a plot about the Pandemic or a story about restrictions and bans been dealt with directly or passively?* **(b)** *How was the feedback you received?*	"There is not much of an epidemic-induced content change in this regard yet. Of course, there have been changes regarding the subject in the advertising industry." *Harun Can* "Although this issue is not directly subsumed in our project, we have tackled the subject of virtual meetings, a process that we all were involved in during the Pandemic, in one episode." *Anonymous* "Everything we did digitally has been successful[2]." *Varol Yaşaroğlu* "We did an innovative episode about staying at home in our animated series titled 'The Lion.' We have demonstrated that some operations have become viable with the support of technology. Apart from that, we have prepared many informative, educational, and short videos and posts about changes in our habits." *Murat Kaya* "We prepared and broadcast a public spot informing children about personal hygiene and social distance with our characters (the Puzzle Tower)." *Ahmet Erdal*

	"Yes. We shared our social media accounts, explaining to children what this process involves and what the future may bring." *Merve Erik* "Informative films on the subject were produced. We received comments and thank you messages that our movies contributed to children's understanding of cleanliness, hygiene, and physical distance." *Kenan Aktaşın* "I handled it directly as a subject. I have characterized the Coronavirus and made a short series of episodes. We have received very positive feedback so far." *Cenk Köksal* "We always prefer to process negative things indirectly. Our hand washing content has reached 50 million views, and we received excellent feedback." *İsmail Fidan* "There were times when I caricatured this process on Instagram. Especially, these posts of mine were loved and shared by others." *Anonymous* "As the new normal culture, 'providing service while observing social distancing' and 'adaptation to the new normal' were invariably included in the project plots, and the works requested from the client. But in my projects, I usually want to avoid 'hype' trends, so I didn't feel like creating something about 'pandemics.'" *Kerim Dündar* "I am working on two projects in progress. Therefore, no feedback has been received yet." *Burak Şahin*

<table>
<tr><td></td><td>“We are working on a project that includes this extraordinary process we are currently experiencing. As we are at the concept stage, no feedbacks yet.”
Yeşim Aktaş

“I did. I covered the issue of hygiene and plastic waste in the second part of ‘Captain Pengu ve Friends.’”
Arzu Yurtseven

“We have worked on face masks, social distance, and hygiene rules in our content to raise awareness of children in particular. Almost all of these attracted great attention and were appreciated and used in other media.”
Bora Durmuşoğlu

“Right, all quite boring. We do not want to deal with the Pandemic.”
Murat Akbulut</td></tr>
<tr><td>7. (a) What kind of a future awaits us in the context of animation after the Pandemic?

(b) Production and consumption conditions, artistic dimension, economy, etc.?</td><td>“I predict that the already diminished sector will shrink even more. Just as even the mighty studios suffer financially, some medium and small studios may terminate their commercial activities. While this may be negative for some of us, it also implies new opportunities. Also, in my opinion, the biggest challenge is that the studios that want to enlarge their team will not be able to find personnel to work as a result of the people working from home during the pandemic period, who have acquired the habit of working freelance and do not want to work inhouse. I think this is when the freelance wind blows the strongest in the sector and will bring high prices.”
Anonymous

“We notice plenty of upheavals in the fairs and summits we attend abroad. But it was time for something to change.”
Evren Yiğit</td></tr>
</table>

	"Production conditions will improve, but as our international circulation will decrease, foreign sales will slow down." *Mehmet Kurtuluş* "I think it's too early to talk about this. I think we are still at the very beginning of everything. It will take a few years for the business to reach its previous levels. I guess bright ideas developed through small teams will stand out." *Harun Can* "I have a positive view. The animation industry is very amenable to digital and online processing. Workwise, both speed and quality will increase technologically. Thus, more time will be left for creativity." *Varol Yaşaroğlu* "Our working methodology will definitely be stretched; we will be as far away from the crowd as possible. We have seen consumption increase all over the world, and this will persist as a trend. Artistic work and financing will proceed hand in hand. There will be no high-budget productions in terms of cinema, and this will affect the creative side." *Murat Kaya* "We have changed our production method permanently. We will continue to work remotely with all our staff after the Pandemic. We predict that the dominance of VOD platforms will increase in consumption." *Ahmet Erdal*

	"Among the new-generation production styles, animation production is a style amenable to almost all. Production processes can be completed successfully even without staff coming together. Animation and similar productions allowed us quickly to mitigate the psychological seclusion that living in closed quarters created to fulfill their needs such as socializing and entertainment. Shortly after the Pandemic, people's desire to spend more time outside will not be curbed. But most of them will still want to stay indoors to avoid risks even if they desire otherwise. A dystopian future awaits us. The animation industry will be cultivated in the field of visual creativity in this dystopian lifestyle. It is evident that consumption will continue without slowing down. The production system will not change much. The need for human labor will increase more. Art is influenced by the conditions of time, or it reflects time. Although there will be variations in the art dimension, I foresee that art and aesthetic understanding in life will decrease and become monotonous. This will be the result of the socio-cultural effects caused by the monotonous Pandemic. The consumption processes that are likely to grow will enable the sector to grow economically. If people reject a digital world and prefer optimum technology, we can talk about a different world and animation." *Kenan Aktaşın* "Even if the Pandemic disappears completely, I think its effects on the psychology of production and form will continue for a while. But ultimately, I feel we will have a more refined animation production environment that is better than before." *Arman Şernaz*

	“Frankly, I don’t think much will change. I think we will start to forget what happened on the very day when everything returned to normal. People will realize that they are a part of one of the few sectors not affected by this crisis. Accordingly, investments may increase. A larger share of the cake can be viable in content production. As for production conditions, I will say how fulfilling it will be if an arrangement can be compromised that would allow for an order to be processed from home at least a few days a week. In this process, I guess that people who have taught themselves production from home may also participate in the production. Therefore, there may be an increase in author-style output. Independent artists may continue to come together and form teams to produce joint works. Artistically, I think it will be as affected as any other art branch. At the most, this will trigger the emergence of creations about difficult times.” *Cenk Köksal* “Working remotely will be our most extensive agenda after the Pandemic. But the need for content is increasing day by day, and people are consuming faster. So there will be more teams for more content, and the economy will grow even more.” *İsmail Fidan*

	"It may be possible that the theoretical courses (and some applied courses) in the department are taught according to a distance education model upon the requests of the relevant instructors. This may provide some relief, especially in departments with crowded quotas like ours (already a similar operating model is applied in compulsory courses such as Turkish Language, Atatürk's Principles, and History of Revolution of Higher Education Institution). Due to the situation we are in, I see that the number of events such as online exhibitions, symposiums, and interviews has increased considerably. I think that online events constitute practical (especially in terms of exhibition participation) and effective premises on behalf of organizing teams, institutions, and participants. Of course, not everything should be evaluated in terms of its usefulness (of course, the feeling of unmediated connection with a work of art cannot be denied), but when the Pandemic is over, the online activities (at least a part of it) that I mentioned above may retain their presence in the art environment to reach a wider audience. It is also a matter of curiosity for me to see whether or how the online working style in the industry will continue in the same manner after the Pandemic." *Can Pekin*

	"Far more than the previous level, the necessity and volume of the animation industry have expanded, as communication now takes place remotely and through digital platforms, and the consumption of digital media for educational and entertainment purposes has also increased significantly. Consumption increased, indirectly production also increased. The economy expanded, new areas were opened where animation would find its place in education, entertainment, and communication. Increased production and consumption generally result in a decrease in quality and quality. I think the artistic dimension can be measured in the longer term." *Kerim Dündar* "I believe that animation will be learned much faster and in a healthier fashion in classrooms/laboratories where instructors and students can physically cooperate. It would not be wrong to say that production will accelerate thanks to digital tools considerably, and therefore consumption will accelerate in parallel. I am not very hopeful about its artistic dimension. I think that with every new generation of theater and other performing arts, the efforts put in for gathering information and conducting research diminish more and more. The economic issue is not very bright either. Especially in the advertising industry, animation is regarded as an inexpensive technique." *M. Korkut Akaçık* "People need morale. I think the production will increase and be subsidized in this direction." *Burak Şahin* "We cannot consider the answer to the question independent of the economic situation of the country. I don't expect an exceptionally bright future in this respect. I guess that the usage areas of animation will expand in the world." *Ayşe Ünal*

	"The advantage of being able to produce remotely in the animation sector has caused the national borders, which had already begun to disappear before the Pandemic, to probably dissipate entirely on account of the experiences attained in this period, and the international work will expand. This will bring the development of the animation industry, especially in our country. At the same time, I believe that animation production can materialize under all conditions to increase the sector's need and interest." *Yeşim Aktaş* "I believe that there will be excellent developments in both production and consumption after these difficult times. I think we will come across many different styles in terms of art." *Bora Durmuşoğlu* "Immediate consumption has increased; with real-time, fast production processes will ensue. If the value of Bitcoin does not drop, the staff will deal with that issue, and the creative quality will decrease." *Murat Akbulut* "Since it cannot be achieved remotely, we will encounter less controlled and less aesthetic productions." *Anonymous* "Production requirements have increased because the content expectations from the digital platforms have increased. I doubt that we will see a movie theater again in the future. Many movie productions are going on now, but all of them are based on digital platforms. Naturally, I guess that this momentum will intensify after the Pandemic. Now the concept of making motion pictures is changing to transferring the business to digital. The era of low-budget productions, such as those on YouTube, is about to end." *Emre Şan*

8. *During the Pandemic, did you apply for and acquired formal support (the Republic of Turkey, Provincial Development Agencies, etc.)?*	"We applied for supporting a demo, no responses yet." *Evren Yiğit* "We are a company of about 50 people. 75 % of this staff is involved with animation. Our application for a short-time working allowance for the remaining staff has been made. Other than that, we did not receive any support. We did not apply for opportunities regarding insurance and tax restructuring." *Murat Kaya* "I live in England. I received support from the state here for the months that I could not work due to the Pandemic. It was God-sent for me." *Anonymous*

During the Pandemic, as it has become challenging to establish new and profound networks as many festivals and travel programs have been postponed, we may have all well realized that walking outside and being social is crucial. Animation is the oasis in a desert. And although our routines were disrupted, human beings are very capable of adapting to different situations. Some of our prejudices disappeared, we gained a new perspective. We all have recognized that the things that we thought impossible to achieve online could be realized. The distance became near, and the old near vanished; our mindset determines our limits. Empathy, justice, good management all make a difference. Health, hope, connection with nature, and good social relations impact a productive output. The necessities and losses during the Pandemic have been unbearable, but fortunately, we have the internet.

Although there has been a massive amount of brain and talent migration to other countries (thanks to many things, including the Ankara Agreement) and the very popular, rapidly growing, and magnified game sector within Turkey, animation has undoubtedly been having a moment in 2020. Homebound audiences are crying out for fresh content[3]. But before the COVID-19 happened, one of the most important things was to encourage people to consider the medium of animation in the first place. Animation needs to stay on top of people's minds in the long term, and animated projects may continue to grow in popularity with governmental funding and private support (there is almost none) and animation education for new talents and workforce to emerge. The cinema funds of the Turkish Republic's Ministry of Culture and Tourism to animation projects and others were awarded late. The process was both problematic and prolonged. Some projects were postponed and canceled. Nevertheless, the implementations such as remote work permits for R&D and Design Centers[4] were helpful.

We expect to see the need and spending continuing in the industry's future, but many belt-tightenings are expected. The value of animation and storytelling art and craft is more visible now. It will be even more visible in the future. The ways to make the dream continue also include tax reduction for the sponsor of the animation productions, at least 50 % IP rights of the creators of animations, collaboration with merchandise and toy industries, know-how for the co-productions, international visibility, and new strategies for the commercial and independent productions and pipelines.

Although online systems will persist, we will return to old habits as soon as the Pandemic is over because we missed them so much. The hybrid system will stand out. The universities and offices took swift relevant decisions and organized the work from home by arranging the delivery of our office computers and online technologies to our homes.

Conclusion

During the Pandemic, when there is no one-on-one communication, the process of persuasion and trust-building suffered, especially throughout the search for resources and networking for the projects. It had been challenging to establish reliable, sincere communication with teammates and students and create mutual acquaintance and belonging. All tried to be resolved by opening all communication channels, inspiring hope, and focusing on the positive aspects. But, it seems that the most critical issue for animation education and the industry will continue to be the "trust." As the administrations return to hybrid operations, they must first gain the trust of their employees; staff, students, workforce, schools, and studios must entrust that safe working conditions are prioritized; educators, managers, remote workers have to trust that they can do their work without direct supervision; students have to be confident that they received a proper education scrupulously under pandemic conditions and that they can corroborate this issue; similar to the security systems that protect the expensive, top-secret IP in-house, customers have to trust that the same IP is securely protected on the non-studio workstations. More importantly, we have to trust that we can return to normal. We have to trust ourselves and our future. And of course, we have to trust the fantastic animation in all of its aspects!

And the Pandemic has reminded us that we are not isolated, and we cannot be solitary[5]. Because, especially under these conditions, "all for one and one for all!" A new golden era rises on the horizon, the golden era of animation. Thus, we can claim: "*Keep Calm and Animate*."

Notes

1 "Turkish Animation Industry During Days of Corona." Interviews with the people of Turkish animation industry from early 2020, the first months of pandemic maybe watched here: https://www.youtube.com/watch?v=oGjymoAyLLo.

2 https://www.google.com.tr/ amp/s/www.hurriyet.com.tr/ amp/kelebek/hurriyet -cumartesi/kim- derdi-ki-cocuklar-bir- gun-uzerinde-sakir-yazan-bir-seyi-gururla-giyecek-41728153

3 UK viewers are watching more than five extra hours of traditional TV each week according to Thinkbox, while streaming services have seen at least a 20 % surge in usage globally (quoted in Sweney, 2020).

4 https://m.sabah.com.tr/ekonomi/2020/07/30/hazine-ve-maliye-bakani-berat-albayrak-mujdeyi-duyurdu.

5 We would like to express our gratitude to the following representatives of animation industry of Turkey who supported our research by responding to our questions, and to the representatives who answered our questions but preferred to remain anonymous: *M. Korkut Akaçık* (BAU Cartoon and Animation), *Murat Akbulut* (1000Volt), *Yeşim Aktaş* (Melon Production), *Kenan Aktaşın* (Netco Animation Studio), *Haki Bal* (Düşlerevi Cartoon Studio), *Harun Can*, *Bora Durmuşoğlu* (TRT Çocuk Channel), *Kerim Dündar*, *Ahmet Erdal* (Yoyo Film Production), *Merve Erik* (Resimli Filim Animation Studio), *İsmail Fidan* (İSF Studios), *Murat Kaya* (Outline Agency), *Cenk Köksal* (Onion Skin Studio), *Mehmet Kurtuluş* (Anima İstanbul), *Can Pekin* (KDÜ Cartoon and Animation), *Burak Şahin* (MU), *Emre Şan* (MGX Studio), *Arman Şernaz* (Lighthouse Animation & VFX), *Ayşe Ünal*, *Varol Yaşaroğlu* (Grafi2000 Production), *Evren Yiğit* (Mako Content and Animation), *Arzu Yurtseven*. Besides, we would like to thank BAU Prep School for their help in translation of this article.

References

Alexander, J. (2020). Trolls World Tour could be a case study for Hollywood's digital future: A debate over what happens when everything returns to normal. *The Verge*. [Accessed on Feb 26, 2021]. Retrieved from https://www.theverge.com/2020/3/18/21184030/universal-trolls-world-tour-hunt-coronavirus-birds-of-prey-warner-bros-disney-paramount-vod-digital.

Black, A. (2020). Why animation could be the answer to advertisers' COVID-19 content production problem. *The Drum*. [Accessed on Feb 18, 2021]. Retrieved from: https://www.thedrum. com/opinion/2020/04/02/why-animation-could-be-the-answer-advertisers-covid-19-content-production-problem.

Cartoon Brew Connect. (2020). SCAD AnimationFest opens a window onto the (new) Golden Age Of Animation. *Cartoon Brew*. [Accessed on Feb 26, 2021]. Retrieved from https://www.cartoonbrew.com/sponsored-by-scad/scad-animationfest-opens-a-window-onto-the-new-golden-age-of-animation-197662.html.

Coggan, D. (2020). Soul is skipping theaters and will debut on Disney+. *Entertainment Weekly*. [Accessed on Feb 26, 2021]. Retrieved from https://ew.com/movies/soul-disney-plus-release/.

Collins, D. (2020). 7 ways COVID-19 could change kid's media drastically. *Kids Screen*. [Accessed on Feb 26, 2021]. Retrieved from https://kidscreen.com/2020/04/21/7-ways-covid-19-could-change-kids-media/.

Edwards, D. (2020). How animation took center stage in 2020. *Shots*. [Accessed on Feb 18, 2021]. Retrieved from https://www.shots.net/news/view/how-animation-took-centre-stage-in-2020.

Kay, J. (2020). Screen talks: VFX leaders on adapting to lockdown, looking to next stage. *Screen Daily*. [Accessed on Feb 26, 2021]. Retrieved from https://www.screendaily.com/news/screen-talks-vfx-leaders-on-adapting-to-lockdown-looking-to-nextstage /5150205.article.

King, D. (2020). Why you're going to see more animation (thanks, Pandemic). *The Wall Street Journal*. [Accessed on Feb 26, 2021]. Retrieved from https://www.wsj.com/articles/why-youre-going-to-see-more-animation-thanks-pandemic-11589724000?redirect=amp#click= https://t.co/L8MWRqLDwA.

Milor, V. (2021). Michelin yıldızı alacak lokantalar niye bizde yok?. [Why don't we have restaurants that may be awarded Michelin stars?]. *Hürriyet Newspaper*. [Accessed on Feb 26, 2021]. Retrieved from https://www.hurriyet.com.tr.

Parisi, K. (2020). Why Blacklist season 7's cartoon ending didn't work. *Screen Rant*. [Accessed on Feb 26, 2021]. Retrieved from https://screenrant.com/blacklist-season-7-ending-cartoon-ending-not-work/.

Romano, N. (2020). The pandemic animation boom: How cartoons became king in the time of COVID. *Entertainment Weekly*. [Accessed on Feb 18, 2021]. Retrieved from https://ew.com/movies/animation-boom-coronavirus-pandemic/.

Sabah Newspaper. (2020). Bakan Albayrak'tan bayram öncesi esnafa ve vatandaşa büyük müjde. [Great good news from Minister Albayrak to shopkeepers and citizens before Eid]. [Accessed on Feb 26, 2020]. Retrieved from https://www.sabah.com.tr.

Sweney, M. (2020). How Coronavirus has animated one section of the film industry. *The Guardian*. [Accessed on Feb 20, 2021]. Retrieved from https://www.theguardian.com/film/2020/may/19/how-coronavirus-has-animated-one-section-of-the-film-industry.

Wunderman Thompson Intelligence. (2020).The future 100: 2021 trends and change to watch in 2021. (Online report). [Accessed on Feb 26, 2021]. Retrieved from https://intelligence.wundermanthompson.com/trend-reports/the-future-100-2021/.

Sinan Aşçı

Decentralizing Media Education in the Post-Pandemic Period: Using the Blockchain Revolution as a Disruptive Innovation

Abstract: Media education in colleges and universities consists of any formal, informal, and connected learning process based on either analyzing media or producing media. During the COVID-19 pandemic, the emergency changes to distance education in any discipline have caused an increase in remote and online forms of teaching and learning. As the COVID-19 pandemic has produced various critical challenges, online education has become a matter of concern worldwide to handle and resolve this crisis at multiple scales, including authorities, schools, teachers, parents, and learners. To find out critical cautions, educational technologies are considered a remedy for such a crisis. The rise of technological advancements, artificial intelligence, big data, machine learning, and blockchain technology has also changed the practice of media education for the last decade. Blockchain technology provides a decentralized infrastructure by supporting users with the autonomy to identify and control over themselves; trust to have enough confidence in its operations, transparency to conduct knowledge transactions; immutability to be permanently written and stored without having any modification or changes; disintermediation for a central authority to check the progress and keep it for itself; lastly, collaboration to connect directly with each other without any need in the third-party applications. In this respect, blockchain technology indeed reveals the potential to change the directions of distance media education in several ways. This chapter explores general course-based aspects of distance media education on theoretical knowledge, technical practices, and artistic productions to enable educators to apply it in different fields of media and communication: for example, advertising, cartoon and animation, cinema and television, communication design, digital game design, photography, public relations, and new media. Particularly, three different bases were taken into consideration, where the use of blockchain technology makes distance education open and decentralized while putting learners in charge of their learning process and the data. Various components regarding a decentralized approach to distance media education are discussed to implement a more creative and innovative approach to educating future media professionals.

Keywords: Blockchain Technology, Media Education, Decentralization, Post-Pandemic Period

Introduction

Educational activities to develop individuals' skills and potentials towards a specific outcome have been controlled mainly by the educational institutions providing quality, governance, and credibility. Due to the COVID-19 pandemic since December of 2019, these activities were nearly interrupted and could not be conducted flexible enough because of all the educators in different fields having scrambled to adapt to self-quarantine and the lockdown decisions made by the government in many countries. During the days of social isolation, some existing virtual alternatives and possible solutions started being used to go on educational activities, not to reveal difficulties in recognizing the achievements and needs of a learner in any formal or informal type of education. Under normal conditions, learners do not have much control over their learning process even if they study in an undergraduate or graduate program. However, such a sharp transition from an in-class and previously defined process to an online and somehow self-governing framework indicated some question marks about the infrastructures of privacy, security, ownership, transparency, accountability, management, and trust through the adaptation of distance education in all the studies, but especially for media studies because media and communication studies consist of theoretical knowledge to comprehend, technical skills to practice and artistic productions to look after their rights.

Well-known platforms in educational tools, social media, and video conference systems have been implemented into any content delivery process. However, it is evident that using different platforms to share educational contents and conduct the communication channels between individuals based on education is considered only as salvaging the day because the process has not been planned very well as required and needed. According to Wiliamson et al. (2020), this type of educational pattern was lifted to an "emergency matter" due to the COVID-19 pandemic. On the other hand, every educator or institution has been obliged to make snap decisions not to interrupt the ongoing processes. This situation indicates a crystal-clear need for reasoning out and offering different solutions for not one perspective on a specific educational basis but all in an inclusive way. Offering solutions to get learners involved in a framework entirely determined by them brings out a decentralized model. Considering the main argument of decentralization (Galiani, Gertler, & Schargrodsky, 2008), it brings decisions closer to the individuals by alleviating information asymmetries and improving accountability. Regarding media education in colleges and universities, a decentralized model allows the learners to fully control how they have been learning theoretical basis, acquiring technical skills, and sharing their qualifications with productions and creations.

Using a decentralized model in educational settings is definitely based on a serious planning and review process. It may lead to a disruptive experience for the individuals who are not fond of such changes or revolutions created with new media technologies in all areas of social life. When the decentralized model is considered on an educational basis during the pandemic era, the emergence of blockchain technology is expected to offer technological means to enable decentralization. A decentralized infrastructure in which previously mentioned components are built can be provided by using blockchain technology. Furthermore, an individual's learning can be experienced from various resources, but we need to form a coherent and understandable picture to create some standards to maintain the quality.

To comprehend this new pattern and suggest a new approach to various areas of distance education in media studies, this chapter aims to critically discuss the existing and future possibilities for media education in the aftermath of the COVID-19 pandemic. A literature review on blockchain technology and a decentralized approach for distance education was presented. Then, different approaches to blockchain technology and its application to distance education by considering media studies were discussed and exemplified. With the results of such a descriptive method used in this chapter, the question about how pandemic experiences regarding media education pave the way for changes in post-pandemic education was critically addressed.

The Applications of Blockchain Technology in Education

Blockchain technology was recently addressed in discussions about crypto money such as Bitcoin or Etheria in Turkey, (Atalay, 2018). However, the interested parties in this technology know that it promises more than changes related to digital currency. The uses of blockchain technology were limited to create cryptocurrencies and making cryptocurrency transactions until 2014, but since then, it has been seen that this technology can be used in many different areas and can lead to significant changes accordingly (ibidem).

Blockchain is a distributed network of computers (nodes) used to maintain the source of information sharing. Each node supports the security and accuracy of the information by keeping a complete set of ledgers of past transactions. A new block is being created by a miner, who is the first to validate all the transactions in the block and solve the problem by generating a digital signature for the block that meets a predefined rule using the hash function. The newly created block will be broadcasting to the whole blockchain network, allowing all nodes to maintain the same complete ledger (Tschorsch & Scheuermann, 2016; as cited in Chen, Xu, Lu, & Chen, 2018). In other words, the Blockchain is cryptographically secured against retrospective manipulations, and it uses a consensus mechanism to keep the database consistent whenever new transactions need to be validated (Beck, 2018).

An information chain created within cryptographically secured and linked blocks is transferred without any central authority because the process consists of the consensus mechanism in the system. That's why it can be inferred that a process depicting such a technology introduces inevitable immutability and trust, but we can use another feature of this technology which is decentralization. Derived from the previously mentioned technical process, some advantages related to blockchain technology can be outlined like publicity based on the ability to see all the transactions, resiliency about containing all transactions that have ever made in the network, security for providing a secure network over untrusted parties, speed in distributing across the web in minutes, cost-saving being not like existing Internet of Things solutions, immutability regarding the verification by the majority of the network nodes, anonymity to process the transaction, and lastly, decentralization without having single authority (Atlam, Alenezi, Alassafi, & Wills, 2018).

Educational applications by using blockchain technology have been started experiencing in different fields at universities and colleges for various reasons and purposes: for example, dealing with the lack of ability to voice and defend preferences (Galiani, Gertler, & Schargrodsky, 2008), academic degree management (Sharples & Domingue, 2016), evaluation for learning outcomes (Skiba, 2017), reformulation of hands-on activities (Machado, Bonan, Perez, & Martelli, 2020). As seen in these examples, blockchain technology is applied to education in various ways beyond the basics to manage and assess. Both educators and learners understandably get benefits from such applications on the design of learning activities and implementation. Such a disruptive technology can solve the problem related to information asymmetry and trust among learners from different backgrounds and in various levels of readiness by using its features like decentralization and immutability.

A Decentralized Approach in Education Ecosystem

Decentralization refers to data verification, storage, maintenance, and transmission on the Blockchain based on a distributed system structure (Chen, Xu, Lu, & Chen, 2018). This feature supports a performance like protecting data because the basis is decentralized rather than the centralized organizations. In other words, such a core principle is based on the fact that data can be published ubiquitously, and the data can be queried and integrated because it is not aggregated into a central location. Keeping the decentralization feature of blockchain technology in mind, it is possible to provide and form this type of Blockchain and its consensus algorithm for different areas and purposes.

The potentials of blockchain technology are based on the fact that all learners' educational data would be integrated into blockchain ledgers if an educational blockchain system were put into use in educational settings (Chen, Xu, Lu, & Chen, 2018). By taking a decentralized approach (Wilson, Liber, Griffiths, & Johnson, 2007, pp. 1386–1395), it is possible to look to delegate technology regulation as far as possible to individuals and self-organizing groups of learners. As understood with the potential integration of blockchain technology into educational settings, using digital technologies cannot be limited to conducting online sessions using specific social media platforms or creating standard files to share and spread the required information.

Sharing the information in the scope of learning outcomes does not mean that the genie will be out of the bottle after the learners get it at will because it consists of at least three different aspects based on theoretical knowledge, technical skills, and artistic productions – especially for media education. Considering these various aspects of the required information, the learning or teaching patterns are expected to contribute to the program outcomes at both undergraduate and graduate levels, like critically interpreting and discussing the theories and fundamentals; attaining written, oral and visual knowledge by using technical equipment and software; getting information about institutional agents and the industry operating in their fields; comprehending the reactions of the audience and users to the changing roles of media environments; grasping global and technological impacts in their areas; developing skills on gathering data and appropriately making use of them; operating collaborative projects by creating a trustworthy environment by getting benefits socially; improving skills on creating works in various formats.

These possible and summarized outcomes pave a must for creating a different educational setting even if we do not experience COVID-19 days worldwide. These new possibilities make it evident that there is no such thing as a free lunch because the decentralized approach highlights learner autonomy and flexibility: however, it brings out some challenges as well – like the interaction between educators and learners or among learners, coordination, and monitoring of the process about whether it is conducted as required or not, and above all guidance about counseling and related services. When these challenges are even considered, the functionality of a decentralized approach in media education can be used for meeting the level of educators' demand from a traditional perspective by considering the possible or general outcomes to contribute to the whole program.

By thinking of the features of blockchain technology, a decentralized approach to be used in the educational settings reveals a need for formulating the whole transcript regarding learning contents and outcomes or learners' achievement and certifications. As is seen, blockchain technology and its possible used features can be used for managing learners' certificates (Sharples & Domingue, 2016), creating a global assessment platform and providing services for storing and managing degree information (Hoy, 2017), designing a digital badge for online learning (Skiba, 2017), and more to focus on matching all kinds of educational information with learners' needs and the new requirements to enhance learning and teaching behaviors. Apart from the evidence of learning or the process-driven (self-)evaluation, a decentralized approach can help learners find ways to fill in the knowledge gap, develop current skills, and create new opportunities to achieve goals in both educational settings industry.

Media Studies with Innovative Educational Applications Using Blockchain Technology

Innovative and disruptive technological advancements for teaching and learning practices mean integrating digital artifacts into content knowledge. According to Hobbs (2011), we as educators cannot afford to ignore the social, intellectual, and emotional functions of digital technologies in the lives of ourselves and our students. That's why thinking about such contemporary technologies brings the idea of "letting students own their credentials (Schaffnauser, 2017)" in the wake because blockchain technology is built for moving and storing knowledge and information rather than value as we focused on communication and collaboration in the previous technological patterns (Tapscott & Tapscott, 2017). As understood in previously detailed explanations, blockchain technology can transform any educational basis and bring out some alternatives to provide diffusive and lifelong learning with the help of a secure ledger where we can store the information.

A decentralized approach to media education by using blockchain technology allows us to replace generic infrastructure according to the primary and expected outcomes, develop the support capacity as in the physical educational settings, and undertake targeted development for both educators and learners to collaborate with the industry. When different course-based aspects are considered, it is fairly to say that all related departments in media education – advertising, cartoon and animation, cinema and television, communication design, digital game design, photography, public relations, and new media – consist of three different angles to focus on theoretically, technically and artistically because communication is based on creativity through the channels. It opens the ways for influencing the individuals' thoughts, perceptions, feelings, decisions, or attitudes toward or against a situation.

Regarding the theoretical basis of media education, the courses to be registered and online resources to engage are available for the learners. In addition to this, educators for guiding the learners and assessing the process are present as needed in any educational environment. By getting learners in the center of their educational approach to show and experience the functionality of blockchain technology regarding their autonomy and flexibility, learners start exploring the basic knowledge, developing technical skills, creating and capturing media productions as artifacts by themselves or with their peers in a group. Considering all types of learning processes based on different knowledge sets in media education, all data about learners, their works, formal and informal feedback they collected with the help of their participation or productions are stored to verify the data. In other words, especially for experiencing technical skills and sharing productions, using a file-sharing system on the Blockchain reduces the storage charges and enables us to check the validity of any document, including the learners' file. According to Sharples and Domingue (2016), we should layer a reputational ecosystem by allowing the learners to rate courses, online resources, and educators based on their specific learning goals.

On top of learners' flexibility about their action taking towards the content, the other collaborators, including other learners and educators, and their planning process on their learning, a decentralized approach cannot be accomplished only as educators have carried out the educational operations physically on the campuses and in the classrooms. Such an approach to media education can be somehow fully completed by adding more components into it to enable students to show their theoretical knowledge with certificates and to exhibit their technical skills and artistic productions as they have been creating an integrated portfolio to be followed by the industry representers also known as employers. By doing so, all transactions regarding a learner in media studies are expected to be visible to any interested party to rate or check.

Two perspectives on taking courses and preparing a portfolio make the learners available to different networks associated with the learners' interests and previous learning sets on blockchain technology. In addition to these, the decentralized approach based on a collection of technologies and standards establishes a process for lifelong learning because it always exists there, and the framework and network which they have created and structured continue to feed the process without stopping. In order to build up different uses for Blockchain at universities or colleges, Clark (2015) highlights "single institution to keep track for project-based education opportunities; shared repository of learning certificate for institutions; global assessment database; continuing professional education; and repository of apprenticeships and corporate learning." Apart from these advantages to implement such technology into media education, there might be some reasons to discuss drawbacks like increasing practices of pressure and censorship on media. According to Atalay (2018), the distributed structure of blockchain technology, which renders the central authority dysfunctional, makes it impossible to censor, destroy, or falsify. That's why a sustainable media production system can be possible to experience before and after getting media education completed in higher education institutions.

Conclusion

This new reality and the post-process, which we are going to experience for sure, can continue revealing different patterns in higher education and mass productions for reaching the audience. Many effective and usable alternatives have been used and available to learners as future media producers worldwide, considering their theoretical knowledge, technical skills, and artistic productions. During the COVID-19 pandemic, all educational institutions were reported access restrictions to their on-campus activities, and the educational content was planned to be provided online immediately.

Replacing on-campus educational materials and activities was not that easy for educators looking for some opportunities to teach in the classrooms and get benefits from digital technologies by ensuring a greater convergence. That's why the content and prospects of media education on different aspects are expected to rethink to make the available content and required needs in adequation with this new reality and up-to-date disruptive technologies. Such a pandemic era highlights a massive demand for further research and practical experiences to educate learners extensively. Looking after some solutions using blockchain technology in higher education is still thought of as in its infancy. The whole patterns we can focus on are that it offers a person-centric view of learning and cuts across different types of learning both in higher education and company training.

Blockchain technology, like all the innovations, is going to be integrated into media education at higher education institutions within a predictable cycle based on "learning is earning" because these kinds of disruptive technologies can foster learners' motivations to be involved in formal learning environments, according to their needs and wills. For educators and learners, adopting blockchain technology to get involved in learning activities can be robust but trustworthy. The decentralization feature of this technology enables learners in media education to plan their journey during their studies and their future profession, which allows them to experience lifelong learning because media is an ever-changing field.

References

Atlam, H. F., Alenezi, A., Alassafi, M. O., & Wills, G. (2018). Blockchain with the internet of things: Benefits, challenges, and future directions. *International Journal of Intelligent Systems and Applications, 10* (6): 40–48.

Atalay, G. E. (2018). Blokzincir teknolojisi ve gazeteciliğin geleceği. [Blockchain technology and the future of journalism]. *Stratejik ve Sosyal Araştırmalar Dergisi, [Journal of Strategic and Social Researches]*, *2* (2): 45–54.

Beck, R. (2018). Beyond bitcoin: The rise of blockchain world. *Computer, 51* (2): 54–58.

Chen, G., Xu, B., Lu, M., & Chen, N. (2018). Exploring blockchain technology and its potential applications for education. *Smart Learn. Environ.* 5, 1 (2018). https://doi.org/10.1186/ s40561-017-0050-x.

Clark, D. (2015). 10 Ways Blockchain could be used in education. *OEB Insights.* Retrieved from https://oeb-insights.com/10-waysblockchain-could-be-used-in-education/.

Galiani, S., Gertler, P., & Schargrodsky, E. (2008). School decentralization: Helping the good get better, but leaving the poor behind. *Journal of Public Economics, 92* (10–11): 2106–2120. doi:10.1016/j.jpubeco.2008.05.004.

Hobbs, R. (2011). *Digital and media literacy: Connecting culture and classroom.* Corwin Press.

Hoy, M. B. (2017). An introduction to the Blockchain and its implications for libraries and medicine. *Medical reference services quarterly, 36* (3): 273–279.

Machado, R. A., Bonan, P. R. F., Perez, D. E. D. C., & Martelli JÚnior, H. (2020). COVID-19 pandemic and the impact on dental education: discussing current and future perspectives. *Brazilian oral research, 34.*

Schaffnauser, D. (2017). Blockchain: Letting student own their credentials. *Campus Technology.* Retrieved from https://campustechnology.com/articles/ 2017/03/23/ blockchain-letting-students-own-their-credentials.aspx.

Sharples M., & Domingue J. (2016). The Blockchain and Kudos: A Distributed System for Educational Record, Reputation and Reward. In Verbert, K.,

Sharples, M., & Klobučar, T. (Eds.), *Adaptive and Adaptable Learning. EC-TEL 2016. Lecture Notes in Computer Science*, vol 9891. Springer, Cham. https://doi.org/10.1007/978-3-319-45153-4_48.

Skiba, D. J. (2017). The potential of blockchain in education and health care. *Nursing Education Perspectives, 38* (4): 220–221. doi:10.1097/01.nep.0000000000000190.

Tapscott, D., & Tapscott, A. (2017). The blockchain revolution and higher education. *Educause Review, 52* (2): 11–24.

Tschorsch, F., & Scheuermann, B. (2016). Bitcoin and Beyond: A Technical Survey on Decentralized Digital Currencies. *IEEE Communications Surveys & Tutorials, 18* (3): 2084–2123. doi:10.1109/comst.2016.2535718.

Wilson, S., Liber, O., Griffiths, D. & Johnson, M. (2007). Preparing for disruption: Developing institutional capability for decentralized education technologies. In C. Montgomerie & J. Seale (Eds.), *Proceedings of ED-MEDIA 2007 – World Conference on Educational Multimedia, Hypermedia & Telecommunications* (pp. 1386–1395). Vancouver, Canada: Association for the Advancement of Computing in Education (AACE). Retrieved December 24, 2020, from https://www.learntechlib.org/primary/p/25557/.

Nisa Yıldırım and *Nilay Ulusoy*

Winners of the Catastrophe: How Streaming Services Proved their Sovereignty during the Pandemic of 21st Century?

Abstract: In the first decade of the 21st century, the way of consumption of films and television shows has changed with the launch of streaming services, firstly Amazon Prime Video, followed by Hulu and Netflix soon after. The introduction of tablet computers in 2010 had also contributed to the popularity of streaming services that allow individual use of their customizable archives. When the COVID-19 pandemic hit the world at the beginning of 2020, public spaces were abandoned globally, impacting the cinema industry. The release dates of already made films had to be delayed, and new projects were canceled despite causing enormous losses for production companies. On the other hand, as the people had to amuse themselves in their houses for months, the value of the corporate audiovisual content that brings the outside to inside unsurprisingly increased. Audiences who did not intend to pay for streaming services until this year had to change their minds. It was announced that Netflix Company, the industry leader, had doubled its net profit even in the first quarter of the year due to a lockdown. Even rearrangements had to be made to reduce the bandwidth due to heavy traffic created by its subscribers. Before the unpredictable pandemic, streaming services were assumed to be threats to the cinema and television industry. And in the post-pandemic era, it can be claimed that these services, which took advantage of their medium, will continue to be advantageous members of the entertainment industry. In this article, we will discuss the pandemic effect on the rise of global streaming platforms. We will also take Turkey as a specific case to make visible the sovereignty of these platforms and the competitive analysis in local and international streaming services in pandemic COVID-19.

Keywords: Streaming Services, Cinema, Television series, Pandemic

Introduction

At the beginning of the 2000s, the internet was considered an utterly distinct medium against other communication technologies such as television, and it used to be defined by the term 'new media' assumed to be a potential threat for the future of television. However, the clear distinction between these two media had begun to get blurred in 2010 with the launch of the 'streaming-only service' of Netflix Company which was established as a DVD rental company in 1997. Introduced with the monthly price of only $7.99, the number of Netflix subscribers had increased 63 percent in its first year, and as a result of its content archive involving a significant number of films and television shows, the service was welcomed as a kind of television which allows it's the user to reach the content via any screen having internet connection (Lotz, 2018, p. 114). It can be claimed that the evolution of television – the primary medium of mass entertainment – is mainly based on the personalization offered by internet technology. As the content was released from the schedules of traditional broadcasting, the control was transferred from the sender to the user, which is interpreted as 'democratizing' characteristics of online communication (Gentikow, 2010, p. 147). The family medium of the last century had been abandoned by a group of audience who prefer to shape their viewing experiences according to their personal choices both for time and content. Besides personal computers, mobile phones had also become television screens with the rise of streaming services, and in a brief period, the computer technology market has gained a new player with the introduction of tablet devices by Apple Company in 2010. Many other electronic companies did not lose time and begun to release their own tablet devices to compete with Apple's iPads in the same year. According to Lotz (2018), the year 2010 can be admitted as the beginning of a new era for the entertainment industry underlines (p. 114). As the tablet technology had reached enough popularity in a short time, Netflix had offered its application to be downloaded on both tablets, mobile phones, and intelligent -TVs allowing its subscribers to customize their profiles according to their preferences. The convenience of the application also contributed to the popularity of streamed content consumption and resulted in new arguments about the 'end of television as we know it. According to Wolff (2015), tablet technology's first aim was to engage a new tool to the audience in the living room as a new version of television or game console. However, the consumers, mostly the members of a young generation, had begun to prefer buying tablets instead of personal computers due to their affordable prices, and the new player had also impacted the electronic industry on the countenance of computer sales. These flat screens with no-physical keyboards had also become one of the primary devices for content consumption of young audiences due to the mobility and flexibility they offer and let these audience groups leave the living room and traditional television.

The launch of streaming services impacted the television industry, and the cinema industry had been met a new competitor treating the potential ticket sales all over the world. As Netflix had become globally available in 2016, the services' libraries, including vast amounts of films, had been appreciated by cinema fans, which resulted in the decrease of the demand for going to movie theaters. However, the experience of going to the movie theater has still been admitted as a ritual, and it is not possible to claim that streaming services had treated the cinema industry as they did for the television industry.

In 2020, when the first decade of streaming services had ended, the pandemic of COVID-19 hit the world and resulted in a global crisis for all business markets. The entertainment industry undoubtedly had been one of the industries impacted by the 'stay home' calls. Movie theaters had been shut down; release dates of the blockbuster movies like the twenty-fifth James Bond movie: *No Time to Die* or Disney's *Black Widow* was delayed; even projects for new movies and new seasons of television like Netflix' *Stranger Things, The Witcher, Grace, and Frankie,* and *Russian Dolls*, Hulu's *The Handmaid's Tale,* Prime Video's *Carnival Row,* or remake of HBO Max' *Gossip Girl* were postponed. There had been some exceptions for blockbusters like *Tenet,* which was released after being delayed three times, but the box-office revenue could not be satisfying as it was predicted. On the other hand, major international festivals were canceled around the world or made via online screenings with a limited number of guests. In April, it was announced that some movies released on streaming platforms would be eligible for the 2021 Oscars because of the COVID-19 pandemic. In the press call, the Academy president David Rubin and CEO Dawn Hudson had made an explanation as: "Our commitment to that is unchanged and unwavering. Nonetheless, the historically tragic COVID-19 pandemic necessitates this temporary exception to our awards eligibility rules" (Alexander, 2020).

As the future of movie theatres began to be discussed in the shadow of global crisis, the company of Warner Bros. made a declaration in December and announced a surprising decision about releasing its new movies, including *Dune* and *The Matrix 4* simultaneously on HBO Max and movie theaters in 2021 (Zeitchik, 2020). Even though an optimistic prediction about possible healing can be made for the future of movie theater in the short run, after the end of the pandemic, however, it can be claimed that movie theaters as space will require arrangements in the middle run to be transformed with renovations and gain new functions to attract the audience with new options.

Supported by the Medium

Even though the cost of the COVID-19 pandemic had been significant for the entertainment industry, it is possible to say that a new era had begun for streaming services due to the advantage of the medium they use. As a result of lockdowns worldwide, people had to amuse themselves in their homes and these services became lifesavers for most of them with their huge archives offering the newest contents and the older ones. Streaming services give a chance to 'old media texts' to meet the audience once again (Derek, 2018, p. 105). Many famous movies and television shows from former decades were discovered by people who did not know them or the younger audience. An offering of these 'old media text' with paying license fees can also be interpreted as a chance for streaming services compared to a new project requiring colossal production costs. Both with the old and new ones, streaming services had managed to make people get busy for hours when they had to 'stay home.'

In the April of 2020, it was announced that Netflix had 15.8 million new subscribers in the first quarter of the year, which was more than the expected number, and reached 182 million subscribers in total worldwide (Alexander, 2020). The second quarter of the year had brought another 10 million new subscribers to the company (Kafka, 2020). According to the data from the U.S.A., "more than 25 percent of consumers had added at least one streaming service during the lockdown in the first half of the year. Hulu saw the biggest growth (25 % to 33 %), followed by Amazon Prime Video (38 % to 44 %). Netflix and Disney both saw a three-percentage point growth—from 60 % to 63 % for Netflix and 29 % to 32 %" (Balderston, 2020).

Before the world hit by the COVID-19 virus, it was known that "Netflix's future is dependent on the take up of high-speed internet by the global middle classes; in the long term, this is where the growth in subscriber numbers will come from. For this reason, Netflix expends considerable energy lobbying for investment in internet infrastructure" (Lobato, 2019, p. 59). The rise of demand on online consumption of audiovisual content had resulted in heavy traffic on networks; Netflix and YouTube had declared that they would reduce the streaming quality in March, followed by Prime Video (Gold, 2020).

In terms of traditional TV, the impact of the COVID-19 pandemic had been observed mainly on the news bulletins instead of fiction content. Hearing about the updates of pandemic nationwide and worldwide became a part of audiences' daily lives all over the world. Besides, comments of health specialists were also followed by larger populations, even the ones who had abandoned watching broadcast television for a while ago. However, the demand to reach the pandemic information could not help traditional television lose its popularity against video-on-demand services. The table below shows the comparison of the "estimated revenue change of TV & video products in 2020 compared to 2019 (in percent)" (Buchholz, 2020).

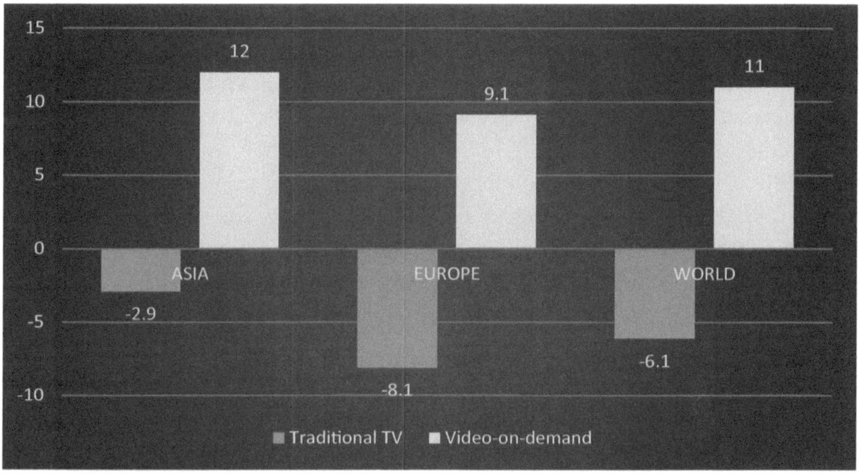

Fig. 5.1: Estimated Revenue Change of TV & Video Productions in 2020 compared to 2019 (in percent). Source: Buchholz, K. (2020). Pandemic gives streaming another boost. (Online report). *Statista*. [Accessed on 27 Apr, 2021]. Retrieved from https://www.statista.com/chart/22968/estimated-annual-revenue-change-of-tv-video-products-selected-countries-regions/.

Even though streaming services have become the game-changer in the entertainment industry lately, the outcomes of their way of content consumption have been criticized for choice fatigue and time famine. In the new era, an audience who does not have to be exposed to the flow of traditional television began to gain more control over the content. Nevertheless, it is not possible to claim, and they are entirely independent in their choices. With the use of recommendation systems, the audience's preferences have been shaped by each service's unique algorithms, which determines the way of their perception of the medium (Uriccho, 2010, p. 37). According to Ellis (2020), it is clear that perception of time had been transformed, and "time itself has become a commodity" (p. 170). Today's audience has more options than ever; however, choosing an infinite amount of content makes them also confused more than ever. People of the modern world feel an obligation to make the best choice, even for entertainment, not to face a time loss which probably would turn into a stressful experience. When the flow of traditional television based on a pre-determined schedule is considered, it can be claimed that its audience had to faceless stressful processes while amusing themselves despite having less agency on their choices (idem, p. 171). As the complaints on 'endless scroll' experiences rise, Netflix announced an upcoming TV channel of scheduled programming in November. The tests of the TV channel planned to be made in France at first (Sharf, 2020). Even though it is too early to predict the results of TV channel attempts yet, it might be succeeded in reaching the target audience who suffer from choice fatigue of online content consumption.

Besides, the tiring effect of endless scroll, users have to make choices among different paid streaming services. If a user prefers to pay for Amazon Prime, he/she has to renounce the huge animation archive of Disney +, or a Netflix user has to decide to pay for the second subscription fee if he/she would like to reach HBO series in HBO Max. At the beginning of 2020, a new home entertainment device called Dabby was introduced in the U.S.A., which offers convenience by combining all paid streaming services in itself and functioning as an "AI-based search engine" for television (Rayome, 2020). However, with its $99 monthly fee, Dabby is far from being a solution for those who do not want to pay high prices to different archives.

The main factor preventing the rise of services is pirated platforms. The data company which has collected the most extensive dataset on digital piracy MUSO reveals significant increases "for film and TV piracy since the lock-down was enforced in March 2020" (muso.com). Despite all precautions of streaming platforms, it is not possible to prevent the consumption of pirated content. "However, it may not be exactly the kind of piracy we know from the past – illegal DivX downloads, torrents vs." (bsgroup.eu). Illegal streaming is a growing industry with big profit margins and its pirate ecosystem. For the pirates targeting the U.S. market, generating $1 billion in annual revenues in the U.S. with profit margins ranging between 56 % to 85 %. The hackers steal subscribers' personal and financial data when installing badware within their free apps (Abdollah, 2020). Pirated content is mainly preferred by the user for being priceless or less expensive and offers more options. Streaming platforms still have limited archives, which depend on the license periods of each content. "No matter how advanced anti-piracy technologies become, completely eradicating the phenomenon is rather an unlikely story. This situation will continue until operators re-bundle their content and services to make them more cost-effective to the consumer" (bsgroup.eu).

Netflix and Transnationalism

At the beginning of the millennium's third decade, Netflix still differs from its competitors like Hulu, Disney+, HBO Max for being the only global streaming service. According to Lobato (2019), it can be defined as a "global television" when the change in the way of digital distribution introduced by the company is considered (p. 23). As internet technology released television from satellite broadcasting and let it go beyond national borders, a globalized industry was born with the rise of online video-on-demand services (Starks, 2013, p. 223). When the history of television is evaluated, it can be seen that cultural production had been impacted and partly shaped by American television, which still protects its dominance in culture industries. One of the main reasons for this dominance can be explained by the cultural heterogeneity of the US domestic market, which made its televisual content embraced by audiences of other countries (Gripsrud, 2010, p. 25). On the other hand, exported contents of American television had impacted the way of narrating local productions worldwide for decades (Curtin, 2009, p. 9).

After being embraced by the audience, the company of Netflix had declared their decision on creating their original content. In March 2011, a political drama named *House of Cards* was announced to be released in 2013. Before *House of Cards*, a Norway-based comedy-crime drama called *Lilyhammer* was released in 2012. With the contribution of *Orange Is the New Black* and the fifth season of *Arrested Development*, Netflix had managed to increase its subscribers by more than thirty million at the end of 2013 (Lotz, 2014, p. 120).

2016 had been the year Netflix became globally available -in 130 countries- and created original content in different countries and languages (Russell, 2016). After becoming an international broadcaster, the company had built its characteristics like releasing content on the same day worldwide (Jenner, 2018, p. 223). These characteristics showed that the company follows a 'grammar of transnationalism' for its original contents (idem, p. 226). According to Broe (2019), "the burst of the dramatic musical phrase accompanied by the logo before each episode of a series" makes the company possible to be defined as a 'super narrator' (p. 174). Functioning as a super narrator also explains the rising popularity of the phrase 'watching Netflix' to define a new viewing experience. The streaming service's growing popularity has given the rise of Netflix-specific slang. Hence, "*Netflix and chill* were the first of much Netflix-related slang. 'Netflix cheating' is watching an episode of your favorite series ahead of your partner. 'Netflastinate' is when you use Netflix to procrastinate" (McCluskey, 2017, np.). The streaming service has become one of the most significant phenomena which change our daily habits and language.

Streaming Services in Turkey

Television has always been a popular form of entertainment in Turkey. However, it is estimated that the growth of SVOD platforms will reach this 30 % over the next four years if we take into account that most of the young people between the ages of 15 and 24 watch television on their tablets, the average age of watching television are also proportional to the level of education (rtuk.gov.tr, 2018). Turkish internet users spend an average of 1 hour and 39 minutes on social media every day. This makes Turkey the ninth country that is more committed to internet networks. It has also been reported that Turks, especially the younger and urbanized generations, are turning to internet media instead of traditional media, keen on alternative programs more in line with their aspirations. The growth of SVOD platforms based on viewer preference continues in a competitive environment to the detriment of traditional televisions. Streaming platforms that are profoundly influencing the television industry are also changing consumer behavior. According to the report by Statista (2020), the overall performance of SVOD platforms with a growth rate of 8.7 % was $ 32.7 billion in 2019. SVOD platforms in Turkey are ranked 19th globally, with an annual return of $ 272 million (statista.com).

The research made by KPMG International on digital broadcasting platforms and consumer satisfaction examined the impact of the pandemic in Turkey. Although participants prefer paid media due to their content quality and ad-free content, free platforms that stand out with their content diversity are also chosen. Although the increase in time spent at home due to the pandemic creates growth opportunities for companies providing online services, retaining users gained during this period can be complex. With the entry of national and global service providers into the market, competition will gain a new dimension. Another detail in the research is the differentiation of device preferences in quarantine, while pre-quarantine television use is more common. Laptop usage increased from 30 % before quarantining to 39 % in quarantine due to the increase in the time spent collectively at home and the tendency of family members to different contents. Television usage stayed at 37 %. The rate of those who spend 6–8 hours a day on digital broadcast platforms increased to 50 % during the quarantine period (KPMG, 2020).

In the first month of 2016, the audience in Turkey had met the first local streaming services, BluTV, besides the arrival of Netflix TR, and in December, the second local streaming service puhutv was introduced. BluTV had raised the first local content produced for online platforms at the beginning of 2017, and the crime drama named *Masum* (*The Innocent*) had been welcomed by the audience and contributed to the numbers of BluTV's subscribers. A few months later, puhutv had released its first original content: *Fi,* which was adapted from a best seller Turkish novel. On the other hand, Netflix TR waited until the end of 2018 before releasing its first Turkish original series *Hakan: Muhafız* (*The Protector*).

Before the COVID-19 pandemic hit the world, streaming services had managed to create their audience by releasing creatively narrated original content that differs from traditional television channels. However, the impact of lockdown also contributed to the demand for these services in Turkey, as it did worldwide. BluTV had added a new crime drama Alef to its library in April, followed by *Yarım Kalan Aşklar* in September and *Saygı* (*Respect*) in October. On the other hand, Netflix TR had released a teen drama named *Aşk 101* (*Love 101*) in April while releasing the second season of *Atiye* (*The Gift*) in September, and the drama called *Bir Başkadır* (*Ethos*) in November. According to the data shared by the content director of BluTV in April, the service had doubled its subscribers after Mar 12 when the first COVID-19 case was approved in Turkey (Ekonomist, 2020). Executives of puhutv, an advertisement-based video-on-demand service, had declared that its users had been doubled in the third week of March (Özöğretmen, 2020). On the other hand, Amazon Prime Video became available in Turkey during the pandemic and was welcomed by the local audience with its affordable price, which is lower than Netflix TR and BluTV. At the end of the year, a competitive attempt came from BluTV, and it was announced that the service would be open-access in the first weekend of December (İçözü, 2020). As a result of over-use caused by the high demand of users, the service was blocked (T24, 2020). Simultaneously, it was revealed that 'free' watching was only available for the first episodes of the series, which was interpreted as a promotional act rather than a favor to the local audience who have to cope with the pandemic. By the beginning of 2021, the audience in Turkey had met two new streaming platforms, which develop a new competition field in Turkey. Exxen was founded by Acun Ilıcalı, who also owns a mainstream channel TV8 and promoted with great media support and began to service with its 9.90 TL monthly price as the third local streaming service of country by offering its first original series like *Şeref Bey* (*Mr. Şeref*), *Hükümsüz* (*Void*) and *Vahşi Şeyler* (*Wild Things*) besides the bonus parts of famous reality-competition *Survivor* (Gazete Vatan, 2020). Different from Exxen, the other new competitor, Gain was introduced as a free 'online content platform' and adopted a unique way by releasing only 'short-length shows like *Oyunlar Holding* (*Conglomeration of Games*), and *Bir Daha Söyle* (*Sing Once More*) or series like *On Bin Adım* (*10 Thousand Step*) and *Terapist* (*Therapist*). The platform that prefers to work with social media celebrities in most of its programs differs from other streaming platforms by allowing its users to watch its whole library only via mobile phones with its application (Koloğlu, 2020).

Although in Turkey streaming platforms were seen closer to the television broadcasting, in terms of cinema, streaming services had also undertaken new roles to distribute movies. Soon after the 'popcorn crisis' which had revealed between primary producers and distributors at the end of 2018 and resulted in regulation for law on cinema films to balance the profit-sharing, the country's leading production company BKM (Beşiktaş Cultural Center), made an unexpected move, and released "*Organize İşler: Sazan Sarmalı*" (*Magic Carpet Ride 2*) on the Netflix two weeks after its theatrical release (Hepdinçler & Tetik, 2020, p. 110). This joint release of the film, which ran for ten weeks with 3.537,429 viewers, as the third most-viewed film in cinemas in Turkey in 2019 on Netflix sparked controversy. The film had already been seen by 2,579,230 box office viewers so far and was a case study in the debate over the future of cinemas in Turkey. In fact, the size of the new television formats and their compatibility with new technologies, and the high picture and sound quality showed that films could be watched much more at home (Takvim, 2019).

During the lockdown, BluTV made a breakthrough in film distribution. In April 2020, during the lockdown, BluTV had announced their arrangement with 'Başka Sinema' which is known as the distributor of independent arthouse movies in Turkey, and new Turkish arthouse movies that could not be released in movie theaters due to pandemic would be available via BluTV by tickets sold online for each film (Ekmekçi, 2020). Netflix had also contributed to the distribution of new Turkish movies like *9 Kere Leyla* (*Leyla Forever*) and *Azizler* (*Saints*) which were released in December. The first releases of the Turkish films on streaming platforms continue to create discussions in Turkey. The debate, therefore, remains open on both the impact of technological innovations and the regulation of these effects on a market that has become more competitive in the Middle East.

When we return to the cinema, according to a recent survey in mid-January 2020, conducted online by DORinsight, the number of spectators watching TV series and movies on online platforms increased in 2020 according to this research conducted around a sample of 5,285 people, representative of different social categories in Turkey. 55 % of participants still prefer to watch new films in theaters, while 45 % prefer online platforms. 54 % of participants believe that online platforms do not will end the habit of watching movies in movie theaters, while 46 % are skeptical about the future of movie theaters (Üçhisarlı, 2020).

Conclusion

Over the last twenty years, there has been a significant change in how films are watched, music is listened to, and television programs are delivered. "The hype around digital film distribution and TV series broadcasting is now at fever pitch, with promises of a brave new world of instant delivery, unfettered consumer choice and new revenue streams for filmmakers" (Lobato, 2014). COVID-19 pandemic made a significant contribution to the adaption of audience and industry to streaming services. In this period, streaming technologies allowed the audience to view television content in long-form, and binge-watching became a regular viewing habit during the lockdown. These technologies also challenged "the temporality of televisual content and different industrial models of distribution. The pandemic demand and supply gap have resulted in different textual programming, and audience reception practices meant to control the market" (Burroughs, 2018). In March 2020, most film production companies decided the best way to have a break to complete their projects; thus, audiences reanimate even the old television series and await new content impatiently. Staying platforms and traditional TV channels used digital media to amuse their audience by 'repeating.' On the other hand, it is not possible to claim that the industry is the only determiner for the fate of movie theatres. There is no inherent reason, other than the pandemic situation, to do first releases of films on streaming platforms. As a communicative, economic, social, and cultural force, Brutal competition between global and local streaming platforms develops its own identity after the COVID-19 pandemic period.

References

Abdollah, T. (2020). Streaming piracy is now a billion-dollar industry. *Dot.* [Accessed on Dec 29, 2020]. Retrieved from https://dot.la/streaming-pirated-content-2647032701.html.

Alexander, J. (2020). Netflix adds 15 million subscribers as people stream more than ever, but warns about the tough road ahead. *The Verge.* [Accessed on Nov 04, 2020]. Retrieved from https://www.theverge.com/2020/4/21/21229587/netflix-earnings-coronavirus-pandemic-streaming-entertainment.

Alexander, J. (2020). Next year's Oscars will allow streaming-only movies to qualify, but with heavy restrictions. *The Verge.* [Accessed on Nov 04, 2020]. Retrieved from https://www.theverge.com/2020/4/28/21240422/oscars-streaming-theaters-rules-2021-netflix-digital-release-academy.

Balderston, M. (2020). More than 25% of consumers added at least one streaming service during the pandemic. *TV Technology.* [Accessed on Oct 22, 2020].

Retrieved from https://www.tvtechnology.com/news/more-than-25-of-consumers-added-at-least-one-streaming-service-during-pandemic.

Broe, D. (2019). *Birth of the binge: Serial TV and the end of leisure*. Detroit, Michigan: Wayne State University Press.

BS Group. (2020). How streaming video providers fight against piracy. [Accessed on Jan 10, 2021]. Retrieved from https://www.bsgroup.eu/how-streaming-video-providers-fight-against-piracy/.

Burroughs, B. (2018). House of Netflix: Streaming media and digital lore. *Popular Communication, 17* (2): 1–17.

Curtin, M. (2009). Matrix media. In G. Turner & J. Tay (Eds.), *Television studies after TV: Understanding television in the post-broadcast era*. London: Routledge.

Derek, K. (2018). Old-time TV's last stand?. In D. Johnson (Ed.), *From networks to Netflix: A guide to changing channels* (pp. 335–336). London: Routledge.

Ekmekçi, N. (2020). Başka sinema, gerçekten sinema salonlarına destek olacak mı?. [Will 'Başka Sinema' really support theatres]. *Novi Cinema*. [Accessed on Nov 25, 2020]. Retrieved from https://www.novicinema.com/yazi/baska-sinema-gercekten-sinemasalonlarina-destek-olacak-mi/.

Ekonomist. (2020). Dijital platformlara iyice yüklendik!. [We overused digital platforms]. [Accessed on Dec 05, 2020]. Retrieved from https://www.ekonomist.com.tr/teknoloji/dijital-platformlara-iyice-yuklendik.html.

Ellis, J. (2000). *Seeing things: In the age of uncertainty*. London: I. B. Tauris Publishers.

Gazete Vatan. (2021). Exxen platform yayına başladı. [The platform, Exxen has stated to broadcast]. [Accessed on Jan 05, 2021]. Retrieved from http://www.gazetevatan.com/exxen- platformu-yayina-basladi-exxen-tv-uyelik-girisi-nasil-yapi-1364239-gundem/.

Gentikow, B. (2010). Television use in new media environments. In J. Gripsrud (Ed.), *Relocating television: Television in the digital context* (pp. 141–156). London: Routledge.

Gold, H. (2020). Netflix and YouTube are slowing down in Europe to keep the internet from breaking. *CNN*. [Accessed on Nov 06, 2020]. Retrieved from https://edition.cnn.com/2020/03/19/tech/netflix-internet-overload-eu/index.html.

Gripsrud, J. (2010). In the digital public sphere. In J. Gripsrud (Ed.), *Relocating television: Television in the digital context* (pp. 3–26). London: Routledge.

Hepdinçler, T. & Tetik, T. (2020). A market on the rise and "the fall": The distribution in the Turkish film industry. In T. Hepdinçler & H. K. Suher (Eds.), *Creative Industries in Turkey* (pp. 99–116). Bern: Peter Lang.

İçözü, T. (2020). BluTV platformunu bu hafta sonu herkese ücretsiz olarak açıyor. [The platform, BluTV is going to provide free access for everyone at the weekend]. *Webrazzi.* [Accessed on Dec 19, 2020]. Retrieved from https://webrazzi.com/2020/12/02/blutv-bu-hafta-sonu-iceriklerini-herkese-ucretsiz-aciyor/.

Jenner, M. (2018). *Netflix and the re-invention of television.* London: Palgrave Macmillan.

Kafka, P. (2020). The pandemic has been great for Netflix. *VOX.* [Accessed on Nov 22, 2020]. Retrieved from https://www.vox.com/recode/2020/7/16/21327451/netflix-covid-earnings-subscribers-q2.

Koloğlu, S. (2020). Yeni İçerik Platformu Geliyor: Gain. [A new content provider is coming: Gain]. *Milliyet.* [Accessed on Jan 05, 2021]. Retrieved from https://www.milliyet.com.tr/cadde/sina-kologlu/yeni-icerik-platformu-geliyor-gain-6384155.

KPMG. (2020). Türkiye'de dijital yayın platformları ve pandeminin etkileri. [Digital streaming services and the influence of the pandemic]. [Accessed on Jan 1, 2021]. Retrieved from https://home.kpmg/tr/tr/home/gorusler/2020/09/turkiyede-dijital-yayin-platformlari-pandeminin-etkileri.html.

Lobato, R. (2019). *Netflix nations.* New York: NYU Press.

Lobato, R. (2014). The politics of digital distribution: Exclusionary structures in online cinema, *Studies in Australasian Cinema,* 3:2, 167–178.

Lotz, A. D. (2014). *The television will be revolutionized.* New York: NYU Press.

Lotz, A. D. (2018). *We now disrupt this broadcast: How cable transformed television and the internet revolutionized it all.* Cambridge, Massachusetts: The MIT Press.

McCluskey, B. (2017). 9 Netflix slang terms besides 'Netflix and Chill' every binge watcher needs to know. *Business Insider.* [Accessed on Dec 30, 2020]. Retrieved from https://www. businessinsider.com/netflix-slang-and-their-meanings-2017–3.

Muso. Film & TV piracy surge during COVID-19 lockdown. [Accessed on Dec 29, 2020]. Retrieved from https://www.muso.com/magazine/film-tv-piracy-surge-during-covid-19-lockdown.

Özöğretmen, T. (2020). Corono günlerinde neyi nereden izliyoruz?. [What we stream from which platform in the Corona days?]. *MediaCat.* [Accessed on Dec 08, 2020]. Retrieved from https://mediacat.com/corona-gunlerinde-neyi-nereden-izliyoruz/.

Rayome, A. D. (2020). Dabby just might be the cure for your streaming subscription fatigue. *C|Net*. [Accessed on Dec 17, 2020]. Retrieved from https://www.cnet.com/news/dabby-might-be-cure-for-streaming-subscription-fatigue/.

RTÜK. (2018). Televizyon izleme eğilimleri araştırması. [TV watching tendency research]. [Accessed on Dec 18, 2020]. Retrieved from https://www.rtuk.gov.tr/assets/Icerik/AltSiteler/televizyon-izleme-egilimleri-arastirmasi-20060053.pdf.

Russell, J. (2016). Netflix launches in 130 new countries, including India but not China. *Techrunch*. [Accessed on Now 28, 2020]. Retrieved from https://techcrunch.com/2016/01/06/netflix-finally-goes-global/.

Sharf, Z. (2020). Can't decide what to stream? Netflix is testing a TV channel of scheduled programming. *IndieWire*. [Accessed on Dec 02, 2020]. Retrieved from https://www.indiewire.com/2020/11/netflix-tests-linear-tv-channel-viewing-1234597287/.

Starks, M. (2013). *The digital television revolution: Origins to outcomes*. London: Palgrave Macmillan.

Statista. (2020). Video on demand in Turkey. [Accessed on Oct 18, 2020]. Retrieved from https://www.statista.com/outlook/201/113/video-on-demand/turkey.

T24. (2020). Hafta sonu kısıtlamasında ücretsiz olan BluTv çöktü. [BluTV's free access collapsed during the weekend lockdown]. [Accessed on Jan 25, 2021]. Retrieved from https://t24.com.tr/haber/hafta-sonu-kisitlamasinda-ucretsiz-olan-blu-tv-coktu.918796.

Takvim. (2020). BKM'den 'Netflix' açıklaması! Organize İşler 2 Sazan Sarmalı neden Netflix'te?. [A statement from BKM: Why *Money Trap* is in Netflix?]. [Accessed on Dec 20, 2020]. Retrieved from https://www.takvim.com.tr/magazin/2019/02/17/bkmden-netflix-aciklamasi-organize-isler-2-sazan-sarmali-neden-netflixte.

Üçhisarlı, C. (2020). Tüketici Netflix kullanıyor ama vizyon filmini sinemada istiyor. *Pazarlamasyon*. [The consumer uses Netflix, but upcoming films are wanted to be released in theaters]. [Accessed on Dec 15, 2020]. Retrieved from https://pazarlamasyon.com/tuketici-netflix-kullaniyor-ama-vizyon-filmini-sinemada-istiyor/.

Uriccho, W. (2010). TV as a time machine. In J. Gripsrud (Ed.), *Relocating television: Television in the digital context* (pp. 27–41). London: Routledge.

Wolff, M. (2015). *Television is the new television: The unexpected triumph of old media in the digital age*. New York: Penguin Press.

Zeitchik S. (2020). In major break from tradition, Warner Bros. moves to debut all its 2021 movies simultaneously on HBO Max and in theaters. *Washington Post*. [Accessed on Now 03, 2020]. Retrieved from https://www.washingtonpost.com/business/2020/12/03/warner-media-movies-hbo/.

Savaş Arslan

Research, Storytelling, and Filmmaking during the Pandemic

Abstract: In the early days of the pandemic, I was working on the post-production of my film, *a Sigmund Weinberg docu-commentary,* and thus had a firsthand experience of the difficulties of filmmaking during shutdowns and curfews. However, since I also released the film and did q&a sessions online, I also had a chance to observe how the pandemic changed the way people consume films and interact with filmmakers, too. While this article touches on such issues, I also present some observations about the interaction between academic research and filmic storytelling. Research involves the posing of a question, data collection, and an attempt to answer the question. Hero-driven storytelling, on the other hand, presents a journey and a gift and a change in the hero during this process. In doing this film, while my research involved multiple aspects of a quest to unearth the story of a semi-forgotten filmmaker, I opted to conceal this journey. Instead, I attempted to bring forward how the inception of cinema brought a change in terms of visual and performative culture at the turn of the twentieth century and in what ways we can recuperate this in contemporary filmmaking while refraining from the traps of anachronism and the fallacies of memory.

Keywords: Research, Storytelling, and Filmmaking during the Pandemic

In a recent article, "Virtual Cinema," David Sterritt notes that due to the changes incurred by the pandemic, "the post-pandemic moviegoing patterns will be significantly different from the paradigms that previously held sway… [and] going to a movie theater will be considered a mildly special event" (2020, p. 507). In one way or another, film theaters and festivals found themselves in a situation to adapt to these new conditions, and streaming films became a habitual practice among filmgoers. Thanks to this change, various new platforms and services appeared, and many art-house or festival films also are made available. Celebrating this change, Sterritt notes, "I hope this temporary alternative becomes a lasting supplement to traditional theatrical moviegoing" (ibidem). It is still unclear whether such an alternative would change our habits, and we will see this in the coming years. But the pandemic also presented a major challenge for me in terms of completing a film project.

I completed the script and the recording of the voiceover for my film, *a Sigmund Weinberg docu-commentary*, before the start of the pandemic in late

2019 and early 2020. But in March 2020, I found myself in a situation to do almost all of the film's post-production online. However, this film project did not start in late 2019. I recorded the first interviews in 2015, then a few others in 2018, and finally the last interview in 2020. But my research on the first Istanbulite filmmaker Sigmund Weinberg, who was also an entrepreneur, photographer, filmmaker, film theater owner, phonograph record maker, and the representative of multiple European companies, dates to 2008. And it is still ongoing because there are many more details about his life and multiple films of him to discover. In this article, I hope to discuss how I conducted a research on the history of the late Ottoman Empire through the life story of Sigmund Weinberg, how I attempted to narrate this by using a combination of a filmic narrative inspired by traditional storytelling conventions, and how such a film is completed and exhibited online.

A simple definition of research, according to Wikipedia, "involves the collection, organization, and analysis of information to increase our understanding of a topic or issue. At a general level, research has three steps: 1. Pose a question. 2. Collect data to answer the question. 3. Present an answer to the question." Faced with such a definition, I looked back onto what I did so far in my research on Weinberg and realized that I simply did not "pose a question." So, then, should a research project feature, as a critical element, a question posed by the researcher? Should it have a thesis, an argument, and/or a hypothesis? Instead, my research on Weinberg started as a "quest" in 2008 when I found myself "positioned in a quest," once again as defined by Wikipedia, as "a journey toward a specific mission or a goal." The quest and the ensuing journey I found myself in was initially about a closure or the realization of a goal. In narratives, this is a simple plot device in which you have a "hero" embarking upon a journey, and at the end of the journey, the hero is changed, experienced, and at a higher level. There are many different blueprints for the hero's journey, and this is one of the basic conventions that is taught to wannabe scriptwriters in Hollywood or other conventional popular cinemas. As Winston Wheeler Dixon puts it, "today, nearly everyone has tried their hand at making a 'film' of one sort or another, but often these projects are parodies of other films, or genre pieces, informed by the history of film itself, existing within the boundaries of conventional narrative, rather than coming from a place entirely outside the dominant culture" (2020, p. 548). Thus, a quest with a closure would put this project and the film itself into this conventional form. Instead, I wanted to present the research in disguise; in my quest, I tried to conceal the journey and attempted to be a storyteller traveling between different forms of narration while staying hidden under a cloak.

But before coming to the point of writing a script and creating a visually moving version of it, my duty was research. The word "re-search" itself means etymologically "to go about seeking" or "searching once again" (of something that happened). In the end, this is all about an "inquiry," being in-a-query. The Latin origin of all these words, "quest," "question," and "query," *quaerere*, brings back a simple act: "to ask." Then, the journey starts when one asks oneself a question as simple as, "Who is Sigmund Weinberg?" This, then, leads one to inquire and to an eventual journey after a quest, which we can alternatively call research in academia. But the academic research demands an answer, a resolution, a cathartic end to please the analytic and rational mind in the least compassionate way. But when turning your research into a film, another thing is necessary. This other thing is not reasonable, nor distanced or staying outside as in empirical research, and not at all objective. Instead, it is subjective in the utmost sense featuring spurts of one's own identity, emotions, and performance – hence communication!

The words "common," "community," and "communication" are all about sharing (*co-*) a duty, task, or gift (*munus*). Then, in this act of sharing, of communing or communicating, my research had the utmost importance for me. This is why I wanted to write a script that attempted to converse or talking together. In this regard, the discursive strength of shadow plays comes to the fore. Karagöz and Hacivat are not only some jokesters, but they are also the epitomes of conversating, quick-witted talkers expressing and interchanging their thoughts and feelings profoundly. I also wanted this feeling to be delivered by the voiceover narrator (dubbed as the "voice outside" in the film), who, in close proximity to classical Yeşilçam films and who, unlike conventional and mainstream Western filmmaking, does not refrain from addressing the audience directly, speaking and asking questions to the spectators, and thus demanding answers from them, as if they are communing. In this regard, this way my attempt to break the fourth wall, to dismantle the imaginary distance between the filmic world and the actual one. This was also an attempt to be subjective at the expense of the objectivity of scientific research presented in the proper form of an authoritative documentary that tells us the facts.

And this subjective quality belongs to a profession, that of a storyteller, which found its death in the face of modernity. Talking about Nikolai Leskov as a storyteller whose profession is coming to an end, Walter Benjamin underlines that storytelling has "the ability to exchange experiences" (1985, p. 83). This exchange and thus communication at the core of the storyteller's work has a longstanding history. Peasants are rooted, they know the tales and traditions, and they stay at home and make an honest living. In contrast, the trading seamen have stories to tell from afar. "If peasants and seamen were past masters of storytelling, the artisan class was its university. In it was combined the lore of faraway places, such as a much-traveled man brings home, with the lore of the past, as it best reveals itself to natives of a place" (idem, p. 85). With the rise of the bourgeoisie and hence the novel, the realist aesthetic and the observing gaze of the novelist – say, like Dickens or Balzac, describing the facts in detail (much like the empirical researcher) – heralded the end of an old profession against the new. But this was done at the expense of the experience itself, as something shared, which one can only realize in his/her imagination when reading a novel in isolation.

Instead, the storyteller is like a "counsel" and in the act of counseling, "the communicability of experience" is at stake. "After all, counsel is less an answer to a question than a proposal concerning the continuation of a story which is just unfolding. To seek this counsel, one would first have to be able to tell the story" (idem, p. 86). For Benjamin (1985), the counsel as a part of real-life presents the epic side of truth, wisdom. With modernity, this communicative experience is dying out with narratives losing their connection to the realm of living speech and hence its beauty. The novel, as a form that is tied to a book and as presenting the facts, is the first departure from the story. A similar thing could be said for the news stories. They rely on the value of information and its newness. They present us the now in an instant, without losing any time. This also explains our contemporary situation enmeshed with the instantaneity of virtual and social media. A similar point about both the novel and news stories may be raised in terms of the documentary genre in cinema. Documentary as a form relies on facts and information, like in the novel's reliance on the book, fastened in the form of a moving picture. This is why, I, in an unnecessarily pretentious way, decided to name the film as a "docu-commentary," instead of a documentary, because the commentary is not only a remark or criticism but also a talk that is shared, like gossip. The word's etymology invites a shared (*co-*) mind, heart, or disposition (*mentis*). The film features documents, the end products of research, that are delivered in an attempt to be a part of a shared discussion, counseling, and communication.

In an article titled, "Research as Storytelling / Storytelling as Research," Patrick J. Lewis (2011) notes: "If story is central to human existence and understanding why, in the research world, is there not more storytelling, particularly in the social sciences?" (p. 506). Unlike information, "[a] story is different. It does not expend itself. It preserves and concentrates its strength and is capable of releasing it even after a long time" (idem, p. 90). In this, Benjamin underlines that both the naturalness of the process and the storyteller's integration into the storyteller's experience are essential in making the story have a place in the memory of and to be repeated by the listener. But does research have such potential? "Can a researcher become a storyteller? Can storytelling become research? Is it enough just to share the story?" (idem, p. 506). For Lewis, the social sciences also started focusing on narrative research, which has the potential to give the marginalized voice and to explain our lives. He also quotes Petra Munro Hendry's emphasis on narrative research to highlight faith than the interpretation with a trust in the storyteller and storytelling. In this sense, according to Benjamin (1985);

> *[t]he storytelling that thrives for a long time in the milieu of work – the rural, the maritime, and the urban – is itself an artisan form of communication, as it were. It does not aim to convey the pure essence of the thing, like information or a report. It sinks the thing into the life of the storyteller, in order to bring it out of him again. Thus, traces of storyteller cling to the story the way the handprints of the potter cling to the clay vessel* (pp. 91–92).

Thus, the story not only gives a chance to narrate the life itself but also opens up a space for a relationship between the self and the other, the storyteller and the listener/reader/viewer. But such a space requires the faith of both sides. With the decline of the idea of eternity (having its source in death) in the modern era, the art of storytelling in terms of the communicability of experience has also started declining. The authority at the source of the story for Benjamin is similar to when all these images go in front of your eyes as you are dying.

Thus, to produce meaning through a story, memory is at work – a recollection of the experiences is shared through stories. Kierkegaard (1983) said that "repetition and recollection are the same movements, except in opposite directions for what is recollected has been, is repeated backward, whereas genuine repetition is recollected forward." It is through genuine repetition, storytelling, that humans narrate ways of knowing and being" (Lewis, 2011, p. 505). This is perhaps what a researcher of history does: take the past and narrate it in novel ways. The same historical epoch or event may be narrated in many different ways by different researchers. Yet, we also do have blueprints for the historian's work, such as Daniel Little's (2007) list of the historian's tasks:

- What happened? "historians are interested in providing conceptualizations and factual descriptions of events and circumstances in the past."
- Why did this event occur? "to provide an explanation of the event or pattern."
- How did this outcome come to pass? "the pragmatic interest of the historian's account derives from the antecedent unlikelihood of the event in question."
- Interpretations of actions, meanings, and intentions: "piecing together the human meanings and intentions that underlie a given complex series of historical actions."
- Archival data: "discovering and making sense of the archival information that exists about a given event or time in the past."

"In short, historians conceptualize, describe, contextualize, explain, and interpret events and circumstances of the past" (Little, 2007). Such a definition or an understanding of the historian's work is indeed a precept for the rules of constructing a narrative of the past based on a set of rules which eventually is expected to be convincing. Yet, there are multiple competing discourses, and the researcher's version belongs to a particular discursive field. It may reproduce the dominant ideology/discourse or present alternative versions by disrupting the dominant narrative. In Little's sense, if then, one may speak of research as the historian's work (be it narrational or not), how would one place the "work" itself? What is the "work" of the historian? Is this not of the two senses of Heideggerian *techne*: the making, the production, as part of the artisan's work, and the making/doing of the artist, which puts us closer to bringing forth or revealing (the truth?). Why does a historian make history? What is the urge behind researching, piecing together a myriad of things to reconstruct the past in our (temporal and spatial) presence?

Hegel (1975) describes history in his *Lectures on the Philosophy of World History* as follows: "History is the process whereby the spirit discovers itself and its own concept" (p. 62). In this sense, the objective history should communicate to and with the subjective consciousness and/or spirit. In this regard, Hegel's recounting of Napoleon's success is illustrative. This was not only a world-historical event, but it also affected Hegel to a great degree, and he placed Napoleon's presence concerning the spiritual aspect of history writing. Through such an experience of the real itself, Hegel introduced the rationale of history, to how knowledge, facts, and reality are contingent upon our given spatio-temporal existence. Though there are some metaphysical and idealistic overtones in this Hegelian rendering, and while it would have been corrected by, say, a materialist like Max Horkheimer, such an understanding of the reality of the "past" is also tied to isolating what one may call as the "facts." In Horkheimer's (1995) sense, the (objective) reality is eventually bound to our particular historical existence: "human activity corresponding to the given social period" (p. 190). Even in this presence, there are competing narratives of the reconstruction of the past. Indeed, both views underline the contingency of the facts and reality, which should be highlighted when a historian is doing her/his work.

What was Sigmund Weinberg's reality in the late Ottoman Empire? How was the human activity in the capital of the empire? As it is well-known and repeated, the Ottoman Empire was a multi-lingual, multi-cultural, and multi-confessional environment. Unlike the demarcations of the contemporary world defined by an ethnic, linguistic, and thus national unity, around half of the population in the late Ottoman era İstanbul was non-Muslim, who were predominantly Greeks,

Armenians, and the Jewish. The city was also demarcated into two significant areas, the predominantly Muslim old İstanbul in the walls and the predominantly non-Muslim another side of the Golden Horn, Pera / Beyoğlu (lit. across). Thus, crossing the Galata Bridge also marked a cultural shift. The arrival of cinema in İstanbul played out in such a backdrop. While the first private screening of films was done at the Imperial Palace, the first public show was done in Pera, where Sigmund Weinberg also had his apartment and stores. It was Weinberg who opened the "first film theater," *Amphithéâtre: Le Cinémathéâtre Pathé* at Les Petits-Champs (Tepebaşı), which made regular film exhibitions in İstanbul on January 30, 1908. Apart from operating Cinéma Orientaux for a while, Weinberg also opened in 1915 the very first proper and luxurious film theater in İstanbul, intended only to showing films, Ciné-Palace (aka. the Weinberg Theater, the Film Theater with Mirrors, and later as Chic/Şık Sineması).

But before such film theaters, it was also Weinberg who started showing films at different theaters or open-air venues from 1897 onwards, immediately after the first public film screening in late 1896 by H. Delavellée, very likely on behalf of the Lumiere representative Louis Janin. Apart from the screenings he did at Concordia Theater and the Taksim Municipal Garden, Weinberg also brought cinema to the Muslim quarters of İstanbul, to Fevziye Kıraathanesi in Fatih, where he used a Karagöz screen to show films, thus connecting the traditional shadow theater with this new visual art. This was especially important in the film because Sigmund Weinberg was not only a witness to the late Ottoman and early Republican process of modernization, he also was recording it visually, through his photographs and films, and hence he turned into an Istanbulite visual chronicler. When one looks at the pre-Yeşilçam Republican era cinema in Turkey until the 1950s, both silent and early sound fiction films were predominantly done by theater actors and directors trained or practicing a more Western-style theater. However, the influx of popular Yeşilçam filmmaking partially departed from these earlier conventions and presented a combination of traditional narrative and performative conventions with the modern vocabulary of filmmaking. A backdrop to this was perhaps this late Ottoman early cinematic connection between Karagöz and Weinberg.

In the film, I wanted to underline and transform this earlier convention of storytelling into shadow plays, combining a conversation through jokes and misunderstandings while in passim touching on touchy sociopolitical issues by using a 2D and stop-motion animation. Naturally, I initially contacted professional Karagöz masters and planned to film their show. However, this did not go through because it was also challenging to film a live Karagöz show and translate its "spirit" or "subjective consciousness" into the filmic language.

Instead, I bought two original handmade and leather Karagöz and Hacivat figures and photographed these. Then, the two editors of the film animated these. For instance, since contemporary audiences start reading from the left-hand side, I switched the places of Karagöz and Hacivat. While in traditional shadow plays, Karagöz is often seen on the right-hand side of the curtain (think of the Ottoman-Arabic script in which you also start reading from the right), he is placed on the left of the screen in the film. Furthermore, I underlined this shift from the traditional storytelling to the modern one through Karagöz-Hacivat dialogues in which Karagöz feels the threat of Sigmund Weinberg's films to take over their profession. Additionally, though there are no guidelines given to the film's audience, the film is divided into four parts of a traditional shadow play: 1. Prologue (*mukaddime*, 00.00–00.03), the opening about the name Weinberg; 2. Dialogue (*muhavere*, 00.04–00.20), the discussion on the first filmmakers (Weinberg, Manakis, and Uzkınay); 3. The main plot (*fasıl*, 00.21–00.85), about who Weinberg was, his family, and Weinberg's stores, photographs, film theaters, and films; and 4. Ending (*bitiş*, 00.86–00.92), the goodbyes by Karagöz, Hacivat, and the voiceover artist followed by Lydia Erdal. This was also an attempt to tell a contemporary rendering of an era by using a traditional narrative and performative partition, which is lost at the expense of a conventional novelistic or cinematic form of storytelling relying upon the hero's journey, the main plotline, and a final climax before the resolution.

In other words, this late Ottoman and Early Republican era marked the death of a form of storytelling. Though I, myself, was briefly exposed to the popularity of Karagöz and some other traditional plays in the Western Anatolian countryside in the late 1970s, the influx of first cinema and then television put an end to these traditional conventions. But this transformation took place in İstanbul during Weinberg's lifetime. Now, it is a simple fact – Karagöz is gone for good. And the past is past; it is gone in an irretrievable manner. It came to an end before the researcher's interest in it. This is why a researcher resorts to language and invites it to come to the rescue. It is the language that gives the researcher the ability to narrate what is recollected from the bygone. "'Language is the house of being' (Heidegger), we reside in that home, and in that house, we possess all that is necessary to engage with the world—the memory of Being, that is, our stories" (Lewis, 2011, p. 507). And our stories re-collect a foreclosed past that has departed from our spatio-temporal presence. Then, the storyteller acknowledges what is lost. Even so that "[d]eath is the sanction of everything that the storyteller can tell. He has borrowed his authority from death. In other words, it is natural history to which his stories refer back" (Benjamin, 1985, p. 94).

Walter Benjamin exemplifies this through a story by Johann Peter Hebel, who talks about an older woman who waited almost all her life for her husband to return. Hebel then chronicles a long list of what had happened during that time of earthquakes, wars, political changes, etc. "Never has a storyteller embedded his report deeper in natural history than Hebel manages to do in this chronology" (idem, p. 95). And the chronicle presents a chance to be close to the epic: "The chronicler is the historyteller" (ibidem). Unlike the historians who tell the happenings in the course of the world, the Middle Age chroniclers base "their historical tales on a divine plane of salvation" (idem, p. 96). "In the storyteller, the chronicler is preserved in changed form, secularized, as it were" (ibidem). And Sigmund Weinberg was the visual chronicler of this transformation – from the divine plane of salvation into a secularized presence.

Sigmund Weinberg, as a photographer and filmmaker, was the visual chronicler of the late Ottoman Empire. He photographed or filmed the crucial events of the era. Weinberg was like Hebel, who chronicled a long list of what happened in the meantime. He was there to take photographs or make films of multiple fires in İstanbul, the Young Turk revolution, the visits of Prince Wilhelm of the Prussian Empire and King Peter I of Serbia, the bullfight in İstanbul, the migration of Muslim Turks from the Balkans, the Balkan Wars, the First World War, the occupied İstanbul, and the arrival of Claude Farrère to İstanbul before he went to İzmit to meet Mustafa Kemal Atatürk. Weinberg also worked as the official photographer and filmmaker for both Sultan Abdülhamid II and Sultan Mehmed V Reşad. Weinberg's *Selamlık*, an "edited" film featuring several shots and pans, is called by Ludwin Brauner as the "first purely Turkish film," since it featured Sultan Abdülhamid II's Friday prayer visit to the Yıldız Mosque (2). Weinberg also filmed Sultan Mehmed V Reşad's visit to the Balkans in 1911 and immediately after the visit showed his film in Salonica. Later, Weinberg was operational in the foundation of the Ottoman Army's initial photography and film operations, and he was also responsible for the first incomplete fiction film projects in Turkey. Thus, in the fold of the chronicler Hebel, Sigmund Weinberg, as a chronicler, was the "historyteller."

But as a researcher and storyteller, I wanted to deliver this in the film and give Sigmund Weinberg his dues. In 1995, Burçak Evren wrote a book and declared in the title of his book that Sigmund Weinberg was "the man who brought cinema to Turkey." However, this catchy title is not anymore valid since some other researchers found that it was not Weinberg who did the first public screening in İstanbul. But such a title invites the reader's memory to be at play. For Benjamin (1985), the memory comes into play if the unaffected listener wants to reproduce the story. "For if the record kept by memory –historiography– constitutes the creative matrix of the various epic forms (as great prose is the creative matrix of the various metrical forms), its oldest form, the epic, by virtue of being a kind of common denominator includes the story and the novel" (p. 97). The storyteller starts with a "web which all stories together form in the end. One ties on to the next, as the great storytellers, particularly the Oriental ones, have always readily shown" (idem, p. 98). Then, what I was after was the story of Sigmund Weinberg, not perhaps as the man who brought cinema to Turkey, but as the man who made cinema in Turkey for the first time.

In this respect, Benjamin (1985) underlines how a novelist whose work is "dedicated to *one* hero, *one* odyssey, *one* battle; the second, to *many* diffuse occurrences" (p. 98), different from the storyteller. Perhaps it is possible to note a similar thing concerning the filmmaker's work as a storyteller attempting to stay away from conventional filmic narrations, be them fiction or documentary films. "Seen in this way, the storyteller joins the ranks of the teachers…He has counsel…for many…For it is granted to him to reach back to a whole lifetime" (p. 109). This, for Benjamin, is a life that combines one's own experience with that of the others by relating and by consuming oneself in the story. This is why in the work of the storyteller, there are episodes in which one's own experiences and memories are displayed, at times, as outbursts. And this was also the case for me through multiple filmic and popular cultural references or binding, says Giovanni Scognamillo to Metin Demirhan (both of whom we lost). Thus, in a way, I encountered myself.

And this encounter also included many others, first the voluntary team of the people who made this film possible, when there were curfews when they were confined in their apartments because of the pandemic. The editing of the film took three months, during when two editors worked at their apartments. Then, I had to do multiple updates to the original script, and thus some additional voiceover recordings were done at home by the film's narrator. In this process, I kept researching visual materials online to use in the film, which features almost 1100 still images and over 200 video bits. After this, I worked with a professional composer for the film's original music. This was followed by the first research on proper sound effects to add to the film and then, the audio mixing of the film is done by yet another professional. Finally, color grading is done by another professional. Once the film was complete, there were no film festivals or exhibition venues available, which led me to premiere the film as part of İstanbul Modern Museum's online film series before showing the film also at the Turkish Cinema Research (TSA) branch of BISAV and the University of Bucharest Turkish Language and Literature Department's seminar series. After each of these three screenings, I did an online question and answer session. As the pandemic continued well into the summer and since there would not be further venues to show the film, I decided to make the film available to members of the International Society for the Study of Early Cinema, Domitor, as well as with many academics working in the field of early cinema and the history and cultures of the Balkans and the Middle East.

But then what? Did memory come into play? Is there anyone who wants to reproduce the story? In our time, we know quite well that "nearly everyone has tried their hand at making a 'film' of one sort or another, but often these projects are parodies of other films, or genre pieces, informed by the history of film itself, existing within the boundaries of conventional narrative, rather than coming from a place entirely outside the dominant culture" (Dixon, p. 548). But can one stay away from that? Is the only way to go rebellious and attempt to break all the existing conventions by producing experimental work? Winston Wheeler Dixon narrates a story about how 1960s New York filmmakers did experimental works which had the potential to stay away from the conventional filmic narratives and then notes, "in a sense, [we have] lost an essential link to our authentic selves, before the technological tidal wave of the twenty-first-century digital detritus washed over us, elevating the trivial to the center of our collective attention, while simultaneously leaving these works – and others equally valuable – behind" (p. 550). However, especially during the pandemic, this digital detritus has come to the rescue. We have observed once again how much we need content, films, television series, news stories, and other social media content. While we were stranded in our own domestic insularity, the stories connected us to the outside world. Thus, at an elementary level, not only do we need stories but also storytellers. If the research, then, has the capacity to turn into a form of storytelling, especially in the case of historical research, then why would not one use that capacity? Furthermore, if one also has a chance to take a written story and turn it into an audiovisual one, why not? Sigmund Weinberg was lived at a moment of significant transformations, from the Empire to the Republic, from the traditional to the modern, but more importantly, from the domination of a narration relying on the spoken or written word to the audiovisual one. This is what I hoped to underline in the film hoping for memory to come into play.

References

Benjamin, W. (1985). The storyteller: Reflections on the works of Nikolai Leskov. In H. Arendt (Ed.), *Illuminations* (pp. 83–109). New York: Schocken Books.

Brauner, W. (1908). Die aussichten der kinoindustrie in der Türkei. [The outlook of cinema industry in Turkey]. *Der Kinematograph*, 92: 1–3.

Dixon, W. W. (2020). Something out of nothing: Or, the essence of cinema. *Quarterly Review of Film and Video*, 6 (37): 543–550.

Evren, B. (1995). *Sigmund Weinberg: Türkiye'ye sinemayı getiren adam*. [*Sigmund Weinberg: The man who brought cinema in Turkey*]. İstanbul: Milliyet Yayınları.

Hegel, G. W. F. (1975). *Lectures on the philosophy of world history*. (H. B. Nisbet, Trans.). Cambridge: Cambridge UP.

Horkheimer, M. (1995). *Between philosophy and science*. (G. F. Hunter, Trans). Cambridge, MA: MIT Press.

Lewis, P. J. (2011). Storytelling as research / Research as storytelling. *Qualitative Inquiry*, *17* (6): 505–510.

Little, D. (2007). Philosophy of history. In *Stanford encyclopedia of philosophy*. Retrieved from online https://plato.stanford.edu/entries/history.

Sterritt, D. (2020). Virtual cinema. *Quarterly Review of Film and Video*, 6 (37): 505–507.

Tuna Tetik

Desktop Cinema as a New Aesthetic Style in the Post-Pandemic Era: Watching the Movie through Protagonist's Computer Screen

Abstract: Cinema has evolved with many technological advances, from the Lumiere Brothers' *Arrival of a Train at La Ciotat* (1895) to the Russo Brothers' *Avengers: Endgame* (2019). Since the inception of cinema, each new technology, such as sound, color, green box, 3-D, CGI, motion capture, virtual reality, and IMAX, has affected both productions and exhibitions of movies. The relation of cinema to technological improvements helps us define cinema's nature as an evolvable art form. When moviegoers were waiting to experience Hollywood's latest big-budget spectacle titled *Tenet* (Christopher Nolan, 2020) on the expanded screens, the world witnessed a pandemic virus that spread worldwide. COVID-19 has changed our way of life. Many new technologies have become our necessities. Undoubtfully, cinema has been affected by COVID-19. The productions of forthcoming movies and all exhibitions have been canceled or postponed to an unknown date. In particular, cinema saloons were closed due to the high possibility of COVID-19 contagion. However, several filmmakers have developed new storytelling ways in the post-pandemic era. Rob Savage's *Host* (2020) was produced during the lockdown that reveals six friends' Zoom meetings. *Host*'s storytelling could be accepted as the latest installments of a particular film language that the audience can see what happens in the movie through the main characters' desktops or mobile screens. With this regard, Aneesh Chaganty's *Searching* (2018), Stephen Susco's *Unfriended: Dark Web* (2018), and Levan Gabriadze's *Unfriended* (2014) could be seen as the ancestor examples of *Host* (2020), which shares similar visual aesthetics with them. I prefer to define this type of film language and narrative aesthetic as "desktop cinema." This chapter investigates how *desktop cinema* could be a new way of storytelling. Specifically, the study focuses on the relation of *desktop cinema*'s narrative aesthetics to diegetic and non-diegetic elements of movies. For this purpose, these movies are analyzed to reveal the function of applications, programs, and webcams in the film language. In this way, *desktop cinema*'s visual and narrative aesthetics are described. Hereby, a broad understanding of cinema's new storytelling way in the post-pandemic era could be gained.

Keywords: Cinema, Aesthetic, Storytelling, Pandemic, COVID-19

Introduction

Cinema as an art form has evolved with many technological advances since 1895. One hundred and twenty-five years after Lumiere Brothers' first screenings at the Grand Cafe in Paris (Loiperdinger & Elzer, 2004), the world has experienced a global pandemic that has changed many crucial things in our lives. According to the World Health Organization, the novel Coronavirus 2019, known as COVID-19, was first recognized and documented in Wuhan, China, on December 31, 2019 (Bruns, Kraguljac, & Bruns, 2020). Significantly, it is proved that COVID-19 is transmitted via the person-to-person contact that people who are within 6 feet of each other (idem, p. 2). During 2020, many different countries have performed several and separate policies against COVID-19. Once for all, many new vocabularies and concepts have entered many lives all around the world. The Oxford English Dictionary has annually selected a particular word to tell a year by it. However, OED has decided to choose sixteen words to disclose 2020 with the tagline of 'Words of an Unprecedented Year' (BBC News, 2020). According to the Oxford Languages report, the words of 2020 are Bushfire, Impeachment, Acquittal, Coronavirus, COVID-19, Lockdown, Social distance, Reopening, Black Lives Matter, Cancel Culture, BIPOC, Mail-In, Belarusian, Moonshot, Superspreader, and Net-Zero. Even though each word in the list is not relevant to COVID-19, as it is seen, COVID-19 and related terms constitute the majority.

COVID-19 has affected many fields and industries during 2020. Unsurprisingly, the cinema industry has been seriously affected by COVID-19. Several productions of forthcoming movies and their exhibitions have been canceled or postponed to an unknown date. Christopher Nolan's latest movie, *Tenet* (2020), has been theatrically released in many countries in August 2020, including United Kingdom, France, Germany, and the United Arab Emirates. After that, the movie was domestically released in the States in September. However, the movie failed the COVID-19 at the worldwide box office. According to Box Office Mojo, whereas the last two movies of Christopher Nolan, *Interstellar*[1] (2014) and *Dunkirk*[2], achieved earn over $1.2 billion at the worldwide box-office, *Tenet*[3], as the savior of the cinema industry, earned only $362 million globally. Nicole Sperling and Brooks Barnes at New York Times (2020) mention that "movie theaters returned and the audiences didn't." According to them, *Tenet*'s release showed that "how much trouble the [cinema] industry is in" (ibidem). Besides, many prestigious and international film festivals have been postponed or organized online, such as 73. Cannes Film Festival and 71. Berlin Film Festival. After the failure of *Tenet* at the box office, Warner Bros. announced its hybrid release strategy for big-budget movies that all movies will be theatrically released and be ready to stream on HBO Max simultaneously. These forthcoming movies are *The Little Things* (John Lee Hancock, 2021), *Judas and the Black Messiah* (Shaka King, 2021), *Tom & Jerry* (Tim Story, 2021), *The Many Saints of Newark* (Alan Taylor, 2021), *Reminiscence* (Lisa Joy, 2021), *Godzilla vs. Kong* (Adam Wingard, 2021), *The Conjuring: The Devil Made Me Do It* (Michael Chaves, 2021), *In the Heights* (Jon M. Chu, 2021), *Space Jam: A New Legacy* (Malcolm D. Lee, 2021), *The Suicide Squad* (James Gunn, 2021), *Dune* (Denis Villenueve, 2021), *King Richard* (Reinaldo Marcus Green, 2021), *The Matrix 4* (Lana Wachowski, 2021), *Mortal Kombat* (Simon McQuoid, 2021), *Malignant* (James Wan, 2021), *Those Who Wish Me Dead* (Taylor Sheridan, 2021), and *Cry Macho* (Clint Eastwood, 2021). The hybrid release strategy of Warner Bros. and HBO Max demonstrates the 2020s would be the competition era of the global and significant subscription video-on-demand services, including Netflix, Hulu, Amazon Prime Video, Apple, Disney+, and HBO Max.

While the cinema industry has experienced such a global crisis during our post-pandemic year, a British movie called *Host* (Rob Savage, 2020) was released on a minor SVODs titled Shudder. *Host* tells six friends and a medium's necromancy session on Zoom during the lockdown. The audience watches the movie through the protagonist's Zoom screen. Al Horner (2020) at BBC Culture states that "Rob Savage's lockdown chiller became one of the year's most talked-about movies. Will its success spark a wave of films about the coronavirus crisis in 2021 and beyond?" However, the categorization of *Host* is quite confusing. Whereas Horner defined *Host* as the Zoom horror, -like a new horror subgenre-several film blogs and Wikipedia called *Host* a found footage horror film. Many scholars and critics describe *The Blair Witch Project* (Eduardo Sánchez & Daniel Myrick, 1999) as a new filmmaking method and a new aesthetic style called the found footage filmmaking (Roscoe; 2000, McDowell, 2001; Telotte, 2001; and many others). Even though the roots of the found footage filmmaking have been based on many years before the release of *The Blair Witch Project*, the movie made this method more popular and well-known worldwide. Besides, *TBWP* used this categorization as the promotion strategy of the movie. However, *Host* has many differences from *TBWP* regarding the production, the post-production, and the exhibition. After the release of *Host,* Netflix released an anthology called *Social Distance* (Hilary Weisman Graham, 2020), which consists of eight episodes. *Social Distance* (2020) shows the connection of a group of people during the Black Lives Matter protests and George Floyd's death in COVID-19 quarantine. Therefore, the audience could watch the anthology through only mobile devices and laptop screens of characters. The creator of the anthology, Hilary Weisman Graham, tells the story via recordings, online meetings, and video calls. Nevertheless, this type of filmmaking and the viewing experience are not related to *TBWP*. *Social Distance*'s filmmaking and the viewing experience could be categorized within the same categorization of *Host*. As seen, there is confusion and ambivalence in defining and labeling these kinds of productions in which all visual materials are combined with the characters' computer, laptop, and mobile devices' screens. The production of these kinds of movies or series and the viewing experience is unique but unusual. With this regard, the audience can watch the movie within the frame of digital screens of characters. I decide to identify these kinds of productions by the categorization as the "desktop cinema" with my own words. COVID-19 demonstrates to us the possibility of new examples of the *desktop cinema*, even the pandemic ends. Because when we investigate other instances of the *desktop cinema* in the last decade, we can find several examples before the pandemic happened. Aneesh Chaganty's *Searching* (2018), Stephen Susco's *Unfriended: Dark Web* (2018), and Levan Gabriadze's *Unfriended* (2014) could be mentioned in this sense. These movies have shared similar visual aesthetics and filmmaking method with *Host*. This chapter examines a new type of visual aesthetic called the *desktop cinema* and how it could be a new way of storytelling. Specifically, the study focuses on the *desktop cinema*'s aesthetics to diegetic and non-diegetic elements of *Host*, *Searching*, *Unfriended: Dark Web*, and *Unfriended*. For this purpose, these selected movies' content is analyzed to reveal the function of applications, programs, digital screens, and webcams in the film language. In this way, the *desktop cinema*'s visual and narrative aesthetics are described. Moreover, a broad understanding of cinema's new storytelling way in the post-pandemic era could be gained.

The Features and the Particularities of the *Desktop Cinema* through the Analysis of *Host*, *Searching*, *Unfriended: Dark Web*, and *Unfriended*

This subchapter traces the visual and narrative aesthetics of selected movies regarding the particularities of the *desktop cinema*. For this purpose, several digital screens, video calls, and Zoom online meeting medium are analyzed to reveal *Host*'s relation to the *desktop cinema*. *Host* displays an online meeting of six friends during COVID-19 quarantine and their online necromancy session. The movie begins with the main character called Haley, who is the main protagonist of *Host*. The audience could learn this information from the Zoom meeting screen in which Haley is the host. In this sense, the protagonist becomes the host in the particular vocabulary of the *desktop cinema*. Therefore, *Host* could be defined as Hayley's meeting on Zoom. Haley invites her friends, including

Jemma, Caroline, Emma, Radina, and Teddy. The names of participants are revealed in the Zoom screen's name taglines. During the meeting, Haley, Emma, Caroline, Seylan, and Radina use their laptops' internal webcams when Teddy participates in the meeting via his cell phone camera. Importantly, Jemma uses both her internal laptop webcam and cell phone camera. That is why Jemma is the only character who leaves her home during the meeting to save her friends from a paranormal entity. Six friends invite a medium to contact with a spirit during their Zoom meeting. *Host* demonstrates many scenes in which a demonic entity terrorizes both the host and the participants. In the fifty-four-minute meeting, the audience watches this online necromancy session and its consequences through Haley's Zoom meeting screen. Thus, viewing experience and visual aesthetics are quite different from traditional storytelling ways in cinema.

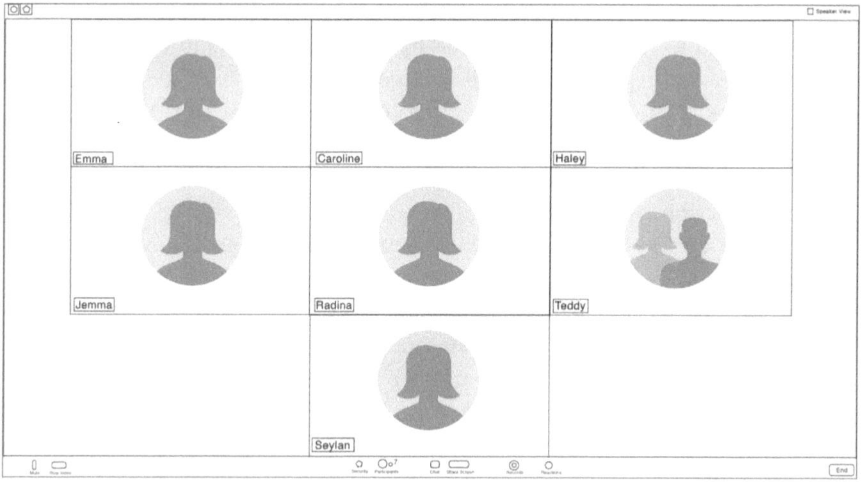

Fig. 7.1: Zoom Meeting Screen as the Main Frame of Host.

Characters of the movie -or the host and participants of the meeting- use the Zoom meeting platform's features. For instance, Emma uses several filters that make her appearance funny via online face applications. However, this application becomes an online prop to increase the tension in the movie. Likewise, Caroline uses the Zoom platform's loop application, which shows the user's action in an endless loop. Nevertheless, this application serves as a narrative device to increase the tension similar to Emma's face app. In general, *Host* tells the story of a group of friends possessed by an unfriendly entity via a technological and online platform.

In the horror genre, a technological device is often used as a possessed tool, such as *One Missed Call* (Takashi Miike, 2004), *Ring* (Hideo Nakata, 1998), and *Poltergeist* (Tobe Hooper, 1984). However, *Host* differentiates itself from them with the help of its visual and narrative aesthetics. *Host* uses the horror genre conventions that the movie is related to the possession via a technological channel. Nonetheless, different productions from various genres could use similar visual aesthetics and narrative devices to *Host*. At this moment, formalistic labeling and another type of categorization are needed to define these productions. Therefore, as the categorization of these kinds of productions, the *desktop cinema* becomes essential to approach them. Because another movie that is analyzed through the particularities of the *desktop cinema*, *Searching*, is not in the same genre as *Host*. In this way, we can call the *desktop cinema* is a new visual aesthetic and a narrative language rather than a genre. Thomas Sobchack (1975) prefers to define the genre that "bound by a strict set of conventions, tacitly agreed upon by filmmaker and audience, the genre film provides the experience of an ordered world and is an essentially classical structure predicated upon principles of the Classical world view in general" (p. 96). Tom Ryall (1975) describes the genre as "patterns/forms/styles/structures which transcend individual art products, and which supervise both their construction by artist and their reading by audiences" (p. 28). Besides, Rick Altman (1999) analyzes the film genre through four concepts: A blueprint, a structure, a label, and a contract (p. 14). Film genres are living ideas that are affected by social formations and industrial trends. However, we can categorize these selected productions under the umbrella of a specific filmmaking method and a unique viewing experience. Therefore, this categorization is different from traditional generic approaches.

Searching is a thriller movie in which the plot is centered on a missing person case. The movie tells the story of a father, David Kim, who tries to find his missing daughter, Pamela Nam Kim. David investigates her daughter's computer to find a clue about her location. Significantly, *Searching* differentiates itself from other mainstream thriller movies or, more specifically, missing person movies by its narrative and visual aesthetics. The movie consists of only digital screen views and mobile camera footage. Therefore, the framing is limited to digital display units. In the beginning sequence of the movie, Pamela uses her laptop in which the configuration is Windows XP. Then, Pam and David's computers are changed from Microsoft to MacOs software. This transformation demonstrates the passing of years. Unlike *Host*, *Searching* contains many visuals, digital screens and documents, websites, applications, and web pages.

Tab. 7.1: Web Pages, Programs, Software, Applications, Social Media, and Types of Cameras in Searching.

<table>
<tr><th>Web Pages</th><th>Programs, Software, Applications</th><th>Social Media</th><th>Types of Cameras</th></tr>
<tr><td>Gmail</td><td>Skype</td><td>Facebook</td><td>Internal Notebook Webcams</td></tr>
<tr><td>Google Searches</td><td>Windows Calendar</td><td>Videolog</td><td>Cell Phone Cameras</td></tr>
<tr><td>www.abc7news.com</td><td>Imessage</td><td>Instagram</td><td>Public Surveillance Cameras</td></tr>
<tr><td>www.evercreekhighschool.org</td><td>Facetime</td><td>Twitter</td><td>Hidden Security Cameras</td></tr>
<tr><td>Yahoo</td><td>AppleSync</td><td>CrowdChase</td><td rowspan="9">Interrogation Cameras</td></tr>
<tr><td>www.namus.gov
“National Missing and Unidentified Person System”</td><td>Cross Messenger</td><td rowspan="8">YouCast</td></tr>
<tr><td>YouTube</td><td>Apple Dialer</td></tr>
<tr><td>Google Maps</td><td>Vehicle Navigation</td></tr>
<tr><td>www.backofamerica.com</td><td>Spotify</td></tr>
<tr><td>http://reddit.com/r/margotkimmystery</td><td>Excel</td></tr>
<tr><td>MemorialOne “Remember Together”</td><td rowspan="2">Apple Screensaver</td></tr>
<tr><td>www.covervatory.upaloalto.org/apply/u/98m844n348i7</td></tr>
</table>

The audience can only watch the movie through digital camera displays of characters. In the movie, five different camera types are used to reveal characters, including laptops' internal webcams, cell phone cameras, hidden security cameras, and interrogation cameras. In *Searching*, the main character's desktop becomes the stage in which investigation is conducted via webpages, programs, software, applications, and social media services. Thus, the frame includes information both for the audience and the characters. Remarkably, the desktop is surrounded by many visuals. Each asset in the desktop serves to the investigation by the main character. David searches for his missing daughter's friends via social media accounts, including Facebook, Instagram, Twitter, Videolog, CrowdChase, and YouCast. He collects data on several websites such as Reddit, Namus, and Bank of America. These assets are contained in the movie as virtual, informative props. Notably, Spotify has a unique usage in the movie. Soundtracks are non-diegetic sounds that characters cannot hear them. However, when a particular character uses Spotify, the music becomes the movie's soundtrack as an extra-diegetic sound. As seen, *Searching* is a convenient and prominent example to demonstrate the particularities and conventions of the *desktop cinema*.

Unfriended is an American thriller movie that tells the story of five teenagers in an online meeting session that an uninvited and supernatural guest terrorizes. The movie was directed by Leo Gabriadze in 2014. The estimated production budget of *Unfriended* is $1 million. According to data in Box Office Mojo[4], the movie's worldwide box-office gross is over $62 million. The movie was premiered at Fantasia Film Festival, 2014 under its original title '*Cybernatural*.' Peter Debruge at Variety mentions *Cybernatural* (*Unfriended*) as an innovative narrative that could be considered as 'found footage 2.0.' As I stated before, there is an ambivalence to categorize these kinds of movies. In the Wikipedia[5] page of *Unfriended*, the movie is labeled an 'American video-meeting footage supernatural horror film.' Amazon PrimeVideo puts the movie between the genres; suspense and horror. In the PrimeVideo catalog[6], several keywords, including found footage, social media, Blair Witch, high school, horror movie, cyberbullying, and the entire movie, are associated with the terms in the movie reviews are mentioned. Rotten Tomatoes Critics Consensus mentions the movie that "Unfriended subverts found-footage horror clichés to deliver a surprisingly scary entry in the teen slasher genre with a technological twist." The movie contains several traditional horror genre conventions in which the horrifying events unfold entirely on the main characters' computer screen. A paranormal and unfriended entity, a victim of cyberbullying, tries to get her revenge on a group of teenagers responsible for her suicide. Each asset takes place on the main character's, Blaire Lily, desktop screen. Skype is used as a meeting medium between characters. When five teenagers start an online meeting, an anonymous guest participates in the meeting and terrorizes them. Likewise *Searching*, many websites, forums, and applications are used as informative and online props in *Unfriended*, such as YouTube, Facebook, iMessage, Facebook Messenger, and ChatRoulette. Types of cameras in *Unfriended* could be listed with internal laptop webcams and cell phone cameras. Spotify playlist of Blaire Lily becomes the main extra-diegetic score of the movie. The desktop of Blaire gives the audience much information about the main characters and the plot. The audience observes that the meeting is made between 20:57 and 22:05. During a seventy-minute haunted and online meeting, the virtual ghost forces the participants to confess their effect on her suicide.

The global box-office achievement of *Unfriended* and good critics cause a sequel titled *Unfriended: Dark Web*, which was directed by Stephen Susco. The movie begins with a MacBook's startup. The audience learns that the computer does not belong to the user, the main character, by startup screen. Critical information, including stolen MacBook and main characters' names, is given during the software's customization. Matias devotes himself to developing an application called Papaya to transform his speech into American sign language to communicate with his deaf girlfriend named Amaya. Matias and Amaya contact each other via Facebook calls and Facebook messenger synchronically. Matias tests his application, but it does not work. Then, Matias and his five friends start a Skype meeting. Matias realizes the MacBook's storage is full of actual abduction and torture video footage during the meeting. The computer owner contacts Matias, and then he begins to terrorize all participants in Matias' personal Skype meeting, including Amaya. Similar to the other examples mentioned before, *Unfriended: Dark Web* includes many overlapped windows in the main character's desktop screen. The audience is limited to get knowledge about characters within their computer screens. For instance, Matias watches his vlogs with Amaya. These videos are presented as narrative tools: flashbacks. The live stream footage is recorded via internal laptop webcams, cell phone cameras, security cameras, and public surveillance cameras.

Host, *Searching*, *Unfriended*, and *Unfriended: Dark Web* allow us to claim that the *desktop cinema*'s narrative aesthetics are suitable to be combined with many conventional horror and thriller elements. However, the ambivalence to define and categorize these examples under a particular genre is explicit. This visual aesthetic and narrative style contains many features from various genres, such as found footage, crime, and mystery. However, innovative styles of directors in these productions are more critical than labeling. The *desktop cinema* includes innovative directorship decisions, visual and narrative aesthetics, and unusual viewing experience regarding framing, diegetic and non-diegetic components, visual surroundings, functions of digital applications, software, and web pages as narrative devices.

Conclusion

After the COVID-19, the number of these productions could be dramatically increased. In the very high-technological age, we are more engaged with our digital screens; thus, we could easily relate ourselves to these productions, which share similar narratives and visual aesthetics. The very first and prominent examples of the *desktop cinema* were associated with thriller and horror genre conventions. However, this particular aesthetic could be applied in a variety of genres or productions. Netflix's anthology, *Social Distance*, is one example that includes important particularities of the *desktop cinema*, although it is not a horror or thriller production. One of the latest examples is *C U Soon* (Mahesh Narayan, 2020) streaming in PrimeVideo catalog that the movie gathers visuals via only cell phone cameras, online meetings, internal notebook webcams. The audience can watch the movie through the protagonist's computer screen, that the storytelling method could be accepted as one of the conventions of the *desktop cinema*. This chapter aims to settle the ambivalence to define these productions and broaden an understanding of a new kind of film language and viewing experience. I want to underline that *desktop cinema* is not a generic term, but it categorizes according to narrative and visual aesthetics. Even though these productions are labeled as 'Zoom horror,' 'found footage 2.0,' or a mixed genre, they could be formalistically categorized under a particular term, the *desktop cinema*. With the incensement in the number of new examples and COVID-19 related changes in the cinema industry, many new installments and sequels could be produced soon. Therefore, the disambiguation to define them is needed. This study could provide insight into further research on the movies that the audience is limited to watching the movie through several characters' digital screens. This study could contribute to film studies because of its focus on an unusual viewing experience, an innovative film language, and a new type of narrative and visual aesthetics.

Notes

1 Worldwide Box-Office Gross of *Interstellar* (Christopher Nolan, 2014). https://www.boxofficemojo.com/search/?q=intersteller [Accessed on January 13, 2021].

2 Worldwide Box-Office Gross of *Dunkirk* (Christopher Nolan, 2017). https://www.boxofficemojo.com/search/?q=dunkirk [Accessed on January 13, 2021].

3 Worldwide Box-Office Gross of *Tenet* (Christopher Nolan, 2020). https://www.boxofficemojo.com/title/tt6723592/?ref_=bo_se_r_1 [Accessed on January 13, 2021].

4 Worldwide Box-Office Gross of *Unfriended* (Leo Gabriadze, 2014). https://www.boxofficemojo.com/title/tt3713166/?ref_=bo_se_r_1 [Accessed on, January 13, 2021].

5 Unfriended. (n.d.). Retrieved from Wikipedia: https://www.wikiwand.com/en/Unfriended.

6 PrimeVideo Unfriended. (n.d.). Retrieved from https://www.primevideo.com/detail/0S7ZICAVSL1HH22ZS2ILI2RUFR.

References

Altman, R. (1999). *Film/Genre*. London: British Film Institute.

Bruns, P. D., Kraguljac, V. N., & Bruns, R. T. (2020). COVID-19: Facts, cultural considerations, and risk of stigmatization. *Journal of Transcultural Nursing, 31* (4): 326–332.

Debruge, P. (August 3, 2014). Film review: 'Unfriended.' *Variety*. Retrieved from https://variety. com/2014/film/festivals/film-review-cybernatural-1201274261/.

Horner, A. (December 1, 2020). The Zoom horror that was 2020's most timely hit. *BBC Culture*. Retrieved from https://www.bbc.com/culture/article/20201130-the-zoom-horror-that-was-2020s-most-timely-hit.

McDowell, D. S. (2001). The method filmmaking: An interview with Daniel Myrick, co-director of *The Blair Witch Project*. *Journal of Film and Video, 2* (3): 140–147.

Loiperdinger, M., & Elzer, B. (2004). Lumiere's Arrival of the Train: Cinema's founding myth. *The Moving Image, 1* (4): 89–118.

OED Word of the year expanded for 'unprecedented' 2020. (November 23, 2020). *BBC News*. Retrieved from https://www.bbc.com/news/entertainment-arts-55016543.

Oxford Languages. (2020). *Words of an unprecedented year*. Oxford: U.K.

Roscoe, J. (2000). *The Blair Witch Project*: Mock-documentary goes mainstream. *Jump Cut*, 43: 3–8.

Ryall, T. (1975). Teaching through genre. *Screen Education, 17*: 27–33.

Sobchack, T. (1975). Genre film: A classical experience. *Literature/Film Quarterly 3* (3): 196–204.

Sperling, N., & Barneys, B. (September 15, 2020). Movie theaters returned. Audiences didn't. Now. What? *The New York Times*. Retrieved from https://www.nytimes.com/2020/09/15/business/media/tenet-movie-theaters-coronavirus.html.

Telotte, P. J. (2001). *The Blair Witch Project* project: Film and the internet. *Film Quarterly, 3* (54): 32–39.

Afra Balcı Arslan

#Stayhomestayhungry: Governmental Use of Social Media and the Economics of Pandemic

Abstract: Since the beginning of the COVID-19 pandemic, in both conventional and social media, there is a general sentiment that the virus is a risk to everyone without discriminating between the rich and the poor and that the virus poses a threat to everyone regardless of one's financial might. While this may seem to true in a sense, it does not present us the full picture of how the virus affects different communities and social groups. Despite, for example, governments ask everyone to stay home and maintain social distancing through variations of official hashtags #stayhome or #stayhomestaysafe in their languages, the economic challenges that the pandemic poses are immense. Multiple layers of the world population continued working since their survival; factories and businesses must be kept in operation. In this article, I will highlight how governmental policies about the pandemic intended for everyone are challenged by the sustainability of the current neoliberal socio-economic system. In this regard, while the global social media campaigns underline that humankind is one big family, we are yet individuals and social actors in an individualistic world. Multiple cultural studies scholars dealt with issues related to the links between economics and media and culture. By keeping in mind how mass culture and mass media indicate a one-way relationship between a central source of the relay, I will investigate whether an all-inclusive hashtag or message is indeed relevant and effective for all of the population or whether there are multiple socio-economic and political factors which demarcate the relay of such messages. In other words, this article will attempt to test how social and economic groups are indeed segregated and how they developed differing responses and practices to the pandemic.

Keywords: Social Media, Class, neo-Liberal Politics, Social Distancing

Will this be the survival of the healthiest, wealthiest, or the most cautious? Or let's put it this way, are we really on the same boat? Since the beginning of the pandemic, in both conventional and social media, there is a general sentiment that the virus is a risk to everyone without discriminating between the rich and the poor and that the virus poses a threat to everyone regardless of one's financial might. Although this claim might be valid in a way, it is far from displaying the full picture or how different parts of the world are indeed affected by the pandemic. The governments and official authorities have been asking everyone to stay home since the beginning of the pandemic with official hashtags; #stayhome and #stayhomestaysafe and highlight the prominence of social distancing, the mask, and hygiene. Yet, how such measures affect the bottom ends of the income spectrum is not considered in employing and maintaining such standards.

Put differently, the risk that the pandemic poses to different sections of the population is not at stake. Ulrick Beck (1992) introduced the theory of 'risk society' in his book *Risk Society: Towards a New Modernity*. To put it simply, the possibility of something going wrong is a risk. It thus entails an uncertainty in terms of an activity's consequences or effects on things that people ascribe value (e.g., health, wealth, prosperity, property, or the surroundings and environment), often focusing on negative, undesirable consequences. This thorough approach toward risk is in understanding post-industrial societies attempts to understand how risk is not anymore local, but global. Accordingly, the "frozen" problems of modernism are regaining functionality, and the natural transformative effects of the globalization process have created an unpredictable and uncontrollable global environment. A series of chaotic developments such as the diminishing influence and control capacities of state structures, especially the nation-state and political institutions, the unpredictability perception caused by technological developments, the deepening global income inequality, and the resulting social tension and conflict potential constitute the basis of the risk society conceptualization. These problematic areas drag all individuals and societies into an atmosphere that they cannot immunize, anticipate, and control themselves in any possible way (Beck, 1992, p. 21).

At the core of the new risk society, the neoliberal economic system is based on a free-market economy and aims at minimizing the state to shield the market from the former's intervention. Neoliberalism is more than merely an economic term and impacts all aspects of human life, including politics, culture, art, and social relations. "Neoliberalism takes diverse shapes and spawns diverse content and normative details, even different idioms. It is globally ubiquitous, yet disunified and nonidentical with itself in space and over time" (Brown, 2015). In addition to its centrality in current political discourse, "neoliberalism is one of the most pervasive and contested concepts of our contemporary era" (Hartmann-Mahmud, 2009, p. 745). Clarke (2008) catalogs a list of the different contexts for which "neoliberal" is deployed as an adjective:

> (...) *states, spaces, logics, techniques, technologies, discourses, discursive framework, ideologies, ways of thinking, projects, agendas, programs, governmentality, measures, regimes, development, ethno-development, development imaginaries, global forms of control, social policies, multiculturalism, audit cultures, managerialism, restructuring, reform, privatization, regulatory frameworks, governance, good governance, NGOs, third sector, subjects,*

> *subjectivities, individualization, professionalization, normalization, market logics, market forms of calculation, the destabilization of government and the degovernmentalization of the state* (p. 138).

Neoliberalism has, in a nutshell, turned hegemonic as a mode of discourse and has pervasive effects on ways of thinking and political-economic actions to an extent where it has become integral to the common-sense manner we interpret, experience, and comprehend the world (Harvey, 2006, p. 145).

For Brown (2015), neoliberalism converts every human realm and attempt, and even the human beings themselves, through a specific economic image. Human activity is based on economic activity, and thus, being on this earth is at the same time encapsulated and measured through the terms and volumes of economic activity, even though activities by themselves are related to monetized modes. In line with the formation of this neoliberal system arrived massive destruction of both the frameworks and power relations of preceding institutions (such as the working of the state is a sovereign manner over economic and political relations) and "the divisions of labor, social relations, welfare provisions, technological mixes, ways of life, attachments to the land, habits of the heart, ways of thought, and so on" (Harvey, 2006, pp. 145–146). In this regard, the current post-industrial and neoliberal system, which in one or another way, diminished the strength of modern mechanisms of governmentality and economic overseeing, can be seen as a warning where one may need to reconsider and reevaluate how and what we make of risk – since, as Beck puts it, the new risks at their core are also posing a threat to some fundamentals of the livelihood, such as health, environment, and property.

In this diminishing of the so-called modern set of political-economic and socio-cultural fundamentals of liberal capitalist societies, the media also plays a critical role. More than being the fourth estate in its modern sense as the estates of the checks and balances, the current influx of social media, which blurred the lines between the imagined reality of a community and its actualities, presented a further risk to individual understandings and/or definitions of imminent spatio-temporal existence, by making it more and more difficult for the general public to have crisp anticipation and control of the events. Apart from social media, such a change in contemporary perception has a historical backdrop also in the changing role of media in the current neoliberal system. The media started losing its power and/or will influence the neoliberal political actors because it has also been the mainstream media channels that promoted the neoliberal idiom. One should not expect everything from the state or the political mechanism.

As with the demand to lessen the role of the state and allow more room for the private capital, the contemporary media environment also works as an extension of the neoliberal system, as a culture industry, which adopts the most novel technologies which at the same time being instrumental in constituting the idealized citizen subjects. In this regard, the social media slogans of the pandemic, especially "stay home, stay safe," has not only become a major part of multiple official discourses, but the conventional media came into the help of the "authorities," in disseminating the slogan. Yet, in this struggle against the virus, staying home comes with an individual price. The discourse of everyone staying home as individuals would result in a collective success story has also helped to augment the existing economic disparities in the neoliberal world. Furthermore, it allowed for the further proliferation of the discourses on more deregulation, welfare reform, and the reinventions of governments based on the technologies of our age (Ouellette & Hay, 2008, p. 472).

In the last few decades, such neoliberalist measures effectively weakened the social welfare states, social security systems, and the increasing violent measures directed toward lower and/or working classes. Yet, in the meantime, a discursive search for lost innocence, family, and religious values came to the fore at the expense of the well-being and safety of the individuals that the neoliberal system claims to give more rights.

Perhaps, this is why it would be more and more time to reconsider and reinvite the earlier or modern notions of social class at such a time of the pandemic when the neoliberal system dynamites the senses of the class. Social classes are made up of groups having a common relation to the means of production and are also divided along those lines. Thus, this creates an unequal property distribution system, power, and material returns even among similar socio-cultural positions. In the Marxist tradition, class relations are fundamental in conceiving the main aspects of culture, society, and history. Classes are essential to social relations determined by the infrastructure and/or economic production and configuration aspects. Marx asserts that the historical procession of socio-economic relations is gradual and may be differentiated by different modes of production. In this regard, the way material goods are produced and distributed also determines the primary conditions of societies and social relations, hence the mode of production. For Marx (1972), as long as society produces more than any amount beyond the subsistence level, then this extra amount sets up the surplus, which should be distributed in a manner. The distribution dynamics of the "base" then start determining the "superstructure" where social institutions and forms of consciousness are at stake. However, the relationship between the two is reciprocal, as although base determines and forms superstructure, superstructure does legitimize and express the base.

According to Hall (2019), there is a political struggle between classes, and culture is precisely in the middle of these struggles. He claims that culture is not subject to the ideologies of the dominant classes. Subordinate classes also have various motivations, and thus, they (can) develop resistance to what dominant types urge them to accept (ibidem). Hall does not necessarily claim that culture can be seen as something separate, and the economic relations do not have any effect on them. However, contrary to what Adorno says, he claims that there can occur a struggle throughout this process of subordination, and the subordinate classes could win it. It is possible to suggest here that, although he does not precisely put aside his ideas which are built on Marx, he (1996) criticizes classical Marxism for "its rigid structural determinacy, its reductionism of two varieties- class and economics; its way of conceptualizing the social formation itself" (Hall, p. 28). According to Hall, Marxism is constantly being transcended and preserved in a way, and this is something he finds problematic. He thinks that classical Marxism is weak and limited in the means of ideology.

In his article, "*The Problem of Ideology: Marxism Without Guarantees*," Hall (1986) proposes that ideological categories are developed, generated, and transformed according to their own laws of development. For these developments to take place, the real indeterminancy of the political must be acknowledged. Thus, it is necessary for Marxism itself as a theory to open up a place for relative openness and relative inter-determinancy. It is only possible to construct a Marxism without final quarantees by understanding 'determinancy' in setting limits, establishing parameters, defining space operations, and social practices. The thing which makes Hall different from Adorno about the relationship between culture and social classes is that Hall tries to open up the way for the reader to quit being strictly attached to an ideology as if it cannot change under any circumstance. He indicates that theories and ideologies should always be theorized to have the possibility to find something of the truth about social realities.

Both Gramsci and Hall insist on the centrality of economic and class relations in any critical analysis of the socio-cultural world, but insisting on their importance does not, in either thinker, mean granting them the position of prime determinant. Both Hall and Gramsci recognize that economic conditions cannot be divorced from cultural conditions and that class struggles must involve cultural struggles, not as secondary, but as integral. It is possible to say that the reason why Hall brought about a new dimension to cultural studies is since he attempted to lay out a non-reductionist theory on the social practices and determination of ideology, politics, and culture. In this, articulation refers to an attempt to reconsider the determination of struggle's dialectical workings. This also points to Hally's move from a Marxist issue toward structuralist theoretical rendering and, at the same time, an underlining of the limits and potentialities of his reconsiderations of Gramsci's work. Here, structuralism highlights a notion or term as something not pre-given but instead the term itself as being in flux, in terms of its production and construction through a system of differences at work in linguistic and social operations (Fiske, 1996, pp. 212–222). As it is underlined by Hall himself, structuralism is the very thing that made him realize that there is no other way of existence beyond living with difference.

Grossberg (1986) mainly proposes that society is a complex unity, and it always bears its determinations in contradictory and multiple terms, which are at the same time historically specific. It is also noteworthy to give place to Raymond Williams, who is accepted as one of the most prominent cultural studies theorists, and his famous article, *"Base and Superstructure in Marxist Cultural Theory*. In the text, Williams (2005) focuses on the proposition of economic base being more crucial and vital for understanding the realities of cultural process. He states that base is never static or uniform since there are deep contradictions in the relationships of production affecting social relations. Thus, the base can be seen as a continuous process and not a "state of being." Williams talks about re-valuing notions to make them realistic and rational when placed in contemporary socio-economic relations (ibidem). He argues that Marxist ideology is based on a certain economic structure that might be ambiguous when placed in the modern cultural scenario changing fastly. One other term which is focused on the text is the concept of totality. Totality can be defined as opposing the structure in which base determines the superstructure but believed that social being determines consciousnesses. Stemming from this point, the question is put forth in the text; "whether the notion of totality includes the notion of intention." On the one hand, Williams puts forth the idea of categorizing work of art as superstructure, but on the other hand, he contradicts himself and says that certain kinds of practices and customs have been so naturalized that they have to be considered as a part of superstructure to understand reality (ibidem). Williams finds the traditional notion of superstructure incomplete, ambiguous and problematic. He also talks about the modern concept of re-inventing, re-modify, and re-work the existing notions and concepts to make them compatible with the contemporary scenarios. Such concepts change from place to place and time to time.

In conclusion, contemporary crisis scenarios such as the one that we have been going through as the COVID-19 pandemic cause turmoil in societies are known. The uncertainty that we are experiencing in all areas of life and social relationships increases the uncertainty in our networks and accelerates the feeling of fear itself to a crisis. As the prominence of individuality is highly promoted and the hashtags #stayhome, #stayhomestaysafe start to seem more difficult to overcome, social and economic groups are segregated and continue to develop different responses to the pandemic.

References

Beck, U. (1992). *Risk society: Towards a new modernity.* California: Sage Publications.

Brown, W. (2015). *Undoing the demos: Neoliberalism's stealth revolution.* New York: Zone Books.

Clarke, J. (2008). Living with/in and without Neo-Liberalism. *Journal of Global and Historical Anthropology,* 51: 135–147.

Fiske, J. (1996). Opening the hallway: Some remarks on the fertility of Stuart Hall's contribution to critical theory. In D. Morley & K. Chen (Eds.) *Stuart Hall: Critical dialogues in cultural studies* (pp. 212–222). London: Routledge.

Grossberg, L. (1986). History, politics and postmodernism: Stuart Hall and cultural studies. *Journal of Communication Inquiry, 10* (2): 61–77.

Hall, S. (1986). The problem of ideology: Marxism without guarantees. *Journal of Communication Inquiry, 10* (2): 28–44.

Hall, S. (1996). The problem of ideology: Marxism without guarantees. In D. Morley & K-H. Chen (Eds.). *Stuart Hall: Critical dialogues in cultural studies.* London: Routledge.

Hall, S. (2019). Cultural studies: Two paradigms. In D. Morley (Ed.). *Stuart Hall: Essential essays vol. 1.* Durham, NC: Duke UP.

Hartmann-Mahmud, L. (2009). Neoliberalism: A useful tool for teaching critical topics in political science. *Political Science and Politics, 42* (4): 745–751.

Harvey, D. (2006). Neo-Liberalism as creative destruction. *Geografiska Annaler: Series B, Human Geography, 88* (2): 145–158.

Marx, K. (1972). *The German ideology.* New York: International Publishers.

Ouellette, L., & Hay, J. (2008). Makeover television, governmentality and the good citizen. *Continuum: Journal of Media & Cultural Studies,* 22: 471–484.

Williams, R. (2005). Base and superstructure in Marxist cultural theory. *Culture and Materialism: Selected Essays* (pp. 31–49). London: Verso.

Dilay Özgüven and *Ece Arıhan*

The Survival of the Turkish Reality Television in the Pandemic Era

Abstract: Reality television is a hybrid television genre that appeared in the late 1980s. It is generally defined as a new trend in which the main subject represents real people and reality. Reality television has many subgenres, also called formats, which combine different elements of other popular genres of television programming. Globally well-known reality television programs in the United States and the United Kingdom include *Survivor, MasterChef*, and *Who Wants to Be a Millionaire* that corresponds to reality-show known as reality game show or gamedoc. These programs were also adapted worldwide in many countries such as Turkey, which will be the focus of this chapter. Starting with the early 1990s, Turkish television began to use a mixture of formats and genres from European and American television. By combining these formats and genres, private TV channels created new shows that became widely popular in Turkey. Building on this foundation, the reality shows such as *Survivor, MasterChef*, and *Who Wants to Be a Millionaire* were directly adapted to Turkish television. In the present, the media is collectively being transformed to accommodate the needs and conditions of the era of the pandemic. Our purpose in this chapter is to explore and analyze the surviving formats of the most popular adaptations of primetime reality shows that adjust to the transformations in the media, which are *Survivor Türkiye* (*Survivor*), *MasterChef Türkiye* (*MasterChef*), and *Kim Milyoner Olmak İster?* (*Who Wants to Be a Millionaire?*). First, we will present the original formats of these programs to showcase how they usually function (before the COVID-19). Afterward, we will examine the Turkish adaptations. Finally, we will compare the normal (before) and new normal (after) versions of the Turkish adaptations and explore the features that were added to accommodate the needs of the new normal, which will reveal the reasons for the endurance of the reality shows and how they can survive in any given condition.

Keywords: Reality Television, Pandemic, Game Show, Turkish Television, Hybrid Television Genre, Adaptation

Introduction

A television program is a content that appears on television, which is produced for broadcasting. Indeed, television programs are more varied than most other forms of media because there is a wide range of formats and genres that can be presented. A television program could be categorized as fictional such as comedies or dramas, and non-fictional such as documentary, news, and reality television. For instance, as Cavender and Fishman (1998) mentions, "[g]ame shows and late-night talk shows (e.g., Letterman & Leno) are not fiction, but neither they are the news; they are entertainment programming" (p. 3). Therefore, it is hard to place a television program in a single genre as they are usually the product of the combination of the elements of many other genres, resulting in hybrid forms.

One of the examples of a hybrid television genre in television programming is reality television. Reality television appeared in the late 1980s as a new television trend that has continued to the present (Cavender & Fishman, 1998, p. 3). There are competing definitions of reality television. However, it is generally defined as a television programming genre where the main subject is the representation of real people and reality. This definition is supported by Penzhorn and Pitout (2008), who point out that reality television focuses on ordinary people, voyeurism, audience participation, and it attempts to simulate real life (p. 62). The essential features of reality television consist of "non-professional actors, unscripted dialogue, surveillance footage, hand-held cameras, seeing events unfold as they are happening in front of the camera" (Hill, 2005, p. 41). The hybridity of reality television enables this format to accumulate several techniques and styles to make it a highly adaptable genre and open to transformation according to the newly emerging trends.

Reality TV, also known as popular factual television, has become exponentially popular and diverse, particularly since the 1990s. According to Annette Hill (2005), reality TV was already "a catch-all category that includes a wide range of entertainment programs about real people" (p. 2). Despite being a hybrid genre, to begin with, reality TV's "popular non-scripted formats have become increasingly specialized and stylistically sophisticated" in recent years (Murray & Ouellette, 2009, p. 5). As reality TV has changed and evolved, the genre has started to include and encourage even more interaction with the viewer and the customization of the content. Besides, reality TV has become increasingly globalized with diverse audiences, as more viewers have started to watch the various formats of the genre all around the world.

The formats or subgenres of reality TV can be generally classified as the docusoap, the reality magazine, and the reality show. This chapter's focus is the reality show format, which is also called reality the game show or the gamedoc. The prime examples of popular programs of the reality show are *Survivor, MasterChef*, and *Who Wants to Be a Millionaire?*, which all air in primetime. These programs can be classified as mega formats, which can be defined as franchises that encompass different formats such as reality television, live entertainment, and, to a lesser extent, filmed series including sitcoms and telenovelas. Because these programs are mega formats, this also makes them global phenomena. Thus, their adaptations emerge in various countries, including Turkey.

This chapter will be centralized on the Turkish adaptations, which are *Survivor Türkiye* (*Survivor*), *MasterChef Türkiye* (*MasterChef*), and *Kim Milyoner Olmak İster?* (*Who Wants to Be a Millionaire?*), and how they survived the pandemic era. We will focus on the adjustments made to fit the new normal (after) and compare it with the normal (before) version. By doing this, the adaptability and durability of reality TV will be presented, highlighting the survival of reality shows in any condition.

Television Formats

In its early beginnings, reality TV was used to classify factual law and order shows, including real-life footage of police (Hill, 2005, p. 2). However, at present, reality TV consists of many formats or subgenres, which are the products of the "hybridization of successful genres" (idem, p. 42), the examples of which include lifestyle and documentary. Even though reality TV is hard to describe with a single, all-encompassing definition, which also applies to its formats and contents, there are three main reality TV formats. These formats can be given as the docusoap, the reality magazine, and the reality show (Bondebjerg, 2002, pp. 171–172).

According to Hill (2005), the first format, the docusoap, as is apparent by its name, is the result of the hybridization of observational *documentary* and *soap opera* (p. 42). This format is also known as the fly-on-the-wall docusoap (idem, p. 7). Some well-known examples of the docusoap are *The Real World, Airport, Jersey Shore, Duck Dynasty,* and *Laguna Beach: The Real Orange County*. Gail Coles (2000) defines the docusoap as the depiction of "everyday experiences of work, family, and relationships… of their 'real' subjects" (p. 27). The distinctive feature of this subgenre is "its link to reality through its characters and settings" (Bondebjerg, 2002, p. 171). Likewise, in a TV series, the experiences of a specific group of people are shown either chronologically or in a "time structured narrative" (ibidem).

Each episode's story usually focuses on the main narrative (or maybe a couple of main narratives) and is supported by multiple smaller ones. Editing these narratives is structured to increase the "dramatic potential" like soap operas (ibidem). Coles (2000) denotes that the centralization of the "extraordinary 'ordinary' people," and the fusion of the "observational film-making techniques," which supports the connection to reality, and "the narrative structure of soap opera" are the reasons for this format's vast popularity (p. 27).

Bondebjerg (2002) classifies the second format of reality TV as the reality magazine, which is a "regularly scheduled journalistic magazine presenting cases from real life, mostly about crime and accidents or other spectacular human-interest stories" (p. 171). So, this format is the result of the hybridization of "a journalistic, informative discourse with dramatic forms related to social melodrama and the crime and detective genres" (ibidem). Popular examples of reality magazines include the court shows such as *Judge Judy* and *The People's Court*.

Each episode of the reality-magazine series consists of "interviews with victims of crime and accidents and the professionals, who take care of and protect our lives and welfare" (ibidem) and the host of the show directs these interviews. The key feature of this format is the use of the actual footage of the incident (crime or accident) or the reenactments of the incident. Bondebjerg (2002) denotes that the narrative of the reality magazine is structured similar to a melodrama in which the daily life of an ordinary person is interrupted by a catastrophe or the person is faced with extreme adversity that is later resolved by the courageous efforts of someone with the result of restoring order (ibidem).

The third and final format of reality TV is the reality show, which is described by Bondebjerg (2002) as "a serialized form of game show where ordinary people are put in extraordinary situations in order both to cooperate with and compete against one another" (idem, p. 172). Hill (2005) also calls the reality show a reality game show or the gamedoc, which she indicates is the combination of the gameshow and observational documentary (p. 42). Usually, there is a prize in this format, which the competitors earn by winning games.

Even though the reality show is structured with rules, according to Bondebjerg (2002), the most crucial aspect of this subgenre is that the "rules being tested are the social and psychological rules and conventions of our everyday life" (p. 172). These shows reveal the true identity, behavior, and relationships of ordinary people under stress and pressure, mainly presented by behind-the-scenes interviews for everyone to see. Although some versions of the reality show may centralize the competition, others may focus more on the social experiment feature, which may provide insight into the human psyche.

The widely popular and renowned examples of the reality show include *Survivor*, *MasterChef*, and *Who Wants to Be a Millionaire?* which have all continued to be produced even with the ongoing pandemic in their countries of origin and globally. Thus, the next section will provide an overview of these programs and their format, followed by information on their adaptations in Turkey and how they have adapted to and are surviving the pandemic.

Mega Formats

The term reality television did not come into use until 2000. However, in the late 1990s, new formatted genres have started to dominate television productions in the representation of real people on television. As Chalably (2016) states, during the TV format revolution, the fastest growing genre became reality programming (this being understood as a broad category that includes talent competitions and factual entertainment shows such as makeovers, coaching, life swaps, etc.) (p. 6). Reality television has been overpowering the television world over the past 15 years; this impact started with the introduction of mega formats such as *Who Wants to Be a Millionaire?* (1998), *Big Brother* (1999) and *Survivor* (2000) and continued with formats such as *Pop Idol* (2001) and the revised format of *MasterChef* (2005). Moran (2014) implied that mega-program franchises had been spread across various formats, including reality television, live entertainment, and, to a lesser extent, filmed series including sitcoms and telenovelas (p. 88).

It was the starting point of introducing one of the mega formats of reality television into the world when ABC had aired *Who Wants to Be a Millionaire?* in 1998. *Who Wants to Be a Millionaire?* was hosted by Regis Philbin. The show's format was based on fifteen questions that the contestants have to pass to win the full prize. Before *Who Wants to Be a Millionaire?*, the reality-show format was a dying genre in the television world. However, "*Who Wants to Be a Millionaire?* instantly became a hit and made Philbin, a longtime entertainment figure, a pop-culture icon. His tagline 'Is that your final answer?' entered the lexicon and was repeatedly endlessly" (Huff, 2006, p. 6).

Later on, a competition began between the two mega formats in reality television. "What CBS did, though, with the first outing of *Survivor* was to force viewers to choose between ABC's strongest show and the much-hyped reality. From a programming standpoint, it was daring of CBS executives to try the new show against *Who Wants to Be a Millionaire?*, proven hit" (Huff, 2006, pp. 6–7). The first aired episode of *Survivor*, "drew fewer viewers than *Who Wants to Be a Millionaire?* but soon, *Survivor* was ahead and stayed ahead. It became a true water cooler show, with people talking about what happened the night before the next day at work" (idem, p. 18).

Survivor became one of the leads in the reality television "when CBS and producer Mark Burnett introduced American television viewers to a newfangled program, in which he shipped 16 regular people off to a small island in the South China Sea where they lived for 39 days, with one getting kicked off every third day, in hopes of being the last person standing and earning a $1 million payday" (idem, p. 11). The main feature of *Survivor* was that it is "nonfiction in nature, and built around regular people, not actors, in the key roles. Before *Survivor*, all but a handful of the television programs were scripted entertainment fare, usually dramas and comedies" (idem, pp. 3–4). According to Bignell (2014) "...*Survivor* welded together the social-experiment documentary and the contest and featured ordinary people in an extraordinary situation. The situation displaced them from their normal milieu and put psychological and social pressure on them that tested their ability to create relationships with fellow participants..." (p. 101). The importance of the format comes from the fact that the participants /contestants were not actors. However, they were "everyday people from all walks of life who were willing to do seemingly anything to win $1 million, even agreeing to be stranded on a small island without basic necessities" (Huff, 2006, p. 167).

It was in 1990 that *MasterChef* first hit the screens. The show ran on television between 1990 to 2001 with Loyd Grossman presenting; each series saw three contestants compete to be crowned Britain's best amateur chef. *MasterChef* was "created by Franc Roddam for the BBC, following a tradition of cookery television where ordinary people would cook a plate of food under time pressure in a studio and be judged on the quality of the food by professional chefs" (Hill, 2019, p. 143). Later, *MasterChef* returned to television with significant adjustments in its format in 2005 as *MasterChef Goes Large*, and in 2008 the name changed back to *MasterChef* with the format remaining unchanged. As Hill (2019) noted, "the original version of the series underwent a major transformation after the wave of competitive reality that dominated the television schedules in the late 1990s. The original British version had followed a typical game show format where ordinary people displayed their practical skills, interacting with the presenter, and competing to win the title of *MasterChef*." However, the revised format of *MasterChef* is a reality show, "where amateurs audition and attend boot camp before being whittled down to a select group who participate in a tough competition judged by professional chefs, where one person is crowned the *MasterChef* winner." In addition to the ongoing *MasterChef*, there are three other formats titled: *Celebrity MasterChef* (2006), *MasterChef: The Professionals* (2008), and *Junior MasterChef* (2013).

Turkish Adaptations of Mega Formats in Pandemic Era

The blend of formats and genres borrowed from Europe or the United States of America into Turkish television. At the beginning of the 1990s, new television formats and genres emerged in Turkish television, including the adaptations of popular reality shows. The first of these that will be focused on is the adaptation of the British reality show *Who Wants to be a Millionaire* whose name changed over the years in Turkey, starting with *Kim Beş Yüz Milyar İster?* (2000–2004), *Kim Beş Yüz Bin İster?* (2005–2006), *Kim Bir Milyon İster* (2008), and ending with *Kim Milyoner Olmak İster?* (2011-present). The second one is the adaptation of the American reality show *Survivor*, named in Turkey *Survivor Türkiye* (2005-present). The third and final one is the British reality show *MasterChef*, adapted as *MasterChef Türkiye*, which aired first in 2011. Even though the show was canceled after a year, it started to be aired again in 2018 and continues today.

Even though their hosts and networks that have aired them have changed over the years, the formats of all of these adaptations follow their originals. Thus, instead of comparing formats of the adaptations versus originals, this chapter will be focused on their survival in the pandemic era. The adaptation, *Kim Milyoner Olmak İster?* was hosted by the famous Turkish actor Kenan İmirzalıoğlu before the pandemic, who still continues to host in the present. The most significant change that is made to adapt to the pandemic era is the removal of the studio audience, hence the removal of one of the jokers, which was "Seyirci Jokeri" (*Ask the Audience*). Instead of *Seyirci Jokeri*, a new joker is introduced called "Uzmana Sor Jokeri" (*Ask an Expert*), and the expert is Arda Ayten, who had previously won a million in this reality show. The final change is made in the introduction of the contestant. Before the pandemic, the contestant's family and friends used to introduce and give information about the contestant. However, the studio audience is removed in the present day; a video montage providing information about the contestant is played before the game begins.

The adaptation *Survivor Türkiye*'s format is not changed at all during the pandemic since the contestants were already on an isolated island. However, an alteration is made concerning the eliminated contestants. Before the pandemic, each eliminated contestant was sent home immediately. Nevertheless, during the pandemic, they had to remain on the island, isolated until the final episode because of the newly introduced government restrictions that had banned traveling worldwide. Another change that is made concerns the location of the finale. Normally before the pandemic, all episodes of *Survivor Türkiye* were shot in the Dominican Republic. However, all the episodes except the finale took place in the Dominican Republic during the pandemic era. The final location was changed due to COVID-19 and moved to Galata Port in İstanbul, Turkey.

The adaptation of *MasterChef Türkiye*'s most considerable alteration in the pandemic era is that the contestants are staying in a house together, isolating themselves from the outside world similar to *Survivor Türkiye*. This may have influenced the contestants' psychology as before they could go home and see their friends and family, but now they have to be in a secure and isolated environment to stay healthy. Another change concerns the location of the challenges. Normally, the challenges were held at various indoor locations in different cities in Turkey. However, when the government restricted traveling, the competition was held only in the *MasterChef* studio, where the contestants prepared meals to be delivered to people to complete a cooking challenge. Later on, when the restrictions were loosened, the challenges are moved to outdoor locations in different cities in Turkey, adhering to the necessary COVID-19 health regulations. The final change concerns checking the taste of a portion of food by the contestants. Because of the pandemic, if a contestant uses a utensil more than once to taste the food, that specific food is immediately disqualified. The contestant is asked to either prepare a new batch or compete without that batch, which would cause a major point loss. To ensure that the contestants are following the health regulations, the production team checks their video footage.

Conclusion

In light of these, the mega formats worldwide, such as *Who Wants to Be a Millionaire*, *Survivor*, and *MasterChef*, were adapted in various countries due to their popularity. The adapted formats in Turkey have followed their originals for the most part. The originals of these formats and their adaptations were compared to explore their durability and adaptability during the pandemic era. It is apparent from the comparison between the normal (before pandemic) and new normal (during and after pandemic) that these adaptations have managed to survive the COVID-19 with minor alterations to ensure the health of the contestants and the production team and to adapt to the government health protocols and restrictions such as the ban on traveling. One of the main reasons for the easy adaptation of these reality shows with minor adjustments in the pandemic era is that the contestants were already in an isolated and controlled environment, so the total isolation was easy to achieve and did not affect the overall format of these programs.

The other main reason for the survival of these reality shows is the nature of the reality shows and the need to connect and identify with real people, especially in the pandemic era and isolation. Moreover, the airing schedules of these reality shows are all in prime time, which coincides with the leisure and relaxation time for families. As a result, the ratings of these shows, which were already high, became even higher, causing a surge in their popularity in Turkey. To conclude, the adaptations of these popular global reality shows have all adapted to and are surviving the era of the pandemic.

References

Bignell, J. (2014). Realism and reality formats. In L. Ouellette (Ed.). *A companion to reality television* (pp. 97–115). New Jersey: Wiley Blackwell.

Bondebjerg, I. (2002). The mediation of everyday life: Genre, discourse and spectacle in reality TV. In A. Jerslev (Ed.). *Realism and 'reality' in film and media* (pp. 159–192). Copenhagen: Museum Tusculanum Press.

Cavender, G., & Fishman, M. (1998). *Entertaining crime: Television reality crime programs*. New York: Routledge.

Chalaby, J. K. (2016). Drama without drama: The late rise of scripted TV formats. *Television & New Media, 17* (1): 3–20.

Coles, G. (2000). Docusoap: Actuality and the serial format. In M. Llewellyn-Jones & B. Carson (Eds.). *Frames and fictions on television: The politics of identity in drama* (pp. 27–39). Bristol: Intellect Ltd.

Hill, A. (2019). *Media experiences: Engaging with reality television*. New York: Routledge.

Hill, A. (2005). *Reality TV: Factual entertainment and television audiences*. New York: Routledge.

Huff, R. M. (2006). *Reality television*. Connecticut: Greenwood Publishing Group.

Moran, A. (2014). Program format franchising in the age of reality television. In L. Ouellette (Ed.). *A companion to reality television* (pp. 74–95). Oxford: Wiley Blackwell.

Murray, S., & Ouellette, L. (2009). Introduction. In S. Murray & L. Ouellette (Eds.). *Reality TV: Remaking television culture*. New York: NYU Press.

Penzhorn, H., & Pitout, M. (2007). A critical-historical genre analysis of reality television. *Communication, 33* (1): 62–76.

Cemal Barkın Engin and *Yahya Burak Tamer*

Evolution of Music Reception: Transformation in the Post-Pandemic Era

Abstract: Music presents a diverse set of functions in society, which are in continuous states of transformation with regard to technological, social, cultural, and economic factors. Music's universal and communicative nature renders it a powerful communication channel which can transmit aesthetic and cultural values, reflect collective memories, and form social communities. Live performances provide an essential medium for this communicative interaction, forming 50 % of the global music industry in 2019, before the restrictions applied due to the COVID-19 pandemic in 2020. The focal point of this chapter is to explore the initial impact which COVID-19 pandemic has implied on music's cultural function and reception. The translation of music education to online platforms and methods is examined, taking technical limitations into consideration. Music has been identified as a continuous process with no limits rather than a fixed object and this aspect of music is embodied by live performances. Representations of live performances as digital streaming media continue to explore ways to reanimate this multi-dimensional sensation. Digital technology has been offering new possibilities regarding musical performance for a significant amount of time, yet the pandemic has accelerated the need to analyze and extend the limits of the online/virtual performance spaces. In spite of the current technical issues such as fidelity and latency, alternative performance spaces and online education will continue to be an integral part of musical reception in the future.

Keywords: Musical Communication, Music Industry, Live Music Performance, Online Performance, Immersive Sound

Introduction

Music's diverse function and role in society have been transformed continuously throughout history, yet its impact as a powerful communication channel persists. A musical work not only transmits the cultural characteristics of its style and tradition but also reflects the collective memory or represents the aesthetic/ideological intention of its composer(s). Music intrinsically carries extra meaning and values saturated by socio-cultural, political, and economic factors surrounding its creation. Emotional attachment to a specific musical composition is often formed by the individual listener's experience and imagination. Thus, music is capable of conducting complex information with varying possibilities of reception. Until the late 19th Century, music could be solely experienced via live performances. The invention of audio recording challenged this paradigm and enabled audiences to witness a specific work, otherwise lost in time, repeatedly. Although this temporal displacement transformed the way audiences perceive music irreversibly, live performances continue to be an integral element for the evolution of the music culture and provide substantial space for human interaction.

In the last decade, social media have been the latest and potentially the most powerful medium to allow musicians an alternative platform to perform. As of 2019, live performances constituted 50 % of the global music industry revenue and were projected to hold their status in the near future. However, the COVID-19 pandemic threatens this estimation due to restrictions regarding social space and physical contact. The numbers of online/virtual music performances have increased dramatically, while music streaming consumption decreased during the successive lockdown periods. This development triggers a series of questions: Could online/virtual concerts become a steady part of our live performance experiences in the future? An analysis regarding the reception of these distinctive experiences might be beneficial for future predictions. Recent audio technologies such as 3D and immersive audio might be the key factors to assess the recent developments since they open up new possibilities to enhance the sensation for the online audience. This chapter aims to investigate the socio-cultural and economic impacts of the COVID-19 pandemic on music reception concerning technological evolution. Current trends in alternative performance spaces and online music education are explored in the following sections.

Music and Communication

Music's universal and communicative nature is a notion that the majority of people will agree upon, although no particular attention has been given to its function as a channel of communication until recently (Cross, 2014, p. 809). The key element to fully capture the extent of music's multilateral status in culture is to analyze its communicational qualities exhaustively. Bloch defines the culture as the complete set of knowledge to function efficiently in a specific form of society which often passes from generation as a non-verbal, empirical set of values (as cited in Widdess, 2012, p. 88). There is often a consensus on the structural similarities between music and language, yet the message or the meaning of music is open to interpretation by the receiver from an emotional perspective compared to the more definitive state of the language. Language is essentially considered as a meaning and information-oriented structure (Ionescu, 2017, pp. 113–114).

"Musicking" is a term proposed by Christopher Small (1998) to define the complex web of human interaction formed around music culture (pp. 1–18). Musicking is an inclusive proposition which efficiently exposes music's potential power to bring people together and form communities in many forms. Nevertheless, focusing on individual parts of this intricate relationship might be helpful to further investigate the extent of communication music is capable of enclosing. Music is an art form written, recorded, performed, and shared with people; thus, its communicative aspect changed significantly concerning different positions concerning musicking (Miell, MacDonald & Hargreaves, 2005, p. 1). A collective musical performance imposes a physical, bodily effect on the performers since they have a mutual dependence and data flow in real-time to compose an abstract, non-tactual sonic outcome. This is a special, closed type of communication. From the listeners' point of view, a musical performance can carry significant meaning to its cultural environment, even more than the linguistic common ground, along with the effect of the musical content, which might resonate distinctively in individuals (Widdess, 2012, p. 89). Whether experienced via live performances, mediatized (live) performances, or studio recordings, music forms a sense of community among its listeners, online or physical, therefore provides people a common space to interact (Sanden, 2012, pp. 11–12).

The emotional reception of a specific piece of music can be quite diverse among the individuals depending on a complex set of parameters such as sociocultural factors. Cross (2012) labels this phenomenon as "floating intentionality" (p. 96). Ionescu (2017) stated that in comparison to the language, music is an expressive form, which is potentially non-representative and does not necessarily make prepositions (pp. 113–114). Miell et al. (2005) approaches the meaning of music from a broader perspective and underlines the fact that music is capable of carrying a varied set of messages and meanings from social and political contexts while not discarding the aesthetic reception or the emotional attachment of the listener (pp. 2–3). In a sense, music not only connects people in a variety of ways as a community but also functions as the actual medium. The exact nature of the message that the musical work proposes varies remarkably due to the complexity of the receiver profiles. It is quite challenging to arrive at a precise definition of music appreciation and reception in a global sense, yet a framework around music's function can be achieved.

Live performances, the most direct and physical form of musical communication in the overall scheme of musicking, continue to be essential and relevant for the culture in the 21st Century. COVID-19 pandemic has interrupted this traditional understanding of performance momentarily. Thus, emerging online platforms and technologies have become crucial alternatives to find new means for performance practices outside of the physical world.

Contemporary Performance Practices & Technology

Traditional Aspects of Live Music Performance

Before the invention of audio recording, there was no contextual differentiation between music and live music. Audio technology has imposed a formerly nonexistent division upon our musical conceptions. The separation between actual live performance and a studio production would later be divaricated with the emergence of mediatized live performances such as radio and TV broadcasts. Today online/virtual platforms offer alternative performance spaces to musicians. The enhanced technological capabilities offered by these platforms enable new aesthetic possibilities in terms of music performance and audience reception (Sanden, 2012, pp. 31–32).

Philip (2004) suggests that music recordings constitute essential information about the shift in performance standards and corresponding audience expectations (pp. 42–49). He points out that there is a significant deviation from the past standards observed throughout the historical recordings. Philip (2004) isolates his analyses to Western Music repertoire recorded in the 20th Century, yet having sonic documentation for a comparative analysis could be beneficial for the research on performance practices of other musical genres (ibidem). Recordings helped to bring local musical traditions to a global platform. The stylistic tendencies merge into each other and establish an international standard despite its negative implications for the monopolization of aesthetic choices. Historical research about musical performance practices before the invention of audio recording offers a great deal of insight into the periodic instruments, the choices of tuning, and other musical attributes, though the general characteristics of a performance such as tempi, intonation, and dynamics could be solely approximated. The increased fidelity of the recordings with impeccable performances often achieved by editing inevitably shaped modern-day listeners' expectations dramatically. Although audience expectations might be genre-specific, there is an overall tendency to anticipate a similar performance and sonic characteristics identical to studio versions. Thus, often live performances are expanded with backing tracks to sound faithful to the studio production without requiring additional musicians.

According to Sanden's categorization (2012) defining networks of liveness, a conventional performance could be labeled as traditional liveness (p. 3).

Nevertheless, a simple categorization such as live (life?) vs. recorded music is not sufficient enough today to express the potential interaction different combinations of liveness networks may establish. Spatial and temporal liveness share the time and space for real-time performances and continue to be an essential part of a public performance. A modern-day performance can be mediatized in various ways with the improved liveness of fidelity, thus diminishing the differences in the perceived sound quality for the physical and non-physical participation. Additionally, recent performances may incorporate enhanced performance strategies and could be using virtual applications. Due to the restrictions on physical distance, online and virtual platforms have gained importance for musicking communities since the start of the COVID-19 pandemic.

Alternative Performance Spaces

Music presents a medium for communicative interaction; thus, listening to music can be considered as a social activity where participants share a "collective intuition" (Cross, 2012, p. 96). Widdess (2012) addresses music as a social symbol featuring a continuous process of meaning creation (p. 88). Bashkow (2004) indicates the dynamic structure of cultures and cultural boundaries as an ongoing process of mutual reformation (p. 454). The interactive and dynamic nature of music as a social activity is one of the prominent factors that condition the evolution of digital music technologies. Spilker (2018) introduces the concept of folding for technological appropriation. Digital music technologies evolve through phases such as development and appropriation, which depend on the interaction of technological, economic, legal, and cultural factors (pp. 4–32). Each aspect's priority is in constant evolution depending on a complex set of circumstances; thus, the upcoming trends in digital music technologies are hard to predict. As of March 2019, the pandemic parameter has been added to this equation, and audiences have been experiencing its effects on live music performance as well as recorded music reception. Due to the social distancing regulations of the pandemic, bands and artists are currently unable to perform live. This reduces the revenue income of the global music industry drastically. The adaptation to the new circumstances introduced by the pandemic occurs through various innovative forms of online live concert experiences.

During the pandemic, artists have been performing live through digital media channels such as social media platforms, online concert venues, global virtual venues, online festivals, and video games. *Spotify* has decided to add live stream event lists to artist pages in collaboration with *Songkick* and *Amazon Music* incorporated a live streaming function to its app via *Twitch* (Nicolaou, 2020). Digital platforms such as *Dice, Stageit,* and *Diuo* serve as online concert venues where artists can organize events as ticketed live streams. *Dice* features partnerships with 109 venues in 14 cities and six countries (Dice, 2020). Nick Cave's solo performance titled "Idiot Prayer" at Alexandra Palace in London was launched as a global streaming event via *Dice*. The performance was produced by the artist's team of sound and video professionals, including a cinematographer, sound engineer, and editor. Following the live stream event in July 2020, the concert has been released as a live album and "concert film" in November (Nick Cave, 2020). *Stageit* allows the artists to monetize their performances via tickets and tips. The platform encourages its audiences to interact with artists and each other through a text messaging interface (Stageit, 2020). *Diuo* has been launched as a streaming concert platform and aims to deliver 10 % of ticket sales as grants to members of the performing industry while providing the much-needed income to performance spaces. The company proposes to supply a production team comprising experienced sound and video engineers (Diuo, 2020). A different approach based on audio streaming with a dedicated playback system is presented by *Oda*. The platform offers an audio-only live music experience played through speakers specifically designed to reproduce live performances. Access to the live streaming program is granted through a seasonal subscription. The stereo speaker system features a wooden front panel design and a control unit. The company suggests that the resonant wood panel similarly radiates musical vibrations to an acoustic instrument which provides dimension, presence, and warmth to the sound, resulting in an immersive live performance experience, as if the performers were in the same room with the audience (Oda, 2020).

Performances in virtual venues are among the new trends explored by musicians and audiences. *Wave* aims to create interactive, immersive, and social virtual concert experiences. The company employs motion capture technology to track artists' body and facial movements and uses this data to create avatars performing in virtual venues. The creation of avatars and venues explores concepts that can go beyond direct digital copies. Via the avatars, the artists can transform into fantastical characters such as giant demons or be digitally recreated via the three-dimensional hologram effect technique so that the avatar can be processed through a series of special effects to emphasize musical expression. The venues can be represented as virtual clubs or otherworldly virtual spaces in continuous evolution during the performance. The audience is provided a gaming-style interaction design (Wavexr, 2020). Live performance events in popular games employ video games as the interaction platform. Travis Scott's virtual concert in *Fortnite* reached 27.7 million players (Ombler, 2020, para. 6). *Block by Blockwest* festival was designed as a virtual music festival in *Minecraft*. The festival featured performances by 30 bands and was able to reach 134000 players (Ombler, 2020, para. 12–13). The incorporation of volumetric capture technology into virtual concerts is one of the recent concepts discussed for the advancement of virtual performance experiences. The technology employs hundreds of cameras assembled in a dome structure, enabling audiences to move around and observe the three-dimensional space in real-time (Hogan, 2020, para. 6).

Festivals and benefit concerts continue to be a part of the live music experience via online concert venues and social media platforms. *Trillerfest* was organized by *Triller* in April 2020 as a live-streaming music festival (Trillerfest, 2020). *Facebook Horizon* presents a virtual social experience, including live concerts, sports, and comedy events (Oculus, 2020). *One World: Together At Home* was curated as a benefit concert featuring 79 popular artists, including Elton John, Paul McCartney, and Stevie Wonder. The event was live-streamed in April 2020 and raised $127.9 million for health care workers and coronavirus relief. The album of the event was released three days after the online concert (Variety, 2020, para. 1–3). Although the *9th St. Petersburg Open-Air International All Together Opera Festival* was able to offer a limited number of spectators for each event, organizations such as *EFG London Jazz Festival, Milano Music Week 2020*, and *the 9th annual celebration of International Jazz Day* have been fully adapted as online events. (Jamshaid, 2020; Efg, 2020; Milanomusicweek, 2020; Jazzday, 2020).

Digital music distributors have begun to promote and initiate live streaming concert channels. This coincides with the emergence of online concert venues and other forms of interactive digital media. The conditions caused by the pandemic act as an accelerant factor for the appropriation process of emerging digital technologies. As a result of the digitization of the performance experience in multiple dimensions, music gets performed and distributed in a new way for which the depth and variety of experiences can differ from a real live performance. Digital performances in popular games allow players to experience the live event via their avatars and an interaction design they are already accustomed to. Virtual venues enable audiences and musicians to interact with the live performance through a gaming-style design. Merging of the game and music industries presents exciting possibilities, yet some of the musical performances in popular games and virtual venues have been pre-recorded live and streamed during the event. Virtual venues offer an enhanced interaction model when experienced via virtual reality headsets. While the musicians are provided the chance to reach a global audience, the social aspect of the interactive designs removes physical boundaries between participants and allows for a new kind of interaction within the audience.

COVID-19 and its Effect on Performance and Education

Economic Impact on the Music Industry

As of 2019, live performances constitute 50 % of the overall music industry revenue. The second-largest financial contribution comes from recordings. Records generate income employing various formats such as digital streaming, downloads, physical formats, and synchronization. Streaming has the biggest percentage among them, establishing 48.6 % of the global market (International Federation of Phonographic Industry [IFPI], 2019). The COVID-19 pandemic has brought limitations in physical forms of interaction, and live performances are among the first sectors to shut down completely. In addition to the loss in physical sales and digital downloads, streaming has been affected unexpectedly during the initial lockdown period. Initial reports have indicated a 7–9 % decrease in overall streaming consumption (Hall, 2020, para. 7). Other research estimates this reduction to be 12.5 %. One theory to examine the rationale of this abrupt reduction suggests that diminished physical mobility and travel bans are crucial factors. Both activities are regarded as the most dominant parameters in digital music consumption. Lockdown has changed consumer habits, and many people turned their attention to other mediums to gather information and communicate (Sim, Cho, Hwang & Telang, 2020, pp. 17–19).

Overall the recent development affects the majority of musicians and other music industry workers profoundly due to the severe financial loss. The initial solution to this problem was to apply a hybrid approach by allowing limited participation to the performance venues and also accept online participation. The recent state of pandemic renders the limited participation option impossible. It has been projected that the complete transition to unrestricted physical activities will be gradual, and the return to limited physical participation and online participation will not be sufficient enough to recover fast (Ombler, 2020, para. 1). Consequently, the music industry is in dire need of finding new means of financial survival. As discussed in the previous section, online and virtual platforms have come into prominence for providing an alternative.

Online Music Education

As worldwide lockdowns and restrictions are executed to slow down the COVID-19 pandemic, face-to-face education adapts to online means of interactive communication. However online conferencing platforms have not been fully optimized for live musical performances as musicians attending from different locations suffer from issues such as latency and poor audio quality, which constitutes an obstacle for music and audio production education (Daubney & Fautley, 2020, p. 109).

It is possible to use a digital patchbay to route high-resolution audio from a digital audio workstation (DAW) into the audio input of an online conferencing platform. This is achieved by sending the output of the DAW to the output bus of the digital patchbay and assigning the streaming application's sound input device to the input bus of the digital patchbay to receive audio. Live microphone and instrument inputs as well as other high-resolution audio on disk can be routed directly to streaming input. This provides a considerable increase in the quality of the streamed audio, but the audio is still being transcoded to lower resolutions by the online conference application for easier transmission. To monitor the audio output, the streamer would have to mirror the digital patchbay input via another DAW running simultaneously. Latency may be inevitable due to high processing power usage caused by the complex routing configuration. More efficient audio streaming methods are presented by digital services such as *Listento, Source Connect, Jamulus,* and *Jamkazam. Listento* operates as a plug-in running on DAWs. The application can stream high-resolution audio and may be used for recording remote performances (Audiomovers, 2020). Simultaneous remote recording sessions from multiple locations can be managed via *Source Connect.* The application features auto replace and restore functions to maintain audio quality and compensate for dropouts caused by bandwidth problems (Source Elements, 2020). *Jamulus* and *Jamkazam* are free audio streaming platforms for remote music rehearsals, recording sessions, and music education (Jamulus, 2020; Jamkazam, 2020). It is possible to say that the use of digital streaming services prioritizing audio quality and performance will continue to spread, and the full potential of online music education and performance is yet to be explored.

Conclusion

The COVID-19 pandemic has transformed the perception of leisure time and social interaction; consequently, music streaming consumption has decreased. Due to the social distancing regulations, the use of social media and online concert venues for live performances has accelerated.

The individual point of view in a physical live performance event includes dynamic audio-visual information. A combination of volumetric capture and immersive audio technologies would present an audio-visual interaction model that the audiences can appreciate. Object-based approaches in immersive audio contain audio and metadata with position information, including azimuth, elevation, distance, and width. Scene-based approaches use the ambisonics format.

A first-order ambisonic stream is formed as a three-dimensional mid-side signal, and higher-order ambisonics increases the number of channels to improve localization accuracy (Kares & Larcher, 2016, p. 3). MPEG-H audio codec supports the coding of audio as channels, objects, or higher-order ambisonics so that various types of immersive audio content can be transcoded. The metadata employed by the object-based representations enables elements from the content to be mapped to specific spatial locations. This feature can be used for interaction via dynamic rendering technologies (Rumsey, 2015, pp. 396–397). Three-dimensional audio presents an improved perception of spatiality as it creates the illusion of being transported to a different acoustic environment. The incorporation of immersive audio techniques in virtual reality applications for live performances presents exciting possibilities.

Scholars have identified music as an activity, a continuous process with no limits rather than a fixed object (Horsfall, Meij, & Probstfield, 2013, pp. 36–39). Live performances embody this aspect of music and representations as digital streaming media explore ways to reanimate the multi-dimensional sensation. The spectral and dynamic content received acoustically forms a significant part of the impact of a live performance experienced by the audience. The transformation of acoustic information into digital media is a lossy process. The codecs applied for streaming reduce the resolution further. Bandwidth limitations may cause low bit rates, which result in a diminished sonic experience. High-quality audio streaming is limited to several digital services which focus on recorded music and remote recording applications.

The implementation of high-resolution audio streaming technology in online applications and improvement in the domestic monitoring systems together could potentially match the fidelity of the physical concert venues. Online music education is subject to further development so that latency issues during online performance sessions can be handled properly. The communicational aspect of the traditional live performances will change inevitably, yet new forms of communication and meaning may emerge and become a part of performance practice.

References

Audiomovers. (2020). Retrieved from https://audiomovers.com/wp/.

Bashkow, I. (2004). A Neo-Boasian conception of cultural boundaries. *American Anthropologist, 3* (106): 443–458.

Cross, I. (2012). Musics, cultures and meanings: Music as communication. *Empirical Musicology Review, 1–2* (7): 95–97.

Cross, I. (2014). Music and communication in music psychology. *Psychology of Music, 42* (6): 809–819.

Daubney, A., & Fautley, M. (2020). Editorial research: Music education in a time of pandemic. *British Journal of Music Education,* vol. 37, 107–114.

Dice. (2020). Retrieved from https://dice.fm/tv.

Diuo. (2020). Retrieved from https://www.diuo.io.

EFG London Jazz Festival. (2020). Retrieved from https://efglondonjazzfestival.org.uk/.

Hall, S. (2020). This is how COVID-19 is affecting the music industry. *World Economic Forum.* Retrieved from https://www.weforum.org/agenda/2020/05/this-is-how-COVID-19-is-affecting-the-music-industry.

Hogan, M. (2020). Where can virtual concerts go after Travis Scott's Fortnite extravaganza? *Pitchfork.* Retrieved from https://pitchfork.com/thepitch/virtual-concerts-travis-scotts-fortnite-100-gecs-minecraft/.

Horsfall, S. T., Meij, J. M., & Probstfield, M. D. (Eds.). (2013). *Music sociology: Examining the role of music in social life.* New York, NY: Routledge.

International Federation of Phonographic Industry. (2019). *Global music report.* Retrieved from https://www.ifpi.org/ifpi-global-music-report-2019/.

Ionescu, D. A. (2017). Music as means of communication. *Lingua. Language and Culture, 1* (16): 111–120.

Jamkazam. (2020). Retrieved from https://jamkazam.com.

Jamshaid, U. (2020). First music festival since start of pandemic in Russia to occur In St. Petersburg in Aug. *Urdupoint.* Retrieved from https://www.urdupoint.com/en /world/first-music-festival-since-start-of-pandemic-984700.html.

Jamulus – Play music online. (2020). Retrieved from https://jamulus.io/.

Jazz Day: International jazz day. (2020). Retrieved from https://jazzday.com/.

Kares, J., & Larcher, V. (2016). *Streaming immersive audio content.* Paper presented at the Audio Engineering Society Conference on Audio for Virtual and Augmented Reality, Los Angeles, CA.

Miell, D., Macdonald, R., & Hargreaves, D.J. (Eds.). (2005). *Musical communication.* Oxford: Oxford University Press.

Milano Music Week. (2020). Retrieved from https://www.milanomusicweek.it/en/.

Nick Cave – Idiot Prayer: Nick Cave alone at Alexandra Palace. (2020). Retrieved from https://www. nickcave.com/news/idiot-prayer-nick-cave-alone-at-alexandra-palace/.

Nicolaou, A. (2020). Spotify to push live streaming concerts in response to COVID-19. *The Financial Times*. Retrieved from https://www.ft.com/content/973f8676-705f-4b88-9394-9c4a8bc08485.

Oculus: Horizon. (2020). Retrieved from https://www.oculus.com/facebook-horizon/.

Oda: Live performances in your home. (2020). Retrieved from https://oda.co.

Ombler, M. (2020). Are video games the future of live music? *GamesIndustry.biz*. Retrieved from https://www.gamesindustry.biz/articles/2020-06-10-are-video-games-the-future-of-live-music.

Rumsey, F. (2015). Immersive audio, objects, and coding. *Journal of Audio Engineering Society, 5* (63): 394–398.

Philip, R. (2004). *Performing music in the age of recording*. New Haven: Yale University Press.

Sanden, P. (2012). *Liveness in modern music: Musicians, technology and the perception of performance*. London: Routledge.

Sim, J., Cho, D., Hwang, Y., & Telang, R. (2020). *Virus shook the streaming star: Estimating COVID-19 impact on music consumption*. SSRN e-library. [Accessed on Nov 8, 2020]. Retrieved from https://papers.ssrn .com/sol3/papers.cfm?abstract_id=3649085.

Small, C. (1998). *Musicking: The meanings of performing and listening. Middletown*, CT: Wesleyan University Press.

Source Elements. (2020). Retrieved from https://www.source-elements.com/products/source-connect/.

Spilker, H. S. (2018). *Digital music distribution: The sociology of online music streams*. New York, NY: Routledge.

Stageit: Your online concert venue (2020). Retrieved from https://www.stageit.com/static/static_pages/what_is_stageit.

Trillerfest. (2020). Retrieved from http://trillerfest.com.

Wavexr. (2020). Retrieved from https://wavexr.com/.

Widdess, R. (2012). Music, meaning and culture. *Empirical Musicology Review, 1–2* (7): 88–94.

Variety. (2020). 'One world: Together at home' 79-song album available now on streaming services. Retrieved from https://variety.com/2020/music/news/one-world-together-at-home-global-citizen-album-lady-gaga-taylor-swift-1234586195/.

Ömer Vatanartıran

New Precariat: Voice-Over Artists Performing at Home in the Time of Global Pandemic

Abstract: As one of the most essential lines of works in the culture industry, dubbing has been facing challenges as well as new opportunities with the developments in recording techniques. While traditional productions are done in the studios, where directors, voice actors, agents, and sound engineers come together for each session, new technologies have allowed different actors of this process to contribute distantly. The convenience and availability of high-quality portable microphones, recording equipment, sound-insulating kits, and digital platforms offering easier production and sharing facilities have already been encouraging the sector to challenge the traditional way of dubbing movies and commercials animations, video games, and documentaries. This shift toward homemade recording has also gained importance after the rise of subscription video-on-demand sites such as Netflix, Amazon Prime, and BluTV or YouTube channels where language diversity and time pressure are enormous. However, neither technological convenience nor market pressure has been able to invalidate the conventional way of recording completely. In-person interaction in the studio and simultaneous co-operation in the same place has kept its indispensability among many people in the field. According to this approach, homemade productions are unfavorable not only because of the insufficient technical hardware but also the quality of artistic performance away from the co-present guidance of the agents, engineers, and directors. Nevertheless, the global pandemic has forced even those people to take up the challenge and adopt distant recording facilities. More and more voice artists are encouraged to record at home, share it online with sound engineers who mix them remotely, and send the file to the telecommuting client. While technology allowed coping with the indefinite and ambiguous global situation, it also reproduces the precarity of dubbing professionals. Artists are falling into a more unclear, unstandardized, unsecured work environment. In this chapter, the challenges and opportunities encountered by dubbing professionals after COVID-19 will be discussed. In other words, it will be questioned whether "new normal" means "new precarious" in this industry in Turkey through a close look at the statistics before and after the pandemic and in-depth interviews with people from the field.

Keywords: Dubbing, Digital Technologies, Recording, Voice Over, Remote, Home-Made, Studio, Precarity, Creative Industry, Telecommuting

Introduction

Creative industries in Turkey have been studied from different perspectives as well as from the standpoint of various fields. From studies on movie sector (Durmaz, Yiğitcanlar, & Velibeyoğlu, 2008; Aktaş et al., 2014; Özkan 2009), to creative clusters in İstanbul (Ekdi, Çıracı 2015; Seçilmiş, 2015), music (Tamer & Engin, 2020), advertising (Töre, 2011), and gaming industries (Binark & Bayraktutan, 2012; Şengün & Öztürkcan, 2020), academia have been paying attention to the evolution of such sectors as creative industries in Turkey. Although most of them show nationwide progress and opportunities they've been generating since the 1990s, the tendency of decline because of the pandemic, as well as recent economic crisis, has been taking attention as well. However, neither the rise of the dubbing industry for several decades nor the threats caused by the pandemic have been much of a matter of debate in academia. Although dubbing has had a growing potential (TÜİK, 2018), especially over the past ten years, its contribution to the progress of creative industries in Turkey has not been sufficiently emphasized. Likewise, the irony of the precarization of its creative class -including not just the voiceover artists but also directors, sound engineers, scriptwriters, translators, redactors, and sound editors- despite its growth has not been widely discussed. Moreover, the transformative power of digital technologies in this specific industry has not drawn much attention even though the threats and opportunities, in general, have been quite popular academic fields of interest (Binark, 2012; Waldfogel, 2018).

Although highly disregarded by academia, dubbing has a glorious history in Turkey. Taking the first steps in the 1930s has accompanied the emergence and the rise of the Turkish cinema, state broadcasting, and advertising. For decades, Turkish movies have been filmed without recording soundtrack, and famous voiceover artists such as Adalet Cimcoz, Ferdi Tayfur, and Sacide Keskin re-enacted the characters. Furthermore, TRT (Turkish State Radio and Television) has functioned as a school for new artists and offered them long-term careers as of the '60s. The scope of the business has remarkably expanded after the launch of private TV channels like Star, Kanal 6, Show TV, and the proliferation of movie theaters in big cities in the '90s. More movies, commercials, and documentaries with dubbed versions both on TV and in cinema halls started taking place. Later on, the emergence of digital media such as new TV platforms in the 2000s followed by online media has offered new channels to voiceover productions, as well. Thematic channels brought by global networks including Discovery Channel, National Geography, Hallmark, MTV, cooking channels, etc.; all of them offered dubbed alternatives in Turkish, which led to the industry's growth.

Finally, streaming services like Netflix, BluTV, Apple TV, Amazon, and puhutv have created brand new opportunities for studios, artists, casting agencies, and all related creative professionals. In short, dubbing has corresponded to all technological developments in accord with all related creative sectors in which it operates: Advertising, marketing, film, TV, podcast, CRM, gaming, e-learning, smartphone applications, etc.

Despite this growth in demand thanks to new operation channels and developing technologies, dubbing gets its share when it comes to the precarization of its creative class. There are more studios, more content for dubbed productions, more technological facilities for in-house recordings, yet more precarized professionals who work without contracts, in growing uncertainties, with decreasing wages and more competitive alternatives which can easily be found online, and thus losing their bargaining power. In fact, this dilemma could be found in many creative industries in Turkey like in other countries. While they contribute to the economy at local and national levels and have a regular rate of growth since the 2000s (Seçilmiş, 2015; Lazeretti, Capone & Seçilmiş, 2014; Yardımcı, 2016); the situation has not been that promising for freelance, non-contractual and unprotected workers since it takes advantage of the myth of bohemian artists (Ross, 2003), deregulated neoliberal state (Kergel, 2016), and non-existent, dormant or inefficacious unions (McRobbie, 2016). Besides, digital technologies enable freelancers to self-promote themselves, get offered a job via online communication, and record at home with the latest facilities such as sound-insulating kits, recording equipment, high-quality portable microphones, and applications of mix and mastering. However, this leads to unsecured self-employment. All these considered voiceover artists suffer from precarization as many other freelancers do in other creative industries. The pandemic has even exacerbated the fragile situation of the creative class working in the dubbing industry. Although digital devices allowing personal recording from home provided continuity of work to a certain degree, it also gave rise to another dilemma for freelancers since networking with agencies, studios, directors and employers are crucial in the sector to create new job opportunities in the future.

Creative Industries: Freedom or Insecurity?

Creative industries are at crossroads where artistic, cultural, and intellectual efforts meet a business perspective to embody commercial value. It is the sum of various subsections such as architecture, design, software, media, performing arts, and advertising where creative labor forms a commercial product or service often registered as intellectual property (NOIE, 2003). Despite the early attempts of defining these industries at the beginning of the 1990s in Australia (Hocaoğlu, 2015), it's been the announcement of the Department for Digital Culture, Media and Sports of United Kingdom towards the end of the millennium which pioneered a vast academic interest and international response by other governments thanks to the encouragement of the British New Labor government (Peuter, 2011; Henry, 2007; Hartley, 2005). While countries may have different categorizations, all of them consider creative and highly skilled labor with the economic prosperity in defining them (Braun; Lavanga, 2007). Moreover, this human capital is also capable of generating new regional attractions by offering 3 T's to economies: "talent, tolerance and technology" (Florida, 2004). In other words, Florida (2004) argues that a creative class of talented and well-educated people leading technological progress who produce high economic value in a tolerant and encouraging environment has a more decisive role in a city's destiny than natural resources or geographical advantages. Thus, creativity has become a critical skill that has been regarded as "the oil of the 21st century" (Ross, 2008, p. 32), considering its ability to increase regional development, destination, and national wealth (Gill, 2002) more than conventional manufacturing industries (Howkins, 2001). Creative human capital invents new technologies which facilitate intellectual, cultural and artistic production with growing business potential. This type of work demands more decentralized structures and networks with a flexible labor force cooperating in fast-changing informal networks (Menger, 1999; Gill & Pratt, 2008). In short, the economy grows following the synergy between culture, knowledge, and creativity (Flew, 2011).

Creative industries unite artistic passion, craving, risk-taking, innovativeness, uniqueness, informality, flexibility, and stand-on-your-own attitude with managerial rationality to increase profitability, sustainability, and entrepreneurship. In other words, bohemia intertwines with a business mindset. Artistic craft, intellectual capital, cultural experience, physical competence, and technological skills are capitalized without hierarchical contracts, strict chain of commands, rigid bureaucracies, and inflexible working hours. In other words, the creative class usually works freelance, and 48 % of the cultural labor in the EU is self-employed (Pasikowska-Schnass, 2020; Menger, 1999). This type of work fits perfectly to artists for whom "collective action" (Becker, 1982) matters more than formal, standardized, and pre-described jobs at companies since it allows more individualism, autonomy, task variety, independency, and creativity (Stimson & Sholette, 2007). However, this freedom has its price; it often comes with instability in an unpredictable professional environment that is imposing temporary short-term projects with continuous fear of a future career and carries a high risk of being dismissed without any social insurance (Christopherson, 2008; Gill & Pratt, 2008; Kunda, 2011).

While this way of work presents emotional and economic difficulties for the creative class, especially for artists (Menger, 1999), it is more attractive for employers, investors, hirers, managers, and shareholders; in short, the business capital, since it offers fewer employee costs, and more "control over working conditions, wages and the pace of work" (Rodgers, 1989). In this neoliberal economic, political and social structure, passionate individual risk-takers are glorified while the failure stories are not seen or heard yet labeled as an individual's own lack of perseverance, passion, and creativity. Thus, there is more to the individual than the state or company in charging responsibility, especially when it comes to the precarity of the working force (Biebricher, 2018; Kergel, 2016).

The dilemma is clear for the creative class, and they keep their independence against bureaucratic hierarchies of companies at the expense of being precarized; that is, maintaining an unstable career without security, protection, and dignity. Guy Standing (2011) draws attention to how the neoliberal global system forces creative labor to work without a stable income, self-enhancement, career advancement and to undertake the fear of arbitrary dismissal, getting ill, or having an accident without the chance of being tolerated and protected, and becoming isolated without a "collective voice." Although Standing (2019) indicates all kinds of "freelancers and self-employed people that work in the creative and knowledge industry" in explaining precariat as a new "transformative class," artistic creative labor especially deserves attention since it by nature involves "deep-commitment, high productiveness, a strong sense of personal achievement and a high degree of risk-taking" (Menger, 1999). Although voluntarily embedded with atypical, non-standardized, and project-based work (Serafini & Banks, 2020), the bohemian way of creation is industrialized (Ross, 2003), artists become "gig-workers" (Alex & Graham, 2018) who are paid per project, performance, session and called on-demand. Thus, independency turns into irregularity, dependency on power networks, and being vulnerable and without formal support when a crisis happens (Foti, 2017). In other words, in a risk society full of financial fluctuations, changing political dynamics, transforming technologies, and the global environment (Beck, 1992), artists are the first to suffer from unsustainable careers, economic uncertainties, and insecurity.

Technology and Artistic Creative Labor

Creative industries are in constant change because of technological developments, and both of them are highly interdependent. They can offer a new type of works to artists, a new space to share their creative efforts, and brand-new business models which transform a whole sector. With the stable growth indicated by GDP's of entertainment media industries, satellite accounts, copyright employments, and household spending numbers on recreation and culture (Van Der Pol, 2007), the way creative labor works changes, too. For example, in the film industry, scriptwriters now use software applications in the pre-production, cameramen shoot with high-quality digital cameras or drones in the production, film editors enjoy improved digital audio and visual effects in the post-production, and finally, the movie gets distributed on various new media. This whole process with new dynamics brings new job descriptions, opportunities, and expertise (Castells, 2002; Lhooq, 2012; Corliss, 2006; Fair, 2006), as well. Transactions among actors at all levels become more flexible, convenient, accessible, and interactive contrary to the offline way of work (Mark, 2018). It even allows consumers or junior artists to become producers by using do-it-yourself audiovisual services and offers them new media such as YouTube, Netflix, or IGTV. Finally, digital facilities made a global interaction among different regions possible; without a Western-centric one-way flow of cultural content, any artist anywhere has the chance to go internationally viral (Van Der Pol, 2007).

As the self-employed artistic labor of the gig economy, artists take advantage of home-production, networking, and performing online independently, reaching various markets with a wide spectrum of the audience, as well as suffering from increasing uncertainty, competition, and invisible work (Vallas & Schor, 2020). In this sense, it can be revealed as another instrument to push artists into the precariat. Despite removing barriers to entry and enabling self-actualization without hard-to-pass filter mechanisms of conventional media, it leads to -usually informal- self-employment with insecurity, asymmetric bargaining, exploitation, and unpaid wage (Standing, 2019; Foti, 2017, Kergel, 2016). Thus, digital technologies offer "free labor" (Terranova, 2000), which is more exploitable by employers than conventional employment relationships. In addition to the lack of social protection, it increases precarization by laying the burden of preparing self-promotion materials online, marketing them constantly through various channels, following communication with prospective employers, presentation of the self on social media with professional purposes, budgeting latest technology, adapting to innovations, access to relevant networking sites, and such. Furthermore, the impact of the "digital divide, high cost of data and limited access to networks" (UNCTAD, 2019) on artists also deserves attention. Not all artists can afford the latest technologies or develop the necessary skills to use them. Thus, those who are not able to adapt to the challenges of new technologies become more vulnerable.

The Pandemic

Despite having a precarizing effect on artistic labor, digital technologies have been functioning as lifebelts in the gig economy during the pandemic. In addition to telecommuting facilities for all types of creative workers, artists have benefited from online gigs such as YouTube concerts or Instagram live shows and used applications that enable different lines of work to connect simultaneously so that a product can be done as if it was happening offline. In other words, "space and time compressions," in Harvey's words (1989), emerged as digitized production, distribution, and selling, virtualized cultural spaces, and experiences such as online museum tours or National Theater YouTube premiers master classes of famous artists paid via PayPal. This means that artificial intelligence, augmented realities and enriched virtual experiences of cultural content responded to the need to spend extended pastime of locked down the audience, and high-quality digital content increased their engagement (OECD, 2020). In short, digitization of creative transactions emerged as an "adapt/evolve or perish" (Ogumbo-Regisford, L., 2020) strategy, and those who could comply with digital means increased their chance to overcome the canceled professional activities because of social distancing measures.

Although there are winners of this process like app developers, popular on-demand sites with high revenues, e-learning platforms with an increasing number of students, artists gaining or reinforcing their popularity on social media, and highly paid celebrities attending online shows, the case is rather more threatening for more and more artists. OECD report (2020) on the effects of the COVID-19 on creative labor displays a stunning result that the pandemic leaves artists alone with their economic problems, without financial support and social security, in their struggle to survive in an "impoverished and downsizing" sector. According to research conducted by the World Federation of Advertisers in October 2020 in 8 companies across 17 sectors with respondents at global positions, budgets dropped at 36 %, 51 % of the respondents have a negative sentiment about the future of the sector despite increasing response campaigns and digital shifts in marketing strategies, and the cuts will not be compensated. Another research conducted by Oxford Economics in the UK (2020) shows that Creative Industries face a turnover loss of 31 % between 2019 and 2020, which means that 409K "jobs are considered at risk." Furthermore, most of them cannot sustain their secondary works, which normally guarantee an income other than creative professional activities. Even worse, most of them attend work as long as it is not restricted by the government to keep their network alive and earn money; however, they risk their health and getting infected in the poorly ventilated studios, lose social distancing measures, and without mask moments of the creative activity. The opposite alternative faces the risk of losing their skills, accumulated network, and hope for a better future. Moreover, they even lack governmental supports arranged particularly for the pandemic since their non-standard and informal self-employment makes it hard to assess according to conventional measures. In short, COVID-19 has been reinforcing the existing trend toward precarization of the artistic creative labor.

Research: Turkish Dubbing Sector and COVID-19

There are several statistical categories in the list of NACE Rev-2, the European Union definition of economic activities, which correspond to the professions composing the dubbing sector: Artists, voiceover artists, scriptwriters, sound engineers, agents, and such. All of these are counted under the creative, entertainment, and performing arts category. Despite the regular increase between 2014–2018 with 5,5 % in 2018, the employment rate in these industries had a decline of 2,6 % in 2019 (TÜİK). This indicates an already existing tendency to go down before the pandemic. Although there are no governmental statistics shared to display the effects of the COVID-19 on creative industries in Turkey yet, it would not be difficult to expect even more dramatic decline considering canceled work, decreasing budgets, and weakening networking opportunities. As discussed above, such considerable outcomes happen not only in employee numbers, industry revenues, and the market size but also individual psychologies.

As described by Merriam (2009), "qualitative researchers are interested in understanding how people interpret their experiences, how they construct their worlds, and what meaning they attribute to their experiences" (p. 5). Our purpose is to understand the meaning people have constructed of their world and their experiences. This qualitative research aims to find out the effects of the pandemic on the Turkish dubbing sector in a less productive and more isolating environment caused by COVID-19 through the experiences of voiceover artists. To have a more comprehensive understanding, different actors of this sector were involved in the study to understand their experiences about how they responded to the pandemic.

As semi-structured in-depth interviews allow to get inside of personal experiences, observations, and feelings concerning social environments (Rubin & Rubin, 2005; Chilban, 1996), this method was used to collect data. Collecting data through interviews involves determining whom to interview. That depends on what the investigator wants to know and from whose perspective the information is desired. Selecting respondents based on what they can contribute to the researcher's understanding of the phenomenon under study means engaging in purposive or theoretical sampling (Merriam, 2009, p. 105). Purposive sampling has been used since the participants were selected according to their level of activity in the sector: Working with leading companies, having a large network, maintaining a successful career in the business. In order to depict what a whole industry has experienced during the pandemic, different occupations in the same sector were selected. This would also provide different standpoints and understandings of the same industry and thus comprehend the gaps among actors working in the same process.

Six professionals from different lines of work were interviewed: One studio owner, one voiceover artist, one union representative, one agent, one sound engineer, and one director. The following questions were prepared in the semi-guided interview protocol:

- How has the amount of work been influenced because of COVID-19?
- How are you satisfied with the performance of digital recording devices and apps which facilitate remote working? Would you continue using technology in the same way after the pandemic?
- What challenges have you been exposed to other than economic difficulties?
- What kind of financial support have you received from the government, companies, or social networks, if any?
- What kind of public policies and alternative support mechanisms do you recommend?

To analyze data collected through the interviews, content analysis was used. As the initial step, organizational categories were formed. The purpose of the initial step is to "fracture the data and rearrange them into categories that facilitate comparison between things in the same category" (Maxwell, 2005, p. 96). Then, using the significant statements of the participants, meaning units were generated, followed by the development of an "essence" description (Bloomberg & Volpe, 2012). At this point, participant quotations were provided to enhance validity.

COVID-19 and Work-Load

Interviews show that workload has been experienced differently. Since voiceover is provided for different content, including advertising, cinema, documentaries, cartoons, trailers, and lectures on different channels such as streaming sites, e-learning platforms, digital TV platforms, movie theaters, and social media; all of them went through different difficulties or opportunities.

One of the interviewees was an agent who brings companies in connection with studios and artists. She said, astounded, that "we even got more work since all the brands are after pandemic campaigns, especially rising sectors, such as online shopping sites, brought more work than usual." However, she admits that this could only be possible thanks to campaigns homed and hosed at post-production tables using stocked content; there has been an enormous fall in brand new commercials produced from scratch. The only field in the decline of work, according to her, has been big events like advertising rewards.

On the other hand, a voiceover artist and the director claim that the march of events in movies, documentaries, and cartoon voiceovers have been different from that of advertising. Especially when studios have been reluctant to serve in the first three months, there has been a stoppage since distant recording synchronized voiceover for feature-length productions full of dialogues is harder than short sessions for commercials. Indeed, the head of the Union of Voice Over Actors of Turkey drew attention to the fact that movie productions were terminated, release dates were postponed, and both national and international flow of content stopped. To illustrate, studios particularly serving to Netflix had a loss of nearly 60 %, "while they had a workload of 2000 minutes before, they now have a maximum of 400. However, a recovery period is on the way, people learned how to cope with it, less or more", he says.

Therefore, fear of losing job was experienced in different ways in different lines of work in the industry. A studio manager stressed that they are more concerned for money-collection for finished work than receiving new ones. The pandemic has been used as an excuse for unpaid budgets for very long periods.

Victory of Digital Skills

The use of digital technologies has been indisputably decisive in coping with COVID-19. All these respondents representing different lines of work emphasized with the same enthusiasm how crucial digital equipment and mastering their use have been from the very beginning of the pandemic. In fact, this determined the level of anxiety since not all the voiceover artists have access to the latest technologies or having the knowledge of using them as required. All of the respondents pay attention to the fact that almost every studio tried to provide microphones to the artists they work with; if they did not have them already, some even offered voice insulation kits.

While clients and agents are satisfied with home-recorded performances, according to the agent working mainly for advertising, the manager states that the expectation went lower with the pandemic, and clients show consent to low-quality performances as long as they "do not sound amateurish." "It is impossible to reach the studio quality, from synchronization problems to providing the right acoustics, there are many insufficiencies," says the agent pointing out the importance of the studio and, above all the sound engineers. Furthermore, the sound engineer points out that "outside-the-studio solutions only kept the quantity assured, while the quality of work is terrible." He also complains about the fact that sound engineers work more to improve the poor qualities of sent items. Indeed, the manager says that "a session which could be operated by listening to the recorded track two times within the surrounded sound systems in the studio, it now takes 10 or 20 times to listen and decide whether there are any sound quality problems with earphones."

Likewise, the voiceover artist also takes attention to the increasing workload of artists since they must prepare the acoustic environment, arrange the microphones' position and other devices' performance, and make at least a basic editing before sharing the content with sound engineers. She also adds that doing this work without a director is very hard, "without a "second ear," without the lead and verification of a higher look, it's anxious to do the work all alone."

Furthermore, the interviewee from the Union underlines the difficulty of synchronization and how extra effort it demands, especially for movies, cartoons, and documentaries. The manager indicates sound engineers' loss from this process, they work more to upgrade the record but paid less since recording sessions normally last longer in the studio, and this increases their wage. Similarly, voiceover artists work more to synchronize their takes with the screen or text, "a session which would normally last 40 minutes now takes almost 2 hours" says the director. "However," she says, "I developed my digital skills, we managed somehow to learn to do remote recording sessions altogether, while one of us speaks, the director gives instructions, and the engineer follows the content technically."

Although digital recording devices, portable complementary kits, and software programs facilitated remote recordings in a time when working in the studio were either banned or avoided because of posing health risks, they created inequality among voiceover artists. First of all, digitally literate young artists have had fewer difficulties, according to all the interviewees. "Many well-experienced and known artists above 60 years old were not able to adapt to the technologies, and therefore they lost their attraction," says the manager. The head of the Union draws attention to another fact which worsens the situation for elder artists: "Even though they admit to work in the studios, they are more fragile because of the obvious reasons, and they feel out of the play." Furthermore, digital literacy or the ability to develop required skills does not suffice, according to the director; many young artists had financial incapability to get them. "Luckier ones got microphones from the studios, some of them made huge sacrifices considering their moderate-income, those without the equipment either were dismissed or forced to take the risk to go to the studio." Similarly, the VO artist says that "it all happened very quickly and harshly, some played the game well, some could not, so it has not been fair." Thus, both materially and cognitively, a digital divide among the artists emerged as a remarkable differentiation point.

Nostalgia for Studios

"Only those who had already big brands in their portfolio got more work in the commercial voiceover side; the rest without ongoing relationships have more difficulties to get new brands," says the agent. Clients prefer to work with those they already know, can rely on the quality of work even accomplished remotely. Thus, networking opportunities are fading away, "artists lose their chance to make acquainted with new clients in the studio environment," she adds. Likewise, the manager points out the lack of networking for the studios as well. "This was the only reason to open our buildings close to ad agencies, we can easily interact in the same neighborhood, once they come for one reason or another to our place, we can offer them help to get another work done, and this has a binding effect for future collaborations." Besides this aspect, touch is lost psychologically as well, according to the voiceover artist. "Studios look like desert islands now, we miss our colleagues, having a word together, offering work to each other less or more, the interaction with other artists." The sound engineer also emphasizes the lack of "catching each other's eye behind the glass wall in the studio," it's not just technical complications but at the same time a feeling that all people involved in this process are used to. Likewise, the head of the Union stresses this feeling of missing each other with the community, "rather than the fear of a sustainable career, and it's this yearning which hurts; however, the sense of security compensates it."

Performance Dependency on the Content

There are certain fields of work that can continue to be done remotely even after the pandemic. All the interviewees point out the fact that clients are happy as long as they can reduce the costs. "They no longer pay for studios; they can get what they want without this expense," says the sound engineer as well as the agent and the manager. Moreover, they all agree regarding the time saved by working remotely. "No longer being stuck in the traffic jam of Istanbul, which could take 2 or 3 hours more than the work in the studio", the agent says. The manager also states that it's relieving for them to work without the stress of urging them to finish the work in the reserved time slot. "They do not complain as long as they do not have to go back and forth between the studio and their office; they save a good amount of time in this way as well as keeping their budget. Sometimes, we keep our artist present in the studio while they insist on working remotely". He argues that commercial and some basic e-learning or CRM voiceovers will likely be done remotely even after the pandemic. The head of the Union adds the audiobooks or audio instructions of product and services to the list, saying that "such work does not demand a studio ambiance to get a better result, one can achieve it easily at home." The sound engineer is more hesitant, "there will always be more complicated texts and campaigns, and clients may always prefer to meet in the studio." On the other hand, the VO artist quite sure that this will be a powerful tendency even after the pandemic. "This all was like a rehearsal, remote recording through digital technologies were already at the door, this accelerated their spread, surely this way of doing is going remain." However, this type of work is not sustainable for content like movies, documentaries, cartoons, they all admit. They require to be present at the same time, allowing artists to be guided instantly, interfering with a technical process in case of any failure on synchronization or following the right of timecodes. Although it is possible to be co-present digitally, any cut-off of someone's internet undermines and complicates the process.

"Precarization"

There is information on studios that went out of business, production companies that could not film new content, and shut down offices because of teleworking facilities in the interview data. These are signs of economic difficulties experienced during the pandemic. However, the precarization of dubbing professionals can be tracked in different aspects. First of all, as mentioned above, the digital divide caused loss of work for elder artists or those without digital equipment and/or who had not sufficient ongoing relations with clients. Besides, there are more and more sound engineers with terminated insurance, and they are forced to work as freelancers. "It was already on their agenda; the pandemic has been the excuse on the right time," says the sound engineer.

The manager points out that the pending payments made it impossible to cover all this labor and freelancing them was inevitable. "Moreover," he says, "they used to earn more since in-the-studio labor was on the books; however, they now waste more time to organize, edit and mix sent items at home, but not paid extra." The agent argues that telecommuting led to a more cutthroat and relentless environment, "all of us, the representatives, agents, artists and sound engineers are exploited more, clients ask for favors which were impossible before, whenever they have a program, they want the artist to be ready no matter what time it is. When we try to protect our artist's privacy or family time, they can counterattack us by saying, "but he did it the last time, what's different now? We can work with someone else who is available!," how can we resist this?". She also underlines that they are impatient to get the work done while under normal circumstances they would tolerate a loss of time to reserve the studio.

Both the agent and the manager draw attention to the fact that clients are more demanding, intolerant to any delay in e-mail replies; they may even ask for newer versions for which they would normally pay more under normal circumstances. Because of the uncertainty of the remote performance, they believe that they deserve this extra labor without additional cost.

Furthermore, agents are expected to respond at any time, night and day, weekend, and national holidays. "Everybody feels exhausted because of the fear of losing job, no one dares to reject any offer, but the price is the order." The manager claims that "extra work without payment regardless its timing got legitimized and it will be hard to break this new normal." The VO artist and the head of the Union emphasizes the depreciation of the artists, "in a deeper isolation, all alone without any official support, being pushed to risk their lives if they are not capable of finding digital solutions, they feel more uncertain, unstable and exposed to danger" says the latter.

Moreover, all of the respondents indicate the hidden loads of this process: Everybody working from home pays higher bills of electricity, wi-fi, food, heating, and none of them are offered to be backed up. "Not just the humble artists working from home," says the manager, "even the studios and agencies have difficulty of coping with increasing fixed costs, we speak on the phone constantly, sometimes send microphones to artists, requesting for another take right after a slight change in the text, all these are not counted as extra costs." Moreover, the copyrights of popular cultural content force agents to work in-the-studio and it poses a risk for the artist who is not in the position to refuse the job. "Although measures taken in the studios and instructions prepared in Turkey have been very successful and even taken as a model internationally, one cannot guarantee to create a zero-risk environment. An artist yearning for creative expression in addition to the desperate need of getting a job makes long confinement at home impossible", the head of the Union says. Moreover, both the VO artist and the manager emphasize how limited networking occasions and artistic development without observing more experienced and proficient veterans are.

Support and Solidarity

Minimum Wage Discussions

All of the respondents show indifference to state subsidies; some of them exactly know the amount of financial support announced by the government; however, they do not believe in its efficiency. In other words, they are not expecting government aid in this sense. However, both the VO artist and the head of the Union believe that basic income is a dream but an inevitable measure that will be taken sooner or later. Moreover, they believe that a minimum wage should be reviewed since people work more to get one job done in this way. Both the manager and the head of the Union appreciate ongoing negotiations to redefine labor per word or minute and reformulate the workload according to time spent remotely or in the studio.

Tax Concessions

The latter also criticizes that VO artists are taken as active labor force and forced to pay their taxes, although they may be inactive for months. In short, tax concessions must be reconsidered by the government, they all say. "The tax deferral announced at the beginning of the COVID-19 did not last long, and when the time of payment comes, it's bitter," says the sound engineer. The VO artist underlines how "providing technology at home" crucial in this process is. The manager adds that creative labor can be supported in terms of getting the right technology as well as the knowledge of using it. Finally, studios must be inspected regularly and encouraged to follow the hygiene instructions, the head of the Unions States.

Conclusion

In this research, the Turkish dubbing sector as a creative industry is revealed concerning threats and opportunities offered by digital technologies, especially during the pandemic. First of all, different lines of work experience the process differently. While the pandemic has been a huge opportunity for commercial voiceovers, other content like movies, documentaries and cartoons had more loss of work at the beginning because of new productions at a standstill. Although digital equipment like high-quality microphones, portable insulation kits, easy-to-use software programs to record and edit offered great help for corporate and individual sustainability, access to these technologies has not been equal for each actor. In addition to affording these devices, having the skills to use them has been decisive on job security. Those who deprive this equipment or have difficulty in learning how to use them were left out of the play or forced to be present in the studio. Furthermore, the pandemic has been used as an excuse to precarize artistic labor, sound engineers pushed to be freelancers, agents, and artists working more and without limitation of time and extra payment. Employers threaten those who resist this formlessness and irregularity with losing the job; thus, fear of dismissal forces them to give any concession. Artists and the Union are more aware of the discussions like basic income or state protection for creative labor; however, such concerns are not shared by all lines of work. On the other hand, as the agent's and manager's emphasis shows, a concern for increasing expenses due to telecommuting is widely shared. Furthermore, these concerns will likely last after the pandemic since working from home can still be preferable.

To conclude, the use of digital technologies for home recording is likely to continue after the pandemic, especially for a certain type of content. Thus, helping artistic laborers to develop their digital skills, minimizing the digital gap, and coping with the increasing costs of teleworking seem essential for any policy considering the dubbing sector in the near future. Moreover, in-the-studio recordings will not disappear as long as demanding synchronization content is produced; therefore, setting hygiene standards for all studios is essential as well. Last but not least, protective mechanisms for self-employment needs to be developed so that artists, sound engineers, and all other freelancers can contribute to the consumption of cultural and creative content in hard times like COVID-19.

References

Aktaş, R., Doğanay, M., Bozdağ, Ş., Karaduman, A. B., Orhan, K., Işıklı, H., ...Altunbaş, A. (2014). National studies on the economic contribution of the copyright-based industries. *Study on the economic contribution of copyright industries in Turkey* (pp. 468–582). vol: 8.

Alex, W., & Graham, M. (2018). *Good gig, bad gig: Autonomy and algorithmic control in the global gig economy*, work. *Employment and Society*, *33* (1): 56–75.

Beck, U. (1992). *Risk society: Towards a new modernity*. Munich: Sage.

Becker, H. (1982). *Art worlds*. Berkeley: University of California Press.

Biebricher, T. (2018). *The political theory of Neoliberalism*. California: Stanford University Press.

Durmaz, B., Yigitcanlar, T., & Velibeyoglu, K. (2008). Creative cities and the film industry: Antalya's transition to a Eurasian FilmCentre. *The Open Urban Studies Journal*, 1: pp. 1–10.

Binark, F. M. (2012). Yeni medya ve yaratıcı endüstri. [New media and creative industry]. *Medya ekonomisi ve işletmeciliği. [Media economy and its managership]*. (pp. 162–191). Eskişehir: Anadolu Ünv: AÖF.

Binark, M., & Bayraktutan, G. (2012). A critical interpretation of a new creative industry in Turkey: Game studios and the production of a value chain. In J. Fromme & A. Unger (Eds.). *Computer games and new media cultures* (pp. 371–391). Berlin: Springer.

Bloomberg, L. D., & Volpe, M. (2012). *Completing your qualitative dissertation: A road map from beginning to end.* Los Angeles: Sage Publications.

Braun, E., & Lavanga, M. (2007). *An international comparative quick scan into national policies for creative industries.* Rotterdam: Euricur.

Chilban, J. (1996). *Interviewing in depth: The interactive relational approach.* California: Sage Publications.

Christopherson, S. (2008). Beyond the self-expressive creative worker: An industry perspective on entertainment media. *Theory, Culture, And Society,* 25: 73–95.

Corliss, R. (2006). Can this man save the movies? (Again?). *Time.* [Accessed on Nov 17, 2020]. Retrieved from http://content.time.com/time/magazine/article/0,9171,1172229,00.html

Ekdi, F. P., & Çıracı, H. (2015). Cultural/creative industries in Istanbul: Beyoğlu case. *A|Z Journal, 1* (12): 67–82.

Fair, J. (2006). *The impact of digital technology upon the filmmaking production process.* [Online published M.A. thesis]. University College Dublin. Retrieved from https://the72project.files.wordpress.com/2011/10/thesis.pdf?&sessionid=6b8246ad01cd6bba198fa4b51f508a5f.

Flew, T. (2011). *The creative industries: Culture and policy.* California: Sage Publications.

Florida, R. (2004). *The rise of the creative class: And how it's transforming work, leisure, community and everyday Life.* New York: Basic Books.

Gill, R., & Pratt, A. C. (2008). In the social factory? Immaterial labor, precariousness and cultural work. Theory, *Culture and Society, 25* (7–8): 1–30.

Gill, R. (2007). *Technobohemians or the new cybertariat?: New media work in Amsterdam a decade after the Web.* Amsterdam: Institute of Network Cultures.

Hartley, J. (2005). *Creative industries.* Oxford: Blackwell Publishing.

Harvey, D. (1989). *The condition of postmodernity: An enquiry into the origins of cultural change.* Cambridge, MA: Blackwell.

Henry, C. (2007). *Entrepreneurship in the creative industries: An international perspective.* Cheltenham: Elgar.

Hocaoğlu, D. (2015). *Yaratıcı endüstrilerin yerel ekonomilerdeki önemi ve tasarımın bu endüstrilere katkısı.* [The importance of creative industries in local economies and contribution of the design to these industries]. *Planlama, 25* (3): 189–194.

Howkins, J. (2001). *The creative economy: How people make money from ideas.* Michigan: Allen Lane.

Kergel, D. (2016). Bildungssoziologie und prekaritätsforschung: Castingshows als Prekaritätsnarration. [Educational sociology and precarity research: Casting shows as precarious narration]. In R.-D. Hepp, R. Riesiger & D. Kergel (Eds.). *Precarity- Shift in the Center of the Society* (pp. 177–196). Wiesbaden: VS Springer.

Kunda, G. (2011). *Gurus, hired guns, and warm bodies: Itinerant experts in a knowledge economy.* New Jersey: Princeton University Press.

Lazzeretti, L., Capone, F., & Seçilmiş, İ. E. (2014). *Türkiye'de yaratıcı ve kültürel sektörlerin yapısı.* [The structure of creative and cultural industries in Turkey]. *Maliye Dergisi,* 166: 195–220.

Lhooq, M. (2012). 9 mind-blowing technologies changing the film industry's future. *Creators Project.* [Accessed on Nov 8, 2020]. Retrieved from http://thecreatorsproject.vice.com/en_aublog/9-mind-blowing-technologies-changing-the-film-industry's-future-2.

Maxwell, J. A. (2005). *Qualitative research design: An interactive approach* (2nd Ed.). Applied social research methods series, vol. 41. Thousand Oaks: Sage Publications.

Menger, P. M. (1999). *Artistic labor markets and careers. Annual Review of Sociology,* 25: 541–574.

Merriam, S. B. (2009). *Qualitative research: A guide to design and implementation.* San Francisco: Jossey Bass.

McRobbie, A. (2016). *Be creative: Making a living in the new culture industries.* Cambridge: Polity Press.

NOIE. (2003). Creative industries cluster study. *National office for the information economy, department of communications, IT and the Arts, Canberra.* [Accessed on Nov 8, 2020]. Retrieved from http://www.govonline.gov.au/publications/NOIE/DCITA/cluster_study_report_28may.pdf.

Ogumbo-Regisford, L. (2020). Our creative economy, science & technology post Covid-19. *Fablstyle.* [Accessed on Nov 8, 2020] Retrieved from https://tinyurl.com/y5gb6ap7 Access: 21/07/2020.

Oxford Economics. (2020). Projected economic impact of Covid-19 on U.K.'s creative industries. (Online report). [Accessed on Nov 8, 2020].

Retrieved from https://www.creativeindustriesfederation.compublications/report-projected-economic-impact-covid-19-uk-creative-industries.

Özkan, E. (2009). Bir ortam olarak yaratıcı endüstri: Film endüstrisi'nin İstanbul'da yer seçim kriterleri. [Creative industry as an environment: Location selecting criteria of the film industry in Istanbul]. *Sigma, 2*: 143–158.

Pasikowska-Schnass, M. (2020). EU support for artists and the cultural and creative sector during the coronavirus crisis. *European Parliamentary Research Service, PE.*

Peuter, G. D. (2011). *Creative economy and labor precarity. Journal of Communication Inquiry, 35* (4): 417–425.

Rodgers, G. (1989). Precarious work in Western Europe: The state of the debate. In G. Rodgers & J. Rodgers (Eds.). *Precarious jobs in labor market regulation: The growth of atypical employment in Western Europe.* Geneva: International Institute for Labor Studies.

Ross, A. (2003). *No collar: The humane workplace and its hidden costs.* New York: Basic Books.

Ross, A. (2008). *The new geography of work: Power to the precarious?. Theory, Culture and Society, 25* (7–8): 31–49.

Rubin, J. H., & Rubin, S. I. (2005). Listening, hearing and sharing social experiences. *Qualitative interviewing: The art of hearing data.* Thousand Oaks, California: Sage Publications.

Seçilmiş, E. (2015). Clustering of creative industries in Turkey. *Ege Akademik Bakış Dergisi, 1* (15): 9–18.

Serafini, P., & Banks, M. (2020). Living precarious lives? Time and temporality in visual arts careers. *Culture Unbound Journal of Current Cultural Research, 12* (6): 1–21.

Standing, G. (2011). *The precariat: The new dangerous class.* London: Bloomsbury Academic.

Standing, G. (2019). The precariat: Today's transformative class?. *Development, 61* (1–4).

Şengün, S., & Öztürkcan, S. (2020). Re-shaped by mobile technologies' disruption: The videogame industry in Turkey. *Pazarlama İçgörüsü Üzerine Çalışmalar. 1* (4): 44–56.

Stimson, B., & Sholette, G. (Eds.). (2007) *Collectivism after modernism: The art of social imagination after 1945.* Minneapolis: University of Minnesota Press.

Tamer, B., & Engin, B. (2020). Turkish independent music industry in the last decade. In T. Hepdinçler & H. K. Suher (Eds.). *Creative industries in Turkey.* Bern: Peter Lang.

Terranova, T. (2000). Producing culture for the digital economy. *Social Text, 18* (2–63): 33–58.

Töre, E. (2011). Türkiye'de reklam endüstrisi değer zinciri ve temel göstergeler. [The value chain of the advertisement industry in Turkey and the main indicators]. *The Turkish Online Journal of Design, Art and Communication. 2* (1).

UNCTAD. (2019). How creative economy can help power development. In The United Nations Conference on Trade and Development. [Accessed on Nov 8, 2020]. Retrieved from https://unctad.org/news/how-creative-economy-can-help-power-development.

Vallas, S., & Schor, J. B. (2020). What do platforms do? Understanding the gig economy. *Annual Review of Sociology, 46* (1).

Van der Pol, H. (2007). *Key role of cultural and creative industries in the economy.* Montreal: UNESCO Institute for Statistics Paper.

Waldfogel, J. (2018). *Digital renaissance: What data and economy tell us about the future of popular culture.* Oxfordshire: Princeton University Press.

WFA. (2020). Culture shock: COVID-19 and the cultural and creative sectors. OECD. [Accessed on Nov 8, 2020]. Retrieved from https://www.oecd.org/coronavirus/policy-responses/culture-shock-covid-19-and-the-cultural-and-creative-sectors-08da9e0e/.

Yardımcı, A. (2016). *İçerdiği faaliyet gruplarına göre Türkiye'deki yaratıcı endüstri üzerine bir çalışma.* [A study on creative industry in Turkey based on its including activity groups]. *Finans Politik & Ekonomik Yorumlar. 613* (53): 65–77.

Çakır Aker

A New Lens Towards Games in Society: *Flaneur*, *Gameur*, and Beyond

Abstract: Until today, conventional communication media have provided somewhat linear and monologue capabilities, yet those methods are giving up their places to interactivity. In parallel to this shift in media practices, the importance of digital games has evolved and placed it among one of the pioneering media. Similarly, some researchers have indicated that the experience is the most important aspect when it comes to interactivity, not the hardware or the software (e.g., Tsekleves et al. 2009). Therefore, in the era in which we live, ubiquitous capabilities and interactivity have started to become the main factors for successful communication. Yet, the notion of those interactive communication technologies and especially digital games have rarely been discussed within the context of its place in society rather than its effects on individuals. Today, when urban areas have evolved into playgrounds in socio-cultural terms, Baudelaire's concept of flâneur is also transforming (Baudelaire, C., 1964). With the development of technology, not only our ordinary daily lives but also our playgrounds undergo radical changes. The usual game board concept from computer games is moving to cover the whole city. Just as flaneur emerged during the transition to modernism, Robert Luke (2005) introduced the character of phoneur during the transition to post-modern society. Following the same footsteps, De Souza e Silva and Hjorth put forward a player persona born of mobile play compatibility and affirmations on the phoneur figure that Luke's definition of phoneur brought. They called it gameur (De Souza e Silva and Hjorth, 2009). Although the transition of the figure of flaneur could be understood as a persona representation, it is also clear that the transition of the definition is ever-changing and adapting, providing a novel perspective on the evolving persona as well. Hence this chapter will be discussing the idea of digital games within the society through the lens of social sciences utilizing perspectives and definitions such as flaneur, phoneur, and gameur (Benjamin, W., 1983; Luke, R., 2005; Silvia e Souza & Hjorth 2009). It aims to provide a structured point of view to observe the evolution and placement of digital games in society as a whole during the pandemic while giving insights into the field for further research.

Keywords: *Flaneur*, *Gameur*, Digital Games, Society, Urban, Play, Cyberspace

How Did We Get Here?

Hevner summarized the traditional approach to informatics by saying that "information systems are organizations that can contribute towards the purpose and efficiency of the organization they are involved in" (Hevner et al. 2004). As can be understood, the perception of information systems has often been tried to be evaluated as it serves a structure above and outside of everyday life. However, media tools, which have presented a monologue and linear communication until today, leave their place to a two-way and interactive structure. The still going pandemic in the year 2020 has underlined the importance of these interactive capabilities within societies and in interpersonal relationships. The widespread utilization of information communication technologies has proved to be invaluable in these times because of the quarantine limitations. To better understand their impact on the situation, one can study the positioning of these media and tools from the perspective of digital games and their role in the pandemic.

Conventional entertainment media are losing the primary role of the household and are replaced by digital games and/or social media tools that offer different interaction methods. Many studies have shown that experience has become a more important factor than advanced hardware and software options. Tsekleves (2009) states that users' desire to interact beyond the possibilities offered by hardware and software is determinant for an effective experience (Tsekleves et al.). One of the most important reasons for this is that these novel tools offer much more interaction possibilities than usual, hence better control over experiences. It is possible to be in various interactions designed for almost every aspect of life with new mobile technologies, which can be explained with the definition of 'simultaneous and ubiquitous' informatics. This innovative approach also has its foundations based on user experience. Regarding the definition of these ubiquitous and all-pervasive opportunities, Youngjin Yoo (2010) indicates that with the inclusion of information communication technologies in our everyday lives, the possibility of leaving the computer that we used to work within the office has disappeared, which not only just blurred the line between work and 'life' but also penetrated to almost every aspect outside of work. Hence A new perspective is required regarding the possibilities and uses of information in nearly every area of our lives. It is necessary to look at information systems from a different perspective and avoid technological reductionism to talk about the experiences of people and their use of new technologies in daily life.

For this reason, the term 'experiential computing' has come to the fore. This concept has been introduced to describe the structures that exist digitally, which can also be intertwined with daily experiences and can be included with the cognitive aspects that we experience in our lives. From this point of view, it is necessary to see that the effects of novel technologies on our cognitive structures influence, change and diversify our experiences. For example, a fitness application that we might install on our mobile device, which would connect us with other runners, will induce a very different meaning for our morning jogging exercise. Now, this exercise may turn into a digital marathon by including a real social experience as well as having a layer on the digital. At the same time, the concept of experiential informatics is against the fact that the knowledge, as stated in conventional approaches, is independent of time and space. Novel pervasive technologies now bring us to the fact that experience, knowledge, and data can be included in the perception of time and space in equal terms with the real world. Regarding this, Yoo (2010) takes the case of being in an '*alternative relationship*' among the existing informatics approaches and gives the example of computer games. Because of their sophistication and relatively closeness to real-life socio-cultural elements, and especially in social science games, MMO (Massive multiplayer online games) genre has been discussed frequently. Although this suggestion on MMO games might sound viable, including only one genre of digital games would not suffice for understanding where we are right now in terms of gaming and its relation to our everyday lives. Regarding this, Corliss (2011) mention that the MMO games might be a good point of entry for analysis and discussions for social sciences research which might provide some means to understand the socio-cultural implications of digital games. However, he also indicates, "MMO games make up only a small portion of the video game genre, and there remains a demand for game studies concerned with the wide range of forms that games take and capable of accommodating games as a far broader socio-cultural phenomenon" (Corliss, 2011). Although we can now experience games anywhere and anytime via mobile phones and/or wireless network capabilities, many of the games mentioned in the literature are subject to mental limitations just like any other digital game. New game approaches start to question how to play is traditionally understood as an activity separate from our ordinary lives (Salen & Zimmerman, 2003; Caillois, 2001; Huizinga, 1955).

According to Huizinga (1955), play is described as a free and meaningful activity, consciously separate from ordinary life bound within either physical or mental borders, which absorbs the player intensely. Yet, in today's world, where technologies might predominate everyday lives, this boundary has begun to blur the border between ordinary life and play. In his definition, Huizinga points out several components of play; the creation of a '*magic circle*,' that is, the boundaries between play and ordinary life; a sense of total immersion; freedom of the activity; and the existence of rules. Nevertheless, the pervasiveness of games, especially into our ordinary lives, has reframed the forms of play in contemporary urbanity. Although Huizinga and several authors also emphasized the separation of those two elements, Salen and Zimmerman (2003) propose a rather more general component of play, including gameplay, ludic activities, and playfulness. Hence it can be possible to analyze the definition of play in contemporary situations from these perspectives. To study and assess both the effects of the pandemic with its implications of isolation from social life and the adaptation of the play in contemporary lives, one can look at playfulness in an urban context.

Flaneur to *Gameur*

To understand the evolution of digital games in the urban context and assess socio-cultural implications, Baudelaire's concept of '*flâneur*' (Baudelaire, 1964) and its shift in meaning can be utilized. The transformation of the icon in 20th century (and late 19th century) modernity, *flâneur*, was the vivid representation of the stroller, and/or the dandy who wanders the streets, observing the ordinary life whom can be defined as; "that aimless stroller who loses himself in the crowd, who has no destination and goes wherever caprice or curiosity directs his or her steps" (White, 2001). Flanarie, which is the act of flâneur, is a recurring motif in literature, sociology, and urban art, and most especially of the metropolitan existence. According to Walter Benjamin (1983), the figure was related to a specific time and place: Paris, the capital of the nineteenth century. This figure in the literature is defined as a male, with no visible income yet fashionable, part of the crowd (while apart from it observing), a strolling observer without specific purpose but to experience the city around him. In its essence, the flâneur figure has the freedom of travel without any worries from the environment. Yet, Musil (1994) indicates that the flanerie cannot be without its dangers in the modern Wien, in which the tramways and running traffic, the flâneur is no longer as safe as he thinks (Tester, 1994). He identifies three distinct points for indicating the necessary shift of the term; the traffic, cities becoming ordinary and boring, and domination of rationality imposed on the city as if by necessity. Musil might not be directly indicating the effects of technological advancement in terms of the shift in meaning; nevertheless, these elements affecting the figure were somewhat related to them. In the developing world, the city also develops along with the people and the experience in it.

Similar to flâneur, Luke (2005) suggests the idea of identifying the postmodern stroller indicating that "the phoneur is the post-modern flâneur: a mobile phone user strolling the cityscape." According to Luke (2005), the cities that turn into an 'information network' (Castells, 1989) emerge more clearly thanks to mobile phones. The phoneur is not that different in terms of creating the reality via observing the everyday life around him/her, but with the mobile technologies, the phoneur is not creating the reality around via utilizing the commercial grids and communication vectors. The identity of the mobile technology user "wanders as (s)he observes the city streets" (ibidem). Although the suggestion of phoneur fits the novel perspective towards understanding flâneur, it also highlights the effects of technology on the term. Luke indicates that the city's physical limits have become functions because of wireless networks, not bindings.

Following the post-modern perspective of phoneur and its ever-ending shift, De Souza e Silva and Hjorth put forward a player persona born of mobile play compatibility. The city, which was once divided into sections by capital and commodity flows, has now turned into random playgrounds. Thanks to digital mobile games, the phoneur has developed towards a person who can prevent his/her normalization by disrupting him from the catalyst position of capitalist and consumption-oriented networks (Silvia e Souza & Hjort, 2009). Hence, De Souza e Silva and Hjorth, based on the phoneur figure, defined by Luke Baudelaire's flâneur concept, revealed a player persona, who was born out of mobile compatibility and affirmation. Just like flanerie, '*gameur*' can turn the daily life ritual in which it lives into a different experience. Moreover, for the playful/ludic approach, games did not need more than the interactions presented by the gameur. As defined by the authors, s/he has a privileged figure that can be found in knowledgeable, urban, and playful spaces. But most different when compared to flâneur and/or phoneur, gameur figure can now equip him/herself with various characters and transitions between new game experiences. The figure is no longer limited by the environmental factors within the city but rather can be the observer, experiencing everyday life from the lens of a digital game. Gameur is capable of "abstracting the concepts of modern game and mobility" as well as the ability to change their game experiences in terms of software and hardware (ibidem). Hence, gameur does not even need to stroll throughout the city streets to drink the joys of everyday life and experience the city, (s)he only needs a screen. The gameur no longer has physical limitations as the flâneur had but also has emancipated from the classical views towards the act of play, such as the borderline differentiating the game and everyday life for which was referred to as the magic circle (Huizinga, 1955). As Moore (2011) puts it, "there is no longer the magic circle for the gameur." In today's world, we play even as we are in public transportation, shifting our perception from the urban towards digital experiences, thus forming digital realities.

Urban Space to Cyberspace

De Souza e Silva (2006) identifies space from three different perspectives; mobile space, social space, and hybrid space (connected space). Although these spaces are 'connected,' no external effort to stay connected is necessary in today's world. We are all connected all the time and the separation is blurred at best. In today's world, in which mobile devices have become a part of daily life, it can be suggested that there is no longer a separation between physical space and cyberspace. The term '*cyberspace*' originally is derived in the 1980s; in his science fiction, "Neuromancer," Gibson (1984) coined the term, which was described as a graphic representation abstracted from each computer's accounts (Gibson, 1984). Since then, the definition has been known prominently as the synonym of the computer-generated digital world and received high attention. So far, the term has been utilized by many researchers, academicians, and experts of the field to determine the separation between the digital and the real. For instance, Wilken (2007) defines cyberspace as a place without any physical necessities in which people can get together via networks, share information, work, exchange, and play. Related theories and innovations are heading towards the definition which the Cyberspace is no longer limited to the digital world alone, but goes beyond to include physical space. For example, with the adaptation of location-based technologies to mobile devices, cyberspace is transferred to the physical space and forms a layer above the physical space. Various location-based mobile games can be seen as both the cause and the result of this transition for instance. As the gameur wanders around the city within a ludic act, the cityscapes and streets remain as reality just as much as the digital cyberspace becomes a layer on top of it. Current mobile technologies, provided that they are always connected, act as a bridge between physical mobility, including transportation technologies, and informational mobility, such as the internet and media (Sheller & Urry, 2006). This bridge has enabled cyberspace to accompany the physical space. Nevertheless, there still is a separation when we think about other digital game platforms such as consoles or desktop computers. The user remains at a fixed place, probably the living room, while interacting with those platforms from which the player can connect to cyberspace and immerse him/herself in the cyber-reality. As some of the authors have put it, the digital information becomes an interface between physical space and the person, expanding the space around him/her while transforming the place's fundamental understanding and the users' perception of the city along with it (Crabtree & Rodden, 2008). Following this, we can indicate that the understanding of place/space from the users' perspective has also changed.

Although the borderline between the digital and the real becomes more blurred each day, the distinction between these two experiences remains the same. The user of the digital technology is aware of its surroundings even though, for instance, while browsing social media and/or playing games on the mobile device. Nevertheless, the transition between these two spaces becomes so frequent and the intuitiveness of novel technologies and user experiences that they provide, any person who decides to change his/her role in a real city to a ludic gameur can do so without a hitch.

Gamer in the Pandemic

It is well indicated that gamers during the pandemic situation started to play digital games more when compared to their previous gaming habits. To say the least, the gaming industry is the one that was not affected by the pandemic, with players joining the ranks more and more each day during this period. For instance, Goslin (2020) indicates that lockdown saw increasing gaming time among gamers in a much more significant proportion than in previous periods. It is possible to say that the increase in time spent playing video games is related to the time that people started to stay at home and started to search for either relief, fun, or enjoyment to pass the time. Moreover, games are not merely for passing the time but also for experiencing novel interactions and the worlds which are presented through digital screens. Hence the figure of the gameur, who was the one who experienced everyday life from a ludic perspective through games, is now stuck at home and/or has limited access to urban life as everybody else.

The perspective towards games has also changed because of the crisis that we are living through. Even the World Health Organization shifted its perspective along with the changes in society. As Kriz (2020) indicates clearly: "In 2019, the WHO called game addiction a sign of mental disorder and warned people against developing game addiction. However, in this year, 2020, the WHO appealed to people to stay home and play games." Moreover, more than 50 game industry leaders have launched a campaign in social media, such as #PlayApartTogether, to promote gamers to keep on playing games following WHO's health guidelines, including precautions such as social distancing. Games may offer some much-needed emancipation and social connection in this time of physical distancing as many studies indicate. As the real space is crushed under pandemic constraints, cyberspace has also taken on the role of a savior. However, the deprivation of the outer city space during the pandemic process disrupted the coming together between cyberspace and real space and redeployed it into two separate parts. Now instead of the real space, people have had to "wander" in cyberspace. To prove this point, Toledo (2020) has conducted a study to investigate gamer behavior and preferences during the COVID-19 pandemic and found that geography played a minimal role in determining gaming behavior during lockdown. While location-based games cannot be played anymore as they are intended, cyberspace takes place entirely for the gameur. The figure now has to exist in a digital reality only, which could alter its intention of experiencing the city from a layered perspective. For the gameur, cyberspace has become the space for ludic wandering without any real space layer underneath.

Observations and Conclusions

This chapter was aimed to discuss the idea of digital games within the society through the lens of social sciences utilizing perspectives and definitions such as flâneur, phoneur, and gameur (Benjamin, W., 1983; Luke, R., 2006; Silvia e Souza & Hjorth 2009) and has aimed to provide a structured point of view to observe the evolution of those figures and what they represent. It has been discussed that although the transition of the figure of flâneur could be understood as a persona representation, it is also easy to notice the transition of the definition, which is ever-changing and adapting to novel technologies and their effects on everyday life. As Wilken (2007) puts it, it is vital to recognize the importance and the impact of metaphors of places/spaces and experiences within them in the discourse on novel technologies and their roles in our lives.

While games may be seen as an adaptive coping strategy in the short term (Russoniello, O'Brien, & Parks, 2009), their role changes. All the changes and shifts through technology have affected the notion of flaneur throughout the time, dragging the figure's meaning to phoneur for which the figure is related to commercial interests and whims of a person who utilizes mobile technologies. Mobility via technology has adapted the act of flanerie towards the foundations of layering the experiences in real life. Similar to this, the novel developments bring about the change of the gameur concept, just like the ways flaneur has passed, with different uses of the term in different periods, yet this time defined by technological capabilities and their ubiquity. In this context, while gameur is a concept that is ascribed to today's urban actors, the situation of being in the street and city life is eliminated due to the pandemic. Now players spend time in virtual cities rather than real cities. Even within the virtual fictions that the games offer them (or try to), the gameur figure prefers to act outside the fiction of the game and by navigating the game world as a real one, replicating the previously described flaneur experience within the cyberspace. It can be suggested that with the influence of technology, the meaning of space evolves towards cyberspace. Hence, the meanings regarding the flâneur are also evolving towards it (**Tab. 12.1**).

Tab. 12.1: The Relationship between the Metaphorical Figure and the Space It Exists.

Figure	***Flâneur***	***Phoneur***	***Gameur***
Space	Real-space	Real and Cyberspace	Cyberspace

Moreover, the deprivation of outer space during the pandemic regulations disrupted the coming together between cyberspace and real space and redeployed it into two separate parts. Now instead of the real space, people have had to wander in cyberspace without necessarily experiencing each layer simultaneously. Essentially, since the real space is crushed under constraints, cyberspace has also taken on the role of a savior for the gameur. S/he now spectates the cyber-cities in a much more playful way. This could indicate a perspective to look at games and their roles in everyday life from the point that cyberspace could replace the real-life experience to some extent. Nevertheless, in reality, the distinction between cyberspace and urban space experiences remains the same for now. It would be beneficial to observe the future from the perspective of '*ur*' figures evolution, to estimate how new technologies might affect the understanding towards space and whose experiencing it.

References

Baudelaire, C. (1964). The painter of modern life. *The painter of modern life and other essays* (pp. 1–40). New York: Phaidon Press.

Benjamin, W. (1983). *Charles Baudelaire: A lyric poet in the era of high capitalism* (pp. 128–129). (H. Zohn, trans.). London: Verso Publications.

Caillois, R. (2001). *Man, play, and games*. Champaign: University of Illinois Press.

Castells, M. (1989). *The informational city: Information technology, economic restructuring, and the urban-regional process* (p. 348). Oxford: Blackwell.

Corliss, J. (2011). Introduction: The social science study of video games. *Games and Culture*, *6* (1): 3–16. doi:10.1177/1555412010377323.

Crabtree, A., & Rodden, T. (2008). Hybrid ecologies: understanding cooperative interaction in emerging physical-digital environments. *Personal and Ubiquitous Computing*, *12* (7): 481–493.

De Souza e Silva, A. (2006). From cyber to hybrid: Mobile technologies as interfaces of hybrid spaces. *Space and culture*: *9* (3): 261–278.

De Souza e Silva, A., & Hjorth, L. (2009). Playful urban spaces: A historical approach to mobile games. *Simulation & Gaming, 40* (5): 602–625.

Goslin, A. (2020, March). Steam sets new records amid worldwide lockdown. *Polygon*. [Accessed on Nov 9, 2020]. Retrieved from https://www.polygon.com/2020/3/23/21191397/steam-highest-active-player-record-coronavirus-covid-19.

Hevner, A., March, S. T., Park, J., & Ram, S. (2004). Design science research in information systems. *MIS Quarterly, 28* (1): 75–105.

Huizinga, J. (1955). *Homo Ludens: A study of the play element in culture.* Boston: Beacon Press.

Kriz, W. C. (2020). Gaming in the time of COVID-19. *Simulation & Gaming, 51* (4): 403–410.

Luke, R. (2005). The phoneur: Mobile commerce and the digital pedagogies of the wireless web. In P. Trifonas (Ed.). *Communities of difference* (pp. 185–204). New York: Palgrave Macmillan.

Moore, C. (2011). The magic circle and the mobility of play. *Convergence, 17* (4): 373–387.

Russoniello, C. V., O'Brien, K., & Parks, J. M. (2009). The effectiveness of casual video games in improving mood and decreasing stress. *Journal of CyberTherapy and Rehabilitation, 2* (1): 53–66.

Salen, K., & Zimmerman, E. (2003). *Rules of play: Game design fundamentals.* Cambridge, MA: The MIT Press.

Sheller, M., & Urry, J. (2006). The new mobilities paradigm. *Environment and Planning* A, *38* (2): 207–226.

Tester, K. (Ed.). (1994). *The flâneur.* London: Routledge.

Toledo, M. (2020). Video game habits & COVID-19. *SSRN,* https://dx.doi.org/10.2139/ssrn.3676004.

Tsekleves, E., Cosmas, J., Aggoun, A., & Loo, J. (2009). Converged digital TV services: The role of middleware and future directions of interactive television. *International Journal of Digital Multimedia Broadcasting, 2009* (4).

Gibson, W. (1984). *Neuromancer.* New York: Ace Books.

White, E. (2001). *The flâneur: A stroll through the paradoxes of Paris.* London: Bloomsbury Publishing.

Wilken, R. (2007). The haunting effect of place in the discourse of the virtual. *Ethics Place and Environment, 10* (1): 49–63.

Yoo, Y. (2010). Computing in everyday life: A call for research on experiential computing. *MIS Quarterly, 34* (2): 213–231.

Elif Engin, Burcu Eker Akgöz, and
Selcan Yeşilyurt

Managing the State of Uncertainty: How to Communicate the Inside during COVID-19?

Abstract: 2020 has started with an unexpected disease, long term, full of questions and worries for humanity. While the health sector and governments were trying to understand and tell the world about this virus, almost every sector in the world was affected by the COVID-19 pandemic. What we are sure of is that the world has 'changed.' 'Communication' has become more critical than ever. Bans and restrictions that come with COVID-19 have changed how we look at the world, life, and ourselves. In addition to trying to keep up with new developments, corporates and brands continued to carry on their communication activities internally and externally. One of the greatest challenges corporations face was about their workforce and how to manage it, both operationally and communicatively. Employees' morale, well-being, health, and safety have become more important than ever as corporations have to protect their employees and work for continued support strategies. The future of the workplace is changing; how employees perceive their work changes, change brings uncertainties that corporations should handle for the well-being of their employees who are the drivers of the businesses. This study will provide an overview of how organizations took and continue to take action during the coronavirus pandemic, what they have done to minimalize the negative effects, their organizational efforts, communication practices, all in terms of internal/employee communications. Global approaches and local workplace practices from Turkish corporations will also be analyzed.

Keywords: Pandemic, Communication Management, International Communication, Organization Communication, Employee Communication

Introduction

The world has gone through many different, complex, and new processes till today and will continue to live through. But today, beginning from late 2019, the industrialized and globalized world is going through something it never had before, a very real and very dangerous pandemic. Every government, institution, organization, and corporation are all working in a way to get out of this period with the least damage possible. This is the age of fast communications, with both physically and virtually connected people, the messages travel faster than the virus itself, which means it is harder to manage people. Corporations suddenly had to figure out new ways of getting the employees to carry on working without being exposed to harm. Also, they had to find the best ways of communicating the necessities of the period to the employees. Corporations carried out research studies with their employees and other organizations carried out researches related to new ways of working. Health and well-being, job performance, and engagement of employees were areas of concern. This study summarizes the concepts related to employee communications in the light of the pandemic period. Then looks at the scenery of corporations going into the new normal with new work practices, areas of concern for employees, and essential points in going back to work with the examination of research studies that have been carried out during the course of the pandemic.

Literature Review

During the year 2020 and the course of the pandemic, businesses faced new challenges and they were obligated to make important and mandatory changes in their business practices as well as communication systems. Employees depend on companies more than ever, both economically and psychologically. Businesses also need their employees to continue working at their best in these turbulent times without losing efficiency. In that sense, keeping the relationships in a stable state with the help of employee communications became important. Communication includes knowledge transfer and knowledge transfer that occurs face-to-face is the best kind but as corporations became larger nationally and internationally in their operations, they had to create knowledge networks that transcend space (Holtz, 2004, p. 223). Before the COVID-19 pandemic, online communication channels included things such as intranets, internal blogs, e-mailing, etc. Now, the primary online internal communication and meeting tools are online meeting programs, which replaced face-to-face communication, making knowledge transfer management harder than before.

Management and employee communications include the critical elements of organizational relationships, which can be counted as trust, credibility, mutual legitimacy, and mutual understanding (Grunig & Huang, 2000). The fulfillment of these elements was hard to handle as the needs created by this unique period brought so many changes. Change is already hard to handle for businesses. Normally, it points out to changes in goals, boundaries, or patterns of activities of the corporations, also involving changing the routines which are already embedded in employee's heads (Nilakant & Ramnarayan, 2006). The dramatic change that is around has brought new routines to all the people inside the corporations bringing the loss of stability. What corporations should do as change management is to help the employees adopt new behaviors, accept and take ownership of change instead of resisting it (Miller & Proctor, 2016). Corporations had to create new ways of keeping their employees stable, so their levels of trust, engagement, well-being, loyalty, and involvement stay stable. Even the changes in work-life balance and the changing safety needs (physical and psychological) of the employees are significant. Improving relationships through employee communication involves morale and relationship-building activities, which can help employees become more effective and efficient in production (Cunconan, 2005), which is something corporations cannot afford to compromise.

One significant transformation happened in workspaces. In a time of mandatory distancing, keeping employees together in workplaces meant risking their safety. Normally, while employees also have some responsibility for their protection and safety, the employers are responsible for providing protective equipment and information, and they should also ensure that employees properly use that protection (Robinson, 2007, p. 691). This time, employers had to protect their employees by keeping them away from the workspaces. Employers found the remote working solution from home, which solved only one part of the problem; psychological safety is still at stake. Psychological safety is the foundation for employee engagement; in team building, it refers to an individual's perception that a team is safe for risk-taking and they will not be labeled as ignorant, incompetent, negative, or disruptive (Peters, 2019, p. 29). Employees need to feel safe first, just as in Maslow's hierarchy of needs. Even the employees who have formerly reached self-actualization goals in terms of their jobs turned back to the very basic needs of safety. Plus, in many sectors, many employees even fell into the first layer by losing their jobs. Employee productivity is dependent on individual needs among other concepts (Smith & Mounter, 2008) and psychological safety needs became hard to manage as nobody feels safe.

The fear of pandemics and the changes in business practices can create problems for employees for their engagement and involvement in their jobs, which may weaken commitment and loyalty loss if they have low levels of trust. Employee engagement is defined as "an emotional commitment to one's work and a willingness to give of one's best at work" (Peters, 2019, p. 9). Employee engagement hinges on three drivers; serving a valuable purpose, being empowered to deliver results, and working in a fulfilling environment (Philips, 2016, p. 11). The last driver mentioned here became somewhat unmanageable by corporations as work environments merged on to home environments. Normally, fulfilling work environments provide a quality setting in which employees can concentrate on their responsibilities and be engaged in their work (Philips, 2016, p. 13). Now it is very hard for employees to do so, as home responsibilities also become primary due to proximity.

A highly engaged but less satisfied employee has a flight risk, they may like their work, but they feel that their company takes advantage of them (Peters, 2019, p. 13). During the pandemic, corporations may have faced this situation in which their employees are still highly engaged, but their satisfaction levels are getting low due to necessary changes and work-life balance getting out of hand. Employee commitment, which becomes important at this point, is related to the employee seeing and acknowledging the company's efforts, then decides to make an effort for the company. Corporations cannot earn employee commitment with just a paycheck; most of the time, it is even not among the top ten reasons for employees being committed (Holtz, 2004, p. 26; Philips, 2016, p. 11). Employee commitment can be gained by trust, involvement, role knowledge, and job satisfaction, trust can be built with open communication with broadly disseminated information (Holtz, 2004). In this equation, more open communication with quality information leads to trust. If employees trust management and leaders, they will focus on the job (thus remain productive) rather than focusing their attention on defensive and self-defensive (covering their backs) risk-mitigation behavior (Stanford, 2007, p. 163). This is especially relevant for the time being of a pandemic, as the employees will be in a state of mind which they will want to protect themselves. While doing so, they might get defensive against the organization's decisions on work practices.

Employee Communications during the Pandemic

Coronavirus Disease (COVID-19) is a virus that was first identified on Jan 13, 2020, due to research conducted in a group of patients who developed respiratory symptoms (fever, cough, shortness of breath) in Wuhan Province in late December[1]. This pandemic, which started to spread rapidly worldwide, brought rapid changes and transformations in work life. According to a report by the International Labour Organization (ILO Monitor: COVID-19 and the World of Work, 2020), as of Apr 22, 2020, 81 % of employers and 66 % of own-account workers were living and working in the countries affected by recommended or required workplace closures. For example, in the US, more than 30 million people have lost their jobs and 62 % of employed Americans were working from home (Friedman, 2020). The effects of the pandemic on corporations and employee communications are examined in the upcoming sections, with results of different research studies made by various organizations. The process is divided into two periods as the first effects and possible going back scenarios.

The First Hit-Shaking Things up for Corporations on Different Dimensions

Effects of COVID-19 on corporations and employee's work-life are in multiple dimensions. Due to the pandemic, many companies worldwide have directed their employees to a digital world where data can be shared and meetings can be held. Building internal networks to reach the workplace, finding out the best applications that enable virtual meetings, and more dependence on cloud services were among the digital transformations. This was one of the transformations from "old normal" to "new normal" which happened when employees were asked to stay at their homes (Herrera et al., 2020). According to the data of SmartMessage (Marketing Türkiye, 2020), in the first month of the pandemic, significant increases were seen in digital communication activities for customers and employees. Also, corporate digital communication increased 70 % in the first month of the pandemic. The pandemic carried the need for the digital world and its communication with employees to a different and unknown world than ever before. The challenge was building the technologies and integrating human beings with them, getting people adapted to the technology, and working with the technology at their hand (Deloitte, 2020).

One possible problem during the pandemic has been seen as employee engagement getting weaker. It is recommended to handle engagement by speaking with clarity, adapting for the audience, showing leadership, considering local needs, being ready to evolve, balancing facts with empathy, and remembering communication works two ways (Edelman UK, 2020). In terms of engagement with employees, the top three topics that have been communicated with the employees were safety guidelines (84 %), COVID-19 updates (79 %), and new organizational policies and procedures (75 %), according to a research study by The Institute for Public Relations and Peppercomm. The research found out that all respondents used e-mails (99 %) and supervisors/managers (91 %) to communicate internally. 75 % of respondents told that in internal communication, the CEO was "very involved." 8-out-of-10 employees stated that the communication function was very involved in terms of COVID-19 related internal communication. One noticeable result was that around 2 out of 3 respondents indicated that employee engagement increased and almost half (49 %) of participants stated that the trust was increased. Briefly, the most-communicated topics to employees were health guidelines and the changes in policies. Another significant result is, although overall productivity decreased, the pandemic had positive outcomes such as trust in companies, collaboration, and employee engagement satisfaction. Communication with employees and their safety are among the most emphasized issues in this period by communication executives and senior leaders. Employee engagement and communication satisfaction are among the most critical issues in the COVID-19 and business process.

There have been changes in employees' level of trust in their organizations during the COVID-19 pandemic in two opposite ends at the same time. According to a research study by Orangefiery (2020), corporations gained trust (17 %) and lost trust (17 %) with equal levels. It is emphasized that some organizations are increasing their level of trust and some others losing; organizations can overcome this crisis by communicating with their employees transparently. According to this research, employees want their organizations to explain how to ensure employee safety as a priority as stay-at-home days, on the issues of when they are expected to turn back, how the workplace is being updated to enable precautions of physical distancing and sanitation, personal protective equipment, and the issue of monitoring for COVID-19 symptoms. Employees expect explanatory and trustworthy information related to the protection of themselves from their organizations in crises.

Another concept emphasized, and perhaps one of the most important ones, is the 'well-being' of employees. To achieve this, it is necessary to build trust first. In a report by McKinsey & Company (Emmett et al., 2020), it is emphasized that continuously listening to the workforce helps build trust. According to their research, there is a "strong correspondence between employees' stated needs and the underlying drivers of their engagement, well-being, and work effectiveness." Those stated needs are on the issues of stable and secure work experience, trusting relationships, social cohesion, inclusion, and individual purpose and contribution. According to the research study, organizations can build trust during the pandemic by making 'credible, feasible, sustainable and personal' key actions.

The corporations also had to reconsider their bottom lines during the pandemic. According to a research study in collaboration with Mercer Turkey and Peryön (2020), the impact of the pandemic on business life in Turkey, 74.3 % of companies stated that they would revise their targets of the year-end goals. 44.9 % of companies stated that they had remote working before the epidemic, whereas 55.1 % of them said that they had not implemented it before. The biggest difficulty brought by remote working had been on employee motivation 40.7 %, followed by employee performance management process, communication, lack of technological infrastructure, and working with children at home. Another significant result that takes attention is that 60 % of companies stated that they take action to support the mental health of their employees.

COVID-19 affected all kinds of sectors and workplaces all around the world. As corporations reactively tried to understand the current situation of their employees in terms of engagement, trust and well-being, they also started to look for possible ways of getting back to the "next normal" (Herrera et al., 2020). An immediate response was critical, but surely corporations want to be more proactive in going back to work.

Getting Back to Work – How is it Going to Be?

Even if the situations created by the pandemic might persist over a certain period, there is no doubt that some employees will return to work, if not all. There are many questions related to going back to work practices, new workplaces that transcend physical spaces, ensuring the employees' protection and safety, among other issues.

At the beginning of the first closures and quarantines, people were anxious about going back to work. After a certain point, as the semi-normalizations started, employees had doubts about returning to workplaces—a research study by Qualtrics XM (2020) found out that 2 out of 3 participants felt uncomfortable returning to work. To feel comfortable returning to the workplace, they expressed three topics as assurance from authorities (63 %); effective medical interventions as treatment (47 %) and vaccine (45 %); safety policies such as wearing a mask (47 %), no handshakes/hugs policies (45 %) and self-quarantine for 14 days after travel for work. As it looks like, the return-to-work concerns and expectations of employees are not only from the corporations.

The practical concerns of employees do not end with the expectations related to the pandemic in general. In a research study by The Harris Poll and the Institute for Public Relations (2020), it has been found out that 80 % of respondents wanted the open space office concept to phase out for social distancing. An important proportion of (83 %) employees thought that employers shouldn't want them to turn back if the job can be done remotely. 81 % agreed to be allowed to work at home until they feel comfortable to turn back, 74 % of them emphasize that workplaces have to have items for protection, 58 % on personal protective equipment, and 56 % insist on redesigned workplaces for social distance. Finally, if corporations show accountability for employee safety, employees are more likely to support legal protection, which includes topics as public safety (56 %) and honest and open communication (47 %).

There is an ongoing re-evaluation in terms of work practices and future needs. This period made employees think about the things they valued and make. A global study commissioned by Kaspersky of 8,000 SME employees from various industries showed that almost three-quarters (82 %) of employees were re-evaluating working methods before COVID-19 (HR Dergi, 2020). Instead of returning to work as they used to, employees wanted to shape the future ways of doing business on their terms, such as spending more time with their loved ones (53 %), making savings (39 %), or working remotely (38 %).

Returning to workplaces is not going to be easy as the pandemic will not disappear from the world suddenly at a point in the future. The usage of offices has been lowered and returning to old capacities does not look very probable for the near future, as the report "The Future of Work after COVID-19" by Deloitte Turkey (2020) has outlined. According to the report, there should be a healthy return not only in terms of physical health but also in terms of mental and spiritual health. The most important considerations according to the report revolve around the issues of detection of disease in the workplace, common practices to be followed with different corporations sharing the same buildings, guest protocols, social distancing at workspaces, eating and traveling protocols, rights of employees who will want to continue remote working, and overall hygiene of the offices. These can be perceived as concerns every corporation should keep in mind while getting their employees back to work. Otherwise, they will be risking the physical and mental safety and well-being of their employees.

Conclusion

The world is not facing a pandemic for the first time. Looking back on history, human beings have struggled with many pandemics. What makes COVID-19 different from the other pandemics is that it coincides with the information age, where technological developments are intense and social media is used worldwide. Besides healthcare professionals, the group that experienced its disadvantages most has been the business and employees. Bans and restrictions which come with COVID-19 have changed the perception of businesses. In addition to trying to keep up with new developments, corporations tried to figure out new ways of communicating with employees. One of the biggest challenges corporations face was about the workforce and how to manage it, both operationally and communicatively. Employees' morale, well-being, health, and safety have become more important than ever as corporations have to protect their employees and work for continued support strategies. The future of the workplace and how employees perceive their work changes, which brings uncertainties that should be handled by corporations for the well-being of their employees who are the drivers of the businesses.

This study has attempted to provide an overview of internal communication-related information on how corporations took and continue to take action during the pandemic, organizational efforts, communication practices, employee expectations, and needs by examining related global reports. When we examined the studies done so far, the most-communicated topics to employees were health guidelines and the changes in policies. Another important result is, although overall productivity decreased, the pandemic had both positive and negative outcomes such as trust in companies, collaboration, and employee engagement satisfaction. Communication with employees and their safety are among the most emphasized issues in this period by communication executives and senior leaders. Employee engagement and communication satisfaction are among the most important issues in the COVID-19 and business process. Crises create uncertainty. Companies need to identify their key publics to overcome the uncertainty with the least damage. Employees are one of the key publics that should be informed properly in times of crisis. The research studies show that employees expect explanatory and trustworthy information related to the protection of themselves from their organizations in crises.

Another prominent issue is the psychological well-being of employees. When the roles in private life and business life intertwined in the house of employees, it created fatigue and exhaustion. In particular, employees with children had difficulties carrying out both work and family life at the same time and made an extra effort. This caused a psychological breakdown. Going back to work will cause another uncertainty that businesses need to overcome. Although the situations created by the pandemic will continue for a certain period, the majority of employees will have to return to work.

At the beginning of the first lockdowns and quarantines, people were anxious about going back to work. After a certain point, as the semi-normalizations started, employees still had doubts about returning to workplaces. Therefore, many problems need to be addressed and resolved, such as returning to work practices, hygiene of physical areas, protecting employees' health, and ensuring their health safety.

As the researches done so far has revealed, the coming years will demonstrate that brand new business models will emerge both for employees and the businesses. The pandemic has also revealed the importance of the increasing number of studies on employee value and employee branding, which have been done over the past few years. Considering that the pandemic period will be in our lives for a while, we can easily say that studies on employees' psychological well-being, new business models, and new working environments will be carried out for a long time.

Note

1 Covid-19 Nedir?. [What is Covid-19]. (2020). Retrieved from https://covid19.saglik.gov.tr/TR-66300/covid19-nedir-.html.

References

COVID-19 Nedir?. [What is COVID-19]. (2020). Sağlık Bakanlığı. [Ministry of Health]. [Accessed on Dec 10, 2020]. Retrieved from https://covid19.saglik.gov.tr/TR-66300/covid-19-nedir-.html.

Cunconan, T. M. (2005). Corporate moral conscience. In R. L. Heath (Ed.). *Encyclopedia of public relations*, New York: Sage Publications.

Deloitte. (2020). Global human capital trends, special report returning to work in the future of work embracing purpose, potential, perspective, and possibility during COVID-19. (Online report). [Accessed on Dec 10, 2020]. Retrieved from https://www2.deloitte.com/content/dam/Deloitte/cn/Documents/human-capital/deloitte-cn-hc-special-report-returning-to-work-in-the-future-of-work-en-200527.pdf.

Deloitte Turkey. (2020). COVID-19 sonrası yeni çalışma hayatına hazır mısınız? İşin geleceğini dayanıklılık ve esneklik temeli üzerine kurmak. [Are you ready to new working life in the post Covid-19? Constructing the future of work on strength and flexibility]. [Accessed on Dec 10, 2020]. Retrieved from https://www2.deloitte.com/tr/tr/pages/human-capital/articles/covid-19-sonrasi-yeni-calisma-hayatina-hazir-misiniz.html.

Edelman UK. (2020). How to guide: employee & internal communications during the coronavirus pandemic. [Accessed on Dec 15, 2020]. Retrieved from https://www.edelman.com/covid-19/perspectives/how-guide-employee-internalcommunication.

Emmett, J., Schrah, G., Schrimper, M., & Wood, A. (2020). COVID-19 and the employee experience: how leaders can seize the moment. *McKinsey & Company*. [Accessed on Dec 19, 2020]. Retrieved from https://www.mckinsey.com/business-functions/organization/our-insights/covid-19-and-the-employee-experience-how-leaders-can-seize-the-moment.

Friedman, Z. (2020). How COVID-19 will change the future of work. *Forbes*. [Accessed on Dec 19, 2020]. Retrieved from https://www.forbes.com/sites/zackfriedman/2020/05/06/covid-19-future-of-work-coronavirus/?sh=4722891a73b2.

Grunig, J. E., & Huang, Y. H. (2000). From organizational effectiveness to relationship indicators: Antecedents of relationships, public relations strategies, and relationship outcomes. In E-J. Ki, J-N. Kim, & J. A. Ledingham (Eds.).

Public relations as relationship management: A relational approach to the study and practice of public relations (pp. 23–53). London: Routledge.

Herrera, S., Wright, B., & Wright, A. (2020). The COVID-19 response playbook, a guide for how to lead and build resilience for the next normal. *SalesForce.* [Accessed on Dec 21, 2020]. Retrieved from https://www.salesforce.com/content/dam/web/en_us/www/documents/e-books/covid-19-response-playbook.pdf

HR Dergi. (2020). Türkiye'de çalışanların dörtte üçü geleneksel çalışma modellerine dönmek istemiyor. [Three out of four workers don't want to return back to the traditional working models in Turkey]. [Accessed on Dec 17, 2020]. Retrieved from https://hrdergi.com/turkiye%E2%80%99de-calisanlarin-dortte-ucu-geleneksel-calisma-modellerine-donmek-istemiyor.

Holtz, S. (2004). *Corporate conversations: a guide to crafting effective and appropriate internal communications.* AMACOM/American Management Association.

International Labour Organization. (2020). *ILO monitor: COVID-19 and the world of work.* (The third edition updated estimates and analysis). [Accessed on Dec 21, 2020]. Retrieved from https://www.ilo.org/wcmsp5/groups/public/---dgreports/-dcomm/documents/briefingnote/wcms_743146.pdf.

Marketing Türkiye. (2020). Korona salgını kurumsal dijital iletişimi daha ilk ayda yüzde 70 artırdı. [Corona pandemic increased corporate digital communication by 70 percent in the first month]. [Accessed on Dec 1, 2020]. Retrieved from https://www.marketingturkiye.com.tr/haberler/korona-salgini-kurumsal-dijital-iletisimi-daha-ilk-ayda-yuzde-70-artirdi/.

Mercer. (2020). Mercer Türkiye ve Peryön işbirliğinde gerçekleştirilen Koronavirüs Salgının İş Hayatına Etkisi Anketi'nin sonuçları açıklandı. [The results of the Coronavirus Pandemic Impact on Business Life Survey conducted in cooperation with Mercer Türkiye and Peryön have been announced.]. (Press release). [Accessed on Dec 28, 2020]. Retrieved from https://www.mercer.com.tr/basin-odasi-haberler/peryon-nisan-2020-koronavirus-turkiye-arastirmasi-basin-bulteni.html.

Miller, D., & Proctor, A. (2016). *Enterprise change management: How to prepare your organization for continuous change.* London: Kogan Page Publishers.

Nilakant, V., & Ramnarayan, S. (2006). *Change management: Altering mindsets in a global context.* California: SAGE Publications India.

Orangefiery. (2020). New research shows employee trust changing during COVID-19; accuracy, appropriate frequency and right channels of communication correlate with higher levels of trust. [Accessed on Dec 7, 2020]. Retrieved from https://orangefiery.com/uploads/Orangefiery_COVID19_Survey2_PressReleaseFINAL_051120.pdf.

Peters, J. (2019). *Employee engagement creating positive energy at work.* Bryanston, SA: KR Publishing.

Phillips, K. E. (2016). *Employee leaps: Leveraging engagement by applying positive strategies.* New York: Business Expert Press.

Qualtrics XM. (2020). Return to work/back to business study. [Accessed on Nov 8, 2020]. Retrieved from https://success.qualtrics.com/rs/542-FMF412/images/Return_to_Work_and_Back_to _Business.pdf.

Robinson, F. J. (2007). Employee protection and work safety. In R. W. Kolb (Ed.). *Encyclopedia of business ethics and society*. California: Sage Publications.

Smith, L., & Mounter, P. (2008). *Effective internal communication*. London: Kogan Page Publishers.

The Harris Poll and The Institute for Public Relations. (2020). Employee expectations are changing due to COVID-19. [Accessed on Dec 1, 2020]. Retrieved from https://instituteforpr.org/wp-content/uploads/Employee-Expecatations-Report-v5-1.pdf.

The Institute for Public Relations and Peppercomm. (2020). Special report: How companies are engaging employees during COVID-19. [Accessed on Dec 1, 2020]. Retrieved from https: //instituteforpr.org/wp-content/uploads /PC_IPR_Coronavirus_Phase2_FINAL-4-22_compressed.pdf.

Nilüfer Geysi, İdil Karademirlidağ Suher, and Çisil Sohodol

Dialogic Communication in the Shadow of COVID-19: An Analysis of How the Largest Turkish Companies Used Twitter

Abstract: This study aims to examine the dialogic communication processes of the largest 50 companies in the Fortune 500 list in Turkey during the COVID-19 pandemic based on four principles: conservation of visitors, the usefulness of information, dialogic loop, and generation of return visits. The data are obtained through the content analysis method. Results indicate that financially leading companies in Turkey did not adopt a completely dialogic communication strategy on Twitter. While "conservation of visitors" was the most implemented principle, "generation of return visits" had the lowest scores in general. The only two items that are identified in more than half of the tweets are "up-to-dateness" by 65.28 % and "use of hashtags" by 54.57 %. "Calendar of events" and "surveys or polls" have the lowest scores among 22 items by 0.34 %. The most common content type of COVID-19 related tweets is "information about operational change or new working conditions" by 34.19 %.

Keywords: Pandemic Communication, COVID-19, Dialogic Communication, Relationship Building

Introduction

The world has coped with various widescale health crises throughout human history. However, the COVID-19 pandemic has been one of the most important struggles for modern people and organizations regarding political, economic, and socio-cultural issues. It is claimed that the COVID-19 pandemic is the most challenging crisis since World War II (UNDP, 2020). The uncertainty and unpredictability of this pandemic time "have put to the test many social structures processes" (Xifra, 2020). Although the COVID-19 pandemic is a health crisis, a considerable amount of companies from different industries were deeply affected by the consequences of the crisis. For example, the limited mobility disrupted tourism and transportation industries or problems in the supply chain put retailing and pharmaceutical industries in trouble (Deloitte, 2020). Corporations have been forced to transform their operational routines due to restrictions, lockdowns, or incipient needs of the societies or governments. Briefly, how corporations carry on business has suffered a change.

The environment created by the pandemic has affected the communication process established by corporations with their publics. It has become even more important for corporations to communicate dialogically to cultivate or strengthen mutually beneficial relationships with their publics (Chen et al., 2020). Organizations needed true stakeholder engagement due to the publics' increased need for clarity, support, and empathy (Camilleri, 2020). Both the restrictions imposed by the pandemic and the usefulness of digital media for dialogic communication (Capriotti & Kuklinski, 2012) made it inevitable for corporations to focus their communication on digital channels.

In this sense, current research focuses on digital and dialogic communication, two essentials created by the pandemic and not examined exhaustively in the previous studies (Liu, Xu & Yi, 2020). This study aims to describe how large companies practice dialogic communication strategies on social media during a widescale health crisis, COVID-19 pandemic. In line with this aim, this chapter is composed of four main parts, including a brief literature review about dialogue, dialogic communication theory and pandemic communication, methodology, results, and discussion and conclusion.

Dialogic Communication Approach

Dialogue, referring to "an orientation that valued sharing and mutual understanding" (Taylor & Kent, 2014, p. 388), is a conversation and interaction between a corporation and its publics in terms of organizational communication (Kent, 2017). The purpose of this conversation "is not to get one's way, but to truly understand and gain deeper knowledge" (Kent & Theunissen, 2016, p. 4042). The interaction between the two parts may not always be satisfying; therefore, dialogue, as a "consensus-building tool" (Romenti, Murtarelli & Valentini, 2014, p. 13), reduces the undesirable outcomes of this interaction that may prevent organizations from achieving certain goals. In this regard, they should enable channels and systems for establishing a dialog-based communication process (Kent & Taylor, 2002).

In contrast to one-way communication, Dialogic communication tries to create a genuine relationship that serves not only the interests of the corporation but also the public' (Park & Reber, 2008). Dialogic communication "represents the efforts of the parties to receive and provide information on the basis of honesty, openness and ethical principles" (Bortree & Seltzer, 2009, p. 317) and is the most effective way in terms of strategic communication practices (Kang et al., 2018).

Pandemic crises are times in which trust and credibility of message sources decline (Glick, 2007), the panic of the publics shoot up (Jones, Waters, Holland, Bevins & Iverson, 2010), rumors circulate uncontrollably (Saliou, 1994), financial issues make people anxious, and social interactions are restricted (Qiu, Rutherford, Mao & Chu, 2017). Managing a pandemic and its chaotic environment requires a well-planned communication strategy (Rogers et al., 2009). Organizations should "disseminate vital information regarding organizational programs and services in disaster situations" (Muralidharan et al., 2011, p. 175), provide guidance to stakeholders to protect themselves, and share clear and scientific data (Reynolds, 2006). Studies show that organizations' tendency to involve in dialogic communication, rather than only disseminating a message, positively affects the audience engagement and reduces negative emotions in crisis times (e.g., Sung-un, Minjeong & Johnson, 2010). When corporations are open to dialogic communication, they can increase their engagement with their target audiences that will affect their post-crisis perceptions (Liu et al., 2020).

Although dialogic communication is not limited to digital media, the nature of dialogic communication complies with digital communication. Thanks to the advancement of Web 2.0 technologies, companies have been increasingly embracing the use of more dialogic communication models (Capriotti, 2017). The lack of gatekeeping process allows them to create an interaction (Wilcox, 2019); the opportunity to share real-time information controls rumors or misinformation (DiStaso, Vafeiadis, & Amaral, 2015). It is asserted that "increasing numbers of the public, as well as professionals, are using social media as a source of news and information" (Hornmoen & McInnes, 2018, pp. 256–257). People are no longer passive message receivers, and they are active information seekers who follow social media (Stephens & Malone, 2009). However, Taylor and Kent (2002, p. 390) discuss that using social media does not always mean that dialogue is ensured; organizations have to understand and apply the rules of interaction to achieve a "real dialogue."

The dialogic communication framework of Kent and Taylor (1998) is extensively used to frame researches related to digital communication studies (Sommerfeldt & Yang, 2018). According to Kent and Taylor, organizations should fulfill five principles to communicate dialogically: (i) ease of interface, (ii), conservation of visitors, (iii) usefulness of information, (iv) maintaining dialogic loop, and (v) generation of return visits. The first principle, ease of interface, is related to the availability of the content that allows visitors to access the digital media easily. The conservation of visitors principle is about encouraging target audiences to stay on the website. The online content should also be tailored to the needs of the target audience, which constitutes the usefulness of the information principle of the dialogic communication approach. In addition, organizations should stimulate a dialogic loop by allowing target audiences to ask questions and get feedback on the digital media. The responsiveness of organizations determines if the dialogic loop principle is applied or not. Lastly, the generation of return visits claims that online content must have encouraging features to revisit the digital channel.

Twitter as a Dialogic Communication Tool

As a microblogging social media platform, Twitter has numerous features for establishing dialogue (Lovejoy & Saxton, 2012) that are useful for health communication planning. It maximizes feedbacks thanks to mechanisms of retweeting, quoting, and liking, replying and mentioning. Retweeting also increases source credibility and visibility (Lim and Lee-Won, 2016) that can help corporations to persuade the target audience and disseminate the message quickly. Chew and Eysenbach's (2010) study presents evidence of how Twitter was used to spread information from credible sources to the public and also was a valuable source to get different ideas and experiences during the H1N1 pandemic.

Hashtags are other notable elements of Twitter that help corporations to create agenda or involve in an agenda (Köseoğlu & Köker, 2014) or build communities (Lovejoy & Saxton, 2012). They can present useful content thanks to photo and video sharing and hyperlinks (Mills, Chen, Lee & Raghov, 2009). Effective management of content may provide opportunities in the long term in terms of strategic communication (Du Plessis, 2017). These characteristics represent Twitter as an environment to fulfill dialogic communication principles.

The pandemic due to novel coronavirus displayed the recent examples of pandemic communication on Twitter. The desire of stakeholders, including customers and employees, for "transparency, guidance, and making sense out of what has happened" has increased (McKinsey, 2020). Users on Twitter focused on the numbers of dead people, anxiety, and stress due to the virus, prevention methods, and the economic impacts of the crisis (Abd-Alrazaq et al., 2020). While people had to deal with helplessness and loss of control (Trougakos, Chawla & McCarthy, 2020), not only health authorities such as the World Health Organization and Ministry of Health but also profit-oriented organizations insistently emphasized the importance of prevention methods via several social media channels. Companies engaged in several corporate social responsibility (CSR) projects and communicated them (He and Harris, 2020). The literature related to the COVID-19 pandemic is not extensive; however, it is claimed that

Twitter can present numerous advantages in terms of dialogic communication due to the aforementioned characteristics.

In the light of the literature reviewed, two research questions (RQ) were developed:

- **RQ1**. How well did Turkey's largest 50 companies implement the dialogic communication principles on Twitter during the COVID-19 pandemic?
- **RQ2**. What type of content do these companies tweet during the COVID-19 pandemic?

Methodology

To address the research questions, the data was collected from the official Twitter accounts of the first 50 companies listed in the Fortune 500 ranking of Turkey in 2019 utilizing the content analysis method. Content analysis is a useful method for researches on interactive media (Skalski, Neuendorf & Cajigas, 2017). On the other hand, Twitter is an increasingly important platform for companies in terms of relationship-building in a dialogic system (Sundstrom & Levenshus, 2017). Furthermore, it was the fifth most visited website in Turkey in 2019, which has a higher ranking than all other news and media sites (We are Social, 2020).

The study was theoretically framed by Kent and Taylor's (1998) dialogic communication theory, which suggests that five principles in a communication process indicate to what extent dialogic it is. The ease of interface principle was not included in the study as a variable since "with the advancement of digital technology and infrastructure, the ease of interface has lost its traction also because it is taken as a given" (Zhou & Xu, 2020, p. 1). Therefore, conservation of visitors, the usefulness of information, generation of return visits, and maintaining dialogic loop principles generated the dimension of the first research question. The usefulness of the information principle was evaluated based on four different target audiences: Employees, customers, media, and the general public. The codebook for the research was prepared based on the previous studies of Chen et al. (2020), Kent and Taylor (1998), Rybalko and Seltzer (2010), and Wang and Yang (2020). For the second research question, 8 types of content were developed at the beginning of the research. Afterward, three different types were identified at the end of the analysis, and the content types were regrouped (see **Tab. 14.2**).

A third months' time period starting from the declaration of COVID-19 as pandemic (11th of March 2020–11th of June 2020) was analyzed. 37 out of 50 companies had an official Twitter account. All tweets related to the COVID-19 or the related issues (restrictions, staying home, changed working conditions, etc.) were included in the analysis. Before the coding procedure started, a pilot study was conducted to ensure reliability. After consensus, two researchers coded the data independently between October and November 2020. The Cohen's Kappa value between two coders across all variables was 0.81, indicating a high level of inter-coder reliability.

Results

In the scope of this research, 2949 tweets from 37 companies (M=79.7) were analyzed in total. 579 of the analyzed posts (M=15.64) were related to the COVID-19 pandemic, and they were included in the study. The number of COVID-19 related tweets from companies varied from 1 to 71. 494 of the tweets (85.31 %) included text, 210 of them (36.26 %) included at least one picture, and 290 of them (50.08 %) included a video. The pandemic-related tweets were retweeted by 142.52 people on average (SD=2214.47), commented by 30.55 people on average (SD=108.68), a liked by 642.35 people on average (SD=6919.75).

RQ1. Implementation of the dialogic communication principles in terms of pandemic communication

The first research question asked how the largest companies in Turkey implement principles of conservation of visitors, the usefulness of information, generation of return citizens, and dialogic loop (see **Tab. 14.1**). "Up-to-dateness of the tweet" (65.26 %) was the most practiced form of *conservation of visitors* principle. "*Usefulness of information*" was mostly ensured by giving information about the organization's services (33.85 %). "Guidance for citizens," which was the second most used item (15.54 %), was added into this research by considering the usefulness of information for the general public in pandemic time. For example, information about how to change tickets for canceled flights or how to use a face mask was included in this item. "Contact information" (0.69 %) and "statement of organization's philosophy or mission" (1.2 %) were rarely shared useful information types. Items related to the *generation of return visits* had the lowest scores in general. Tweets consisting of "discussion forums and FAQs on the organization's website" had the highest frequency of all (4.66 %).

Tab. 14.1: Occurrence of Dialogic Communication Principles on COVID-19 related Tweets.

Dialogic Communication Indices	**n**	%
Conservation of visitors		
Link to other organizational social media accounts	112	19.34 %
Link to the official website	70	12.08 %
Up-to-datedness of the tweet	378	65.28 %
Usefulness of information		
Link to news/media room/annual reports/policies	48	8.29 %
Graphics/infographics	9	1.55 %
Guidance for citizens	90	15.54 %
Information about the organization's services	196	33.85 %
Audio-visual publications	73	12.6 %
Statement of the organization's philosophy or mission	7	1.2 %
Contact information	4	0.69 %
Summary of the activities	11	1.89 %
Other	65	11.22 %
Generation of return visits		
Calendar of events	2	0.34 %
News about the organization issued by the external media	10	1.72 %
Discussion forums and FAQ's on the organization's website	27	4.66 %
Use of retweets to add information published by other users	9	1.55 %
Use of links to add external information	22	3.79 %
Dialogic loop		
Use of hashtags	316	54.57 %
Surveys or polls	2	0.34 %
The use of the "@" function	117	20.2 %
Responding a question	80	13.81 %
Posing a question	6	1.03 %
No dialogic loop	148	25.56 %

In terms of the *dialogic loop,* "hashtags" (54.57 %) were the most frequent way to start a conversation with target audiences. 316 of the tweets (54.57 %) had at least 1 hashtag; the number of hashtags varied from 1 to 7. The average number of hashtags per tweet that include a hashtag is 2.09 (*SD*=1, 56). The most popular ones used by the companies were related to solidarity (#iyileşeceğiz by 9.37 %, #birliktebaşaracağız by 8.01 %). The second most used hashtags were warning the target audience to stay home by 7.11 %. The hashtags that include "coronavirus" or "COVID-19" were used in 2.39 % of all tweets. 23.44 % of all hashtags included the name of the company which posted the tweet. Although 13.81 % of tweets were responding to a question, only 1.03 % asked a question.

RQ2. Type of the Content

To answer the second research question, types of tweets' contents were categorized as presented in **Tab. 14.2**. The most frequent content type was "information about operational change or new working conditions" by 34.19 %. The announcements about new working hours or working styles were counted in this type. "Solidarity," referring to messages about unity and recovering together, was mentioned by 24.17 % of the tweets. "Information about CSR activity" (17.09 %) included information such as donation of money, medical equipment, and internet. "Guidance for stakeholders," consisting of information on how to be safe from coronavirus and ways to maintain positive mental health, was contained by 15.54 % of tweets. The companies also posted suggestions to do at home (e.g., training, recipes, book recommendations) at the rate of 13.81 %.

Tab. 14.2: Types of COVID-19 related Tweets' contents.

Type of Content	**n**	%
Information about operational change or new working conditions	198	34.19 %
Information about the current news regarding pandemic	9	1.55 %
Guidance for stakeholders (to prevent virus and protect mental health)	90	15.54 %
Suggestions to do at home	80	13.81 %
Appreciation to medical services	54	9.32 %
Appreciation to employees	41	7.08 %
Solidarity	140	24.17 %
Information about CSR activity	99	17.09 %
Advertisement	23	3.97 %
Celebrating special days	28	4.83 %
Other	31	5.35 %

9.32 % of all tweets appreciated medical services and 7.08 % of them appreciated employees. "Celebration of special days" (4.83 %) mostly included mother's day, feast, world health day, and 1st May worker's day. Tweets that advertised a product or service established 3.97 % of the posts. "Information about the current news regarding pandemic" had the lowest score by 1.55 %.

"Other" (5.35 %) included announcements about live broadcasts, appreciation to other stakeholders, collaborations with other companies, and job advertisements. There was only one company that made a reactive statement about the pandemics. The crisis that required an explanation was about the working conditions of employees of a retailing company.

Discussion and Conclusion

This study aimed to present how the largest Turkish companies' during the COVID-19 crisis implemented the dialogic communication theory and what type of content they shared. Overall results indicated that they did not adopt a dialogic approach strictly on social media, which is vital in crisis communication (Cheng, 2020), and focused on changing operational conditions while giving the message.

Among the findings, the most prominent principle was the *conservation of visitors* due to the up-to-dateness of the tweets. The most common use of *usefulness of information* principle was related to the "information about organization's services," and the second most frequent use was "guidance for citizens." Since this study examined the first three months, namely the first wave of the pandemic, this situation can be explained with the view that "in the early stages of a pandemic, communications should focus on increasing awareness of the disease and communicating important, but simple, protective behaviors to reduce the risk of transmission" (Jones et al., 2010, p. 131).

The companies poorly adopted the generation of return visits principle. However, if corporations want to establish a dialogue with their publics, they need to encourage them to revisit the website (Wang & Yang, 2020). The results reflected that companies cannot benefit from the technical opportunities of Twitter regarding the *dialogic loop*. They predominantly focus on hashtag usage. From a dialogic approach, "hashtags contribute to maximizing the easiness of Twitter and facilitating easy search and discovery for its users" (Park, Reber & Chon, 2016, p. 189).

In line with the usefulness of the information principle, the most frequent content type was about announcing an operational change or new working conditions. Furthermore, the study indicated that "appreciation to medical services" had a higher score than "appreciation to employees," which is consistent with the view that the "COVID-19 pandemic has raised the visibility of health care workers to the level of public heroes" (Hennekam, Ladge & Shymko, 2020, p. 1088). Twitter could provide an opportunity to the companies in terms of internal communication as Yuan, Ye, and Zong (2020) claimed, "when employees physically return to work, they also need to be mentally prepared to dive into their upcoming work" (p. 6).

Considering all findings, this study revealed the fact that financially leading companies in Turkey did not adopt a completely dialogic communication strategy on Twitter during the COVID-19 pandemic. This finding supports Rybalko and Seltzer's (2010) conclusion about Twitter's underutilization for dialogic communication purposes. Similarly, in their study about nonprofit organizations, Waters and Jamal (2011) found that organizations mostly rely on the public information model of public relations rather than two-way symmetrical communication. They overlook social media's great potential for dialogic communication at the organizational level (Lovejoy & Saxton, 2012).

The present study has several limitations in terms of the sample and time frame. Further studies may examine a larger sample of the companies in a longer time frame or include the pre-pandemic period into the analysis. The second wave of the pandemic should also be studied. Moreover, other social media accounts such as Instagram and Facebook should be analyzed in further research.

Despite the limitations, the study contributes to the dialogic communication literature regarding pandemic communication in Turkey. It also has practical implications for communication professionals by presenting information about dialogic social media strategies during a health crisis. Undoubtedly, the COVID-19 pandemic is neither the first nor the last health crisis for the global public. Furthermore, it is also obvious that the need for stakeholder engagement will be on the agenda for a long time for both proactive and reactive communication strategies. Considering the results of this study, strengthening the dialogic social media strategy of the companies may provide several opportunities for the prospective global health crises.

References

Abd-Alrazaq, A., Alhuwail, D., Househ, M., Hamdi, M., & Shah, Z. (2020). Top concerns of tweeters during the COVID-19 Pandemic: Infoveillance study. *Journal of Medical Internet Research, 22* (4). doi: 10.2196/19016.

Bortree, D. S., & Seltzer, T. (2009). Dialogic strategies and outcomes: An analysis of environmental advocacy groups' Facebook profiles. *Public Relations Review*, *35* (3): 317–319. doi: 10.1016/j.pubrev.2009.05.002.

Camilleri, M. A. (2020). Strategic dialogic communication through digital media during COVID-19 crisis. In M.A. Camilleri (Ed.). *Strategic corporate communication in the digital age* (pp. 1–25). Emerald. https://ssrn.com/abstract=3663873.

Capriotti, P., & Kuklinski, H. P. (2012). Assessing dialogic communication through the Internet in Spanish museums. *Public Relations Review, 38* (4): 619–626. doi:10.1016/j.pubrev.2012. 05.005.

Capriotti, P. (2017). The World Wide Web and the social media as tools of CSR communication. In S. Diehl, M. Karmasin, B. Mueller, R. Terlutter, & F. Weder (Eds.). *Handbook of integrated CSR communication* (pp. 193–210), Berlin: Springer.

Chen, Q., Min, C., Zhang, W., Wang, G., Ma, X., & Evans, R. (2020). Unpacking the black box: How to promote citizen engagement through government social media during the COVID-19 crisis. *Computers in Human Behavior,* 110. doi: 10.1016/j.chb.2020. 106380.

Cheng, Y. (2020). The social-mediated crisis communication research: Revisiting dialogue between organizations and publics in crises of China. *Public Relations Review, 46* (1). 101769.doi: 10.1016/j.pubrev.2019.04.003.

Chew, C., & Eysenbach, G. (2010). Pandemics in the age of Twitter: Content analysis of Tweets during the 2009 H1N1 outbreak. *PloS one, 5* (11). e14118. doi: 10.1371/ journal.pone. 0014118.

Deloitte. (2020, May). COVID-19 sonrası tedarik zincirlerinde kazananlar ve kaybedenler. [Winners and losers in the supply chains after COVID-19]. [Accessed on Nov 12, 2020]. Retrieved from https://www2.deloitte.com/content/dam/Deloitte/tr/Documents/consumer-business/Covid19 sonrasitedarikzinciri.pdf.

DiStaso, M. W., Vafeiadis, M., & Amaral, C. (2015). Managing a health crisis on Facebook: How the response strategies of apology, sympathy, and information influence public relations. *Public Relations Review, 41* (2): 222–231. doi: 10.1016/j.pubrev.2014 .11.014.

Du Plessis, C. (2017). The role of content marketing in social media content communities. *South African Journal of Information Management, 19* (1): a866. doi:10.4102/ sajim.v19i1 .866.

Glick, D. C. (2007). Risk communication for public health emergencies. *Annual Review of Public Health*, 28: 33–54. doi:10.1146/annurev.publhealth.28.021406.144123.

He, H., & Harris, L. (2020). The impact of COVID-19 pandemic on corporate social responsibility and marketing philosophy. *Journal of Business Research.* doi: 10.1016/ j.jbusres.2020.05.030.

Hennekam, S., Ladge, J., & Shymko, Y. (2020). From zero to hero: An exploratory study examining sudden hero status among nonphysician health care workers during the COVID-19 pandemic. *Journal of Applied Psychology, 105* (10), 1088–1100. doi: 10.1037/apl0000832.

Hornmoen, H., & McInnes, C. (2018). Social media communication during disease outbreaks: Findings and recommendations. In H. Hornmoen. and H. Backholm (Eds.). *Social Media Use in Crisis and Risk Communication* (pp. 255–275). Emerald. doi:10.1108/978-1-78756-269-120181016.

Jones, S. C., Waters, L., Holland, O., Bevins, J., & Iverson, D. (2010). Developing pandemic communication strategies: Preparation without panic. *Journal of Business Research, 63* (2): 126–132. doi.org: 10.1016/j.jbusres.2009.02.009.

Kang, M., Kim, J. R., & Cha, H. (2018). From concerned citizens to activists: A case study of the 2015 South Korean MERS outbreak and the role of dialogic government communication and citizens' emotions on public activism. *Journal of Public Relations Research, 30* (5–6): 202–229. doi: 10.1080/1062726X.2018.1536980.

Kent, M. L. (2017). Principles of dialogue and the history of dialogic theory in public relations. In X. Chen (Ed.). *Prospect of public relations science* (pp. 2–51). Peking University Press.

Kent, M. L., & Theunissen, P. (2016). Discussion, dialogue, discourse | Elegy for mediated dialogue: Shiva the destroyer and reclaiming our first principles. *International Journal of Communication, 10* (15).

Kent, M. L., & Taylor, M. (1998). Building dialogic relationships through the world wide web. *Public Relations Review, 24* (3): 321–334. doi: 10.1016/S0363-8111(99)80143-X.

Kent, M. L., & Taylor, M. (2002). Toward a dialogic theory of public relations. *Public Relations Review, 28* (1): 21–37. doi: 10.1016/S0363-8111(02)00108-X.

Köseoğlu, O., & Köker N. (2014). Türk üniversiteleri Twitter'ı diyalogsal iletisim açısından nasıl kullanıyor: Beş Türk üniversitesi üzerine bir içerik analizi. [How Turkish universities use twitter from the perspective of dialogic communication: A content analysis on five Turkish universities]. *Global Media Journal: Tr Edition, 4* (8): 213–239.

Lim, Y. S., & Lee-Won, R. J. (2017). When retweets persuade: The persuasive effects of dialogic retweeting and the role of social presence in organizations' Twitter-based communication. *Telematics and Informatics*, 34: 422–43. doi: 10.1016/j.tele.2016. 09.003.

Liu, W., Xu, W., & Tsai, J. Y. (2020). Developing a multi-level organization-public dialogic communication framework to assess social media-mediated disaster communication and engagement outcomes. *Public Relations Review, 46* (4): 1–9. doi: 10.1016/j.pubrev .2020.101949.

Lovejoy, K., & Saxton, G. D. (2012). Information, community, and action: How nonprofit organizations use social media. *Journal of Computer-Mediated Communication, 17* (3): 337–353. doi: 10.1111/j.1083-6101.2012.01576.x.

McKinsey. (2020). A leader's guide: Communicating with teams, stakeholders, and communities during COVID-19. Retrieved from https://www.mckinsey.com/business functions/organization/our-insights/a-leaders-guide-communicating-with-teams-stakeholdersand-communities-during-covid-19#.

Mills, A., Chen, R., Lee, J., & Raghav Rao, H. (2009). Web 2.0 emergency applications: How useful can Twitter be for emergency response?. *Journal of Information Privacy and Security, 5* (3): 3–26. doi: 10.1080/15536548.2009.10855867.

Park, H., & Reber, B. H. (2008). Relationship building and the use of web sites: How Fortune 500 corporations use their web sites to build relationships. *Public Relations Review, 34* (4): 409–411. DOI: 10.1016/j.pubrev.2008.06.006.

Park, H., Reber, B. H., & Chon, M. G. (2016). Tweeting as health communication: health organizations' use of Twitter for health promotion and public engagement. *Journal of Health Communication, 21* (2): 188–198. doi: 10.1080/10810730.2015.1058435.

Reynolds, B. (2006). *Crisis and emergency risk communication: Pandemic Influenza*. Atlanta, GA: Centers for Disease Control and Prevention.

Rybalko, S., & Seltzer, T. (2010). Dialogic communication in 140 characters or less: How Fortune 500 companies engage stakeholders using Twitter. *Public Relations Review, 36* (4): 336–341. doi: 10.1016/j.pubrev.2010.08.004.

Rogers, W. A., Street, J. M., Braunack-Mayer, A. J., Hiller, J. E., & FluViews Team. (2009). Pandemic influenza communication: views from a deliberative forum. *Health Expectations, 12* (3): 331–342. doi: 10.1111/j.1369-7625.2009.00562.x.

Romenti, S., Murtarelli, G., & Valentini, C. (2014). Organizations' conversations in social media: Applying dialogue strategies in times of crises. *Corporate Communications: An International Journal, 19* (1): 10–33. doi: 10.1108/CCIJ-05-2012-0041.

Qiu, W., Rutherford, S., Mao, A., & Chu, C. (2017). The pandemic and its impacts. *Health, Culture and Society, 9*: 1–11.

Saliou, P. (1994). Crisis communication in the event of a flu pandemic. *European Journal of Epidemiology, 10*: 515–517.

Skalski, P. D., Neuendorf, K. A., & Cajigas, J. A. (2017). Content analysis in the interactive media age. In K. A. Neuendorf (Ed.). *The content analysis guidebook* (2nd edition) (pp. 201–242). Thousand Oaks, CA: Sage Publications.

Sommerfeldt, E. J., & Yang, A. (2018). Notes on a dialogue: Twenty years of digital dialogic communication research in public relations. *Journal of Public Relations Research, 30* (3): 59–64. doi: 10.1080/1062726X.2018.1498248.

Stephens, K. K., & Malone, P. C. (2009). If the organizations won't give us information...: The use of multiple new media for crisis technical translation and dialogue. *Journal of Public Relations Research, 21* (2): 229–239. doi:10.1080/10627260802557605.

Sundstrom, B., & Levenshus, A. B. (2017). The art of engagement: Dialogic strategies on Twitter *Journal of Communication Management, 21* (1): 17–33. doi: 10.1108/JCOM-07-2015-0057.

Sung-Un, Y., Minjeong, K., & Johnson, P. (2010). Effects of narratives, openness to dialogic communication, and credibility on engagement in crisis communication through organizational blogs. *Communication Research, 37* (4): 473–497. doi: 10.1177/ 0093650210362682.

Taylor, M., & Kent, M. L. (2014). Dialogic engagement: Clarifying foundational concepts. *Journal of Public Relations Research*, 26 (5): 384–398. doi:10.1080/1062726X .2014.956106.

Trougakos, J. P., Chawla, N., & McCarthy, J. M. (2020). Working in a pandemic: Exploring the impact of COVID-19 health anxiety on work, family, and health outcomes. *Journal of Applied Psychology, 105* (11): 1234–1245. doi: 10.1037/apl0000739.

UNDP. (2020). Coronavirus. Retrieved from https://www.undp.org/content/undp/en/home/coronavirus .html.

Wang, Y., & Yang, Y. (2020). Dialogic communication on social media: How organizations use Twitter to build dialogic relationships with their publics. *Computers in Human Behavior*, 104. https://doi.org/10.1016/j.chb.2019.106183.

Waters, R. D., & Jamal, J. Y. (2011). Tweet, tweet, tweet: A content analysis of nonprofit organizations' Twitter updates. *Public Relations Review, 37* (3): 321–324. doi: 10.1016/j .pubrev.2011.03.002.

We are Social. (2020). Global digital report 2020. Retrieved from https://datareportal.com/reports/ digital-2020-turkey.

Wilcox, D. L. (2019). Dialogic communication theory in the age of corporate activism: A postmodern perspective. *Communication and Media in Asia Pacific, 2* (1): 1–10.

Xifra, J. (2020). Corporate communication, public relations and reputational risk management in the days of Covid-19. *Profesional de la Informacion*, *29* (2): 1–18. doi: 10.3145/ epi.2020.mar.20.

Yuan, Z., Ye, Z., & Zhong, M. (2020). Plug back into work, safely: Job reattachment, leader safety commitment, and job engagement in the COVID-19 pandemic. *Journal of Applied Psychology*, Advance online publication. doi: 10.1037/apl0000860.

Zhou, A., & Xu, S. (2020). Digital public relations through the lens of affordances: A conceptual update of the "ease of interface" dialogic principle. Available at SocArXiv. doi: 10.31235/ osf.io/uzhk9.

Deniz Denizel

Conclusion: From Cybernetic Eschatology to Pandemic Theology

As the late-information age has formatted the collective consciousness at a speed that has never been seen before, it also made the previous social, psychic, ideological, operational, and aesthetic definitions of the concept of 'communication' inadequate.

First, Pyrrhon doubted his senses, then René Descartes spoke of an *evil demon* that could manipulate him in an incomprehensible way. Science was then an esoteric field where the *demons* of Pierre-Simon Laplace and James Clerk Maxwell competed. With structural linguistics, thought (thus emotions) was limited to language. Friedrich Nietzsche announced God dead, and all generalizations 'including this one' were wrong. The meaning was fragmented with Ludwig Wittgenstein's *language games*. Vannevar Bush was not so wrong when he doubted that technology would bring more evil than good as he might have thought. Marshall McLuhan declared the world a *global village*, and Michel Foucault's *panopticon* has turned into a *synopticon*. The reality was a rock, and the rhizomatic solutions of Gilles Deleuze and Felix Guattari are a breeze that takes the dust off from it. The age we live in was then the *age of uncertainty*, as John Kenneth Galbraith suggested. Jean Baudrillard would introduce us to *hyper-real*, which replaces itself with real even though it is not real. While Kenneth Gergen declared the fragmentation of the self with *multiphrenia*, Samuel Huntington heralded a new paradigm shift with the *clash of civilizations*. After Nick Bostrom made an unfalsifiable *simulation argument*, we welcomed the *post-truth* only one decade later.

Then the apparent, right/wrong, reality, and the truth were so intertwined that it was almost impossible to separate them from each other in the regular flow of daily life. Thus was born '*homo pragmasis*,' who acts upon a mechanical and entropic impulse with sensing the shortest path on daily things that must be done as quickly as possible; and prefers cognitive emptiness and psychic nothingness in the rest. The collective truths were so systematically distorted that the post-information and pre-super-intelligent societies were constantly faced with the fact that they 'got things wrong.' The ancient men, who had been evolving through the spiritual faculties, transformed into something else that desires to manifest on the mortal toys of the material world. Thus, *homo pragmasis* had chosen to be in an imaginary timeline that he did not remember the beginning and forgot the reason as in *Vanilla Sky* (Cameron Crowe, 2001), instead of drowning in that dark and vast ocean where he can understand what the interactional equations were and how the laws of the scientific and metaphysical universe could have been infiltrated.

Moreover, this enigma and suspense continued to evolve with four extraordinary works, such as the *Dark City* (Alex Proyas, 1998), *Truman Show* (Peter Weir, 1998), *The Matrix* (Wachowskis, 1999), and *13th Floor* (Josef Rusnak, 1999), were released in the late-postmodernism where cinema has come of dominance over other art forms and everything in creative flow manifests for the last time but in its highest quality. In the same year, another significant thing happened: *Half-Life* (Sierra Studios, 1998), perhaps still the best game in video game history, hit on the retail stores and, just as Socrates in the history of philosophy or *Citizen Kane* (Orson Welles, 1941) in history of the cinema, brought a new shift in the history of video games. The eschatological message of the first game turned into an 'eschatological nightmare' in the second game when the calendar pages showed October 2004. Since the late 90s, works of the visual arts, especially films and video games, have continued to transmit such false-reality and eschatological messages through primarily self-directed natural/organic or artificial/synthetic settings and fictive worlds with momentum.

Apocalyptic scenarios decorated with the themes of suspense, enigma, and non-existence/reality that are described through cybernetic structures such as fictional worlds based upon conspirative plots and over cybernetic devices like television and computer, caused eschatology, which is one of the branches of theology and examines the possible ending theories of the world, to welcome cybernetics. Therefore, *cybernetic eschatology* also welcomed us with all the semantic dimensions.

In a more generalized summary on the rest... Along with the definitions and practical outcomes of such concepts as 'normal' and 'social' became ambiguous, the phenomena such as *New Media* and *Industry 4.0* redefined and even set the standards of new sets of information and communication structures in the evolutionary flow. The new literal and metaphorical discourses of communication told new stories, the message areas changed within all the layers, the concept of 'information' then gained consciousness with the support of cybernetic systems such as artificial intelligence, machine, and deep learning.

Ultimately, all those things were happening in the '*pale blue dot*' as the science prophet Carl Sagan once pointed out...

At this very stage of history, all these factors have become a brief history of the recent past.

The COVID-19 outbreak shocked many constants and variables of the vital parameters in evolutionary flow, as well as causing some structures and systems to decline and some others to irreversibly deteriorate. Since the beginning, the Coronavirus has taken a total of above three million lives.[1] Although this amount is a small percentage of the entire lives that the Black Plague had taken in over five years, the Coronavirus may have triggered the events that lead to one of the most significant paradigm shifts in history. The main reason is not the virus or the disease itself, but the inevitable development of and the irreversible dependence on technology, the rapidly increasing world population since the end of modernity in the face of the consumed resources, along with the accustomed predominance of late-capitalism which has advanced within the national and geopolitical axis of ideology, and, finally, is that we did not fully understand, trivialized, and/or completely forgotten the lessons that we learned from the previous pandemics.

The pandemic has long been able to pull personal attention from the fragmented delusion grounds and gather the collective perception in one spot. As former American President Ronald Reagan has reminded several times in the past, in the face of a common global threat, the potential of humanity to forget its differences and fight this threat has manifested itself. This also signaled that Niles Eldredge and Stephen Jay Gould's *punctuated equilibrium* (1971) model, even as a metaphor, was not too distant to humankind as a species. A similar leap was also experienced in the systems used by official educational institutions in terms of quantity and quality, and thus it would not be wrong to claim that education on a global scale continued with minimum loss. Although the cinema industry had to slow down more than ever, we are not left behind from classic and new qualified films upon the breakthroughs made by the platforms. Moreover, upon Tuna Tetik's words, we welcomed new cinematographic aesthetic styles in the process too.

Interestingly, sometimes artists or writers manage to forecast the future in their 'fictional' literary works, themes, or concepts as an irony of fate. Although he might not have known where the concepts of *futurecasting* or *futurology* fit in the big picture, Robert Heinlein, who is one of the most significant science fiction writers in all times, coined the term '*new normal*' in his novel, *The Moon is a Harsh Mistress* (1966) to describe the conditions of a new free world desired by the revolutionists in a dystopian universe. On the other hand, this term refers to the conditions of the pandemic that tear the world and systems down and the constraints that have become prerequisites for everyday living.

In the end, it was such a realm that the universal truths had become transparent and disappeared from our blurry eyes like a vessel vanishing on the horizon before the pandemic; however, the vessel turned back in the same way, carrying a vital message from a global threat. The apparent, right/wrong, hyperreal, reality, and the truth have left their places altogether to nothing but 'real and truth.'

Upon this threat, new communication syntagms and paradigms continued to evolve and generate new structures and systems until this time. The meanings of informatics and communication models are changing, the boundaries of educational sciences are expanding with new media that have gained importance and produced, individual and social standards are being redefined. In all this complexity, digital rhetorics' theoretical and practical foundations gain brand new identities through new channels. Ultimately, social structures find themselves on a new ground that is almost impossible to be defined with even the recent ones. The vertical and horizontal progression of information no longer communicates with monosemic and synonymic codes but transcends with polysemic and antonymic patterns. Thus, the collective consciousness is advancing.

Towards the end, it would be proper to declare that the pandemic conditions, within which the COVID-19 outbreak pushed us together and the struggle to survive in many layers of the global crisis gave us an original motivation to ask new epistemological and theological questions and a natural intuition to follow the traces to the very end where the truth lies. This quest for answers, which are brand-new for us but old for the knowledge system, shows that the theological search in philosophy will progress through and over the pandemic codes, patterns, indexes, and structures for a certain period. Therefore, this path of theology upon the pandemic would lead further an ontological field of *pandemic theology*.

Finally, as individuals of the world civilization, as long as we choose to keep progressing the history in a decisive manner and become united as is now, we shall prevail and are likely to advance to the next level of spiritual and technological development.

Deniz Denizel
Res. Assist. at Bahçeşehir University,
Cartoon and Animation Department.

Acknowledgment:

As editors, we thank the dear academics who relayed valuable information on the new forms, models, and theories of communication through countless hours of study and with an invaluable academic devotion; thus, contributing scientific knowledge in the heart of the pandemic.

Note

1 Retrieved at https://covid19.who.int/ (Accessed on 4 May, 2021).

List of Figures

List of Tables

Author Biographies

(In Alphabetical Order)

Afra Balcı Arslan is a doctoral candidate at Bahçeşehir University, Cinema and Media Research program, working currently on her thesis titled "Culinary Capital and Food Culture in the Turkish Food Show *Yemekteyiz*." After completing the bachelor's program at Yeditepe University, English Language and Literature program, Balcı Arslan received a master's degree from Galatasaray University, Political Science program. Since 2017, she is a part-time lecturer at Bahçeşehir University. She previously worked as a lecturer and as the International Relations and Erasmus coordinator at Plato Vocational School and as an editor and coordinator for Fanatik Film and SinemaTürk Website.

Burcu Eker Akgöz is an associate professor in Public Relations and Publicity at Bahçeşehir University. She earned her Ph.D. in Public Relations from Marmara University. She has started working as a research assistant at the Faculty of Communication in Bahçeşehir University in 2005. She is currently teaching several classes on Public Relations and Publicity. Her areas of interest include event management, corporate culture, organizational commitment, crisis communication, and corporate social responsibility.

Cemal Barkın Engin received M.A. & Ph.D. degrees from Advanced Studies in Music (MIAM) program at İstanbul Technical University. He recently works as an assistant professor at Bahçeşehir University in the Communication Design Department and Audio Technologies Graduate Program. His research areas include music production, sound design for various media, and sonic arts. He has been a performing musician since 1998. He continues to release records with diverse musical projects titled Replikas, Reverie Falls On All, Pitohui, and Yerçekimi, besides featuring as a solo artist on various albums. He has contributed to multi-cultural musical projects such as Verklaerte Zeit, Yolda, and Breath Song as a composer and performer. Engin has also been working as a freelance sound engineer and designer for music and film productions since 2005.

Çakır Aker is currently working as an assistant professor at Faculty of Communication, Department of Digital Game Design in Bahcesehir University, and as the coordinator of Bahçeşehir University Game Lab. He has a Ph.D. in Media and Communication Studies (2018) from Galatasaray University, an M.Sc. (2010) from University of Pompeu Fabra, an MBA (2008) from Bahçeşehir

University, and a B.A. in Advertisement (2005) from the same university. His research areas include gamification, interaction design, player experience, and user experience. Aker has been working on experience in advertising and teaching experience in the areas of interaction design, user/game experience, player psychology, and gamification.

Çisil Sohodol has been working as a professor in the Public Relations and Publicity Department in the Faculty of Communication at Bahçeşehir University. She received her bachelor's, master's, and Ph.D. degrees in Public Relations at Ege University. Her researches and courses focus on media relations and crisis communication.

Deniz Denizel is a research assistant in the Cartoon and Animation Department and a graduate student in Game Design at Bahçeşehir University. After having his B.F.A. in Photography from Dokuz Eylül University, he exhibited in and curated solo and group exhibitions; published, edited, and reviewed various types of articles; and lectured on photography, film, and video games. His research interests gather around narrative theory, intertextuality, film criticism, and postmodern theories. He is also the co-editor of *Multidisciplinary Perspectives on Narrative Aesthetics in Video Games* (2021).

Dilay Özgüven is a Ph.D.(c) in Cinema and Media Research program at Bahçeşehir University, and working on her dissertation on Critical Cases in the History of Turkish Reality Television. She has work experience in painting, illustration, video, and photography. She received her M.A. degree at Sabancı University and has experience in movies as the first assistant director. Her interests are reality television, crime, memory studies, and game theory.

Ece Arıhan is a Ph.D.(c) at Bahçeşehir University, Cinema and Media Research program. She has written and directed her own short animation film called *Never After*, which has won awards. Presently, she is teaching Advanced Game Development courses at the Department of Digital Game Design at İstanbul Bilgi University. Furthermore, she is writing her doctoral thesis on the representation of women in animated films, focusing on gender and women's studies.

Elif Engin is an associate professor in Public Relations and Publicity at Bahçeşehir University. She earned her Ph.D. in Public Relations from Marmara University. She has started working as a research assistant at the Faculty of Communication in Bahçeşehir University in 2001. She is currently teaching several courses on Public Relations. Her research interests include corporate storytelling and narrative, corporate social responsibility, corporate culture, and strategic public relations management.

Görkem Bir is a research assistant in the Advertising Department at Bahçeşehir University, where he is currently conducting doctoral studies. He has a bachelor's degree in Sociology from Middle East Technical University, and he holds a master's degree in Sound Technologies from Bahçeşehir University. He has several published and ongoing translations in the fields of sociology and marketing. His diverse research interests include consumer culture, media technologies and audio branding.

Haluk Gürgen is a member of the Public Relations and Publicity Department at Bahçeşehir University. He received his Ph.D. in Advertising and Public Relations from Anadolu University. Gürgen served as the dean of the Faculty of Communication at Bahçeşehir University for seven and a half years. He has five books on public relations, advertising, and copywriting among many international and national kinds of research and journal articles. Gürgen has conducted many communication campaigns for private and public institutions; he has managed communication projects for several ministries and the General Directorate on Women's Status. Gürgen is the executive committee member of Bahçeşehir College. He is currently teaching several undergraduate and graduate courses on public relations, advertising, advertising and society, social campaigns, and reputation management & PR.

Hasan Kemal Suher is a member of the Advertising Department in Bahçeşehir University. He is the Dean of the Communication Faculty and the head of the Department of Advertising. He received his Ph.D. in Advertising and Public Relations from Anadolu University, Turkey. He is currently teaching several undergraduate courses on media planning, research in advertising, advertising campaign, and graduate courses on historical and social research, mass communication theories and research. He has edited many inter/national books. His research interests include creative industries, new trends in communication education, and data analysis with SPSS. He continues his researches at national and international levels.

İdil Karademirlidağ Suher is a professor and the head of Public Relations and Publicity Department at Bahçeşehir University since 2006. She received her bachelor's, master's, and Ph.D. degrees in public relations and communication from Anadolu University. Karademirlidağ Suher teaches both graduate and undergraduate courses on public relations management and strategy. Her research interests include issues management and source credibility. She holds seminars about persuasive communication. Besides her academic studies, she has contributed to the field by being involved in several sectoral research projects.

Murat Cöpçü is an instructor in Cartoon and Animation Department at Bahçeşehir University. He received a Ph.D. from the Graduate School of Digital Design, Kyungsung University in South Korea, 2012. His research interests are the quality of moving images and experimental moving images.

Nazlı Eda Noyan is a professor and the founder head of the Cartoon and Animation Department of Bahçeşehir University. She is the author and designer of 13 children's books; writer and director of awarded short animations *The Children of the Other Lands* and *A Cup of Turkish Coffee* (supported by ARTE and CNC); director of İstanbul Animation Festival Animist and founder of animasyonunkadinlari.org – an archive project for women of animation in Turkey and owner of *Girl Saw the Sea Productions.*

Nilay Ulusoy is a professor at Bahçeşehir University. She graduated from Marmara University's Communication Faculty in 1997. She finished Marmara University's Communication Sciences Master's Program in 2000 and her doctoral studies in 2006. In the same year, she conducted research at the National Center of Cinematography and the Moving Image (CNC) in Paris with a scholarship from the French Institute of İstanbul. She teaches courses on the history of narrative film (M.A. level), film theory, visual culture, and Turkish cinema (Ph.D. level). Her research interests include the language of fashion and Turkish cinema history. She is the head of the Film and TV Department at Bahçeşehir University.

Nilüfer Geysi has been working as a research assistant for five years in the Faculty of Communication at Bahçeşehir University. She is a Ph.D.(c) in the Advertising and Public Relations program of the same university. She has completed her undergraduate degree in Public Relations and Advertising, and master's degree in Marketing Communication and Public Relations at İzmir University of Economics. Her academic interests include corporate culture, digital media, and sustainability.

Nisa Yıldırım had a B.S. degree in Computer Science and M.A. degree in New Media from Kadir Has University. As a CGI artist in post-production, she began her professional career and continued as a producer in television and executive editor in leading Turkish cinema websites. She had a Ph.D. degree in Cinema and Media Research from Bahçeşehir University. Currently, she works as an assistant professor in Radio, Television, and Cinema department in İstanbul Gelişim

University, and continues to write research articles – primarily based on 'the evolution of audiovisual fictional narratives in the digital era,' besides novels and screenplays.

Ömer Vatanartıran has a Ph.D. in Organization Studies with a dissertation titled *A Discourse Analysis of the Communicative Action of Strategy Professionals on Social Media*. He is a multi-dimensional communicator: TV presenter; university lecturer in theater, ethics, media, and communications; experienced voice-over artist, specialized in commercials, movies, and animations; and theater actor with international experience.

Öykü Türkeli is a research assistant in Advertising Department at Bahçeşehir University. She received her master's degree from Marmara University, Advertising Department in 2017. She is a Ph.D.(c) in Advertising Department at Marmara University.

Savaş Arslan is a professor in the Film Design Department and the Director of the Fine Arts Institute at Dokuz Eylül University. Apart from contributing various articles on cinema, arts, and culture to different international journals, magazines, and edited volumes, he has four books: *Cinema in Turkey: A New Critical History* (2011), *Balkan Cinema and the Great Wars* (co-editor, 2020), *Media, Culture and Identity in Europe* (co-editor, 2009), and *Melodrama* (2005, in Turkish). He is also the founding editor of the journal Studies in World Cinema.

Selcan Yeşilyurt is an instructor, Ph.D., working in the Faculty of Communication, Department of Public Relations and Publicity at Bahçeşehir University for ten years. Her main areas of teaching include corporate communications, corporate social responsibility, public relations research, and persuasion. Her main areas of research interest are public relations professionalism, ethics, social responsibility, and corporate communications.

Sinan Aşçı is an assistant professor in the Department of New Media at Bahçeşehir University, and he is working with an international research team as a PDRA for SDI München. He completed his B.A. in English Language Teaching (2010) and received his M.A. degree in General Journalism (2013) with a thesis on the representation of LGBT individuals in newspapers in Turkey and the U.S. Then, he earned his Ph.D. in Media and Communication Studies with a thesis work mainly focusing on *Cyberbullying and Youth in Turkey* under the supervision of Prof. Dr. Michel Bourse from Galatasaray University (2018). He has been teaching courses related to media studies at the associate and undergraduate level both in Turkey and Germany, providing his services as an editor and manuscript reviewer of peer-reviewed journals, and doing research on social media, social media and kids, cyberculture, digitization, digital journalism, and digital literacy.

Şafak Şahin graduated from Anadolu University, Public Relations and Advertising Department. Şahin has completed his master's program in Advertising Brand Management at Bahçeşehir University. He completed his Ph.D. thesis titled *Personality Features, Creative Thinking Processes and Advertising Creativity Relation* in Bahçeşehir University, Department of Advertising and Public Relations. He was a sales manager at Boyner Holding. He lectures on advertising, text writing, and creative communication in the Advertising Department. He is the head of Bahçeşehir University, the Center of Creative Industries, BAUKEM.

Tolga Hepdinçler is an assistant professor in the Communication Design Department at Bahçeşehir University. He received his Ph.D. on Film and Television from Ankara University and worked at the same university as a research assistant between 1998 and 2001. He also directed short documentaries and received nominations and awards in many festivals. He is currently teaching several undergraduate courses on photography and video production and graduate courses on visual culture and memory studies. His research interests include contemporary photography, art history, visual culture, and European film studies. He is the editor of the book titled *Creative Industries in Turkey.*

Tuna Tetik is a member of the Film and Television Department at Bahçeşehir University. He received his doctoral degree at Bahçeşehir University, Cinema and Media Research program, and directed short films and a documentary that received international awards. His research interests are superheroes, comics, transmedia, film genres, video-on-demand services, and video games. He is the co-editor of the book titled *Multidisciplinary Perspectives on Narrative Aesthetics in Video Games* (2021). He is currently lecturing several undergraduate courses on digital editing and film production.

Yahya Burak Tamer is an associate professor in the Department of Communication Design and Audio Technology Graduate Program at Bahçeşehir University. Tamer's recent studies focus on music production, interactive sound design, and music information retrieval. He received a B.S. degree in electronics and communication engineering from Yıldız Technical University in 2001, M.A. and Ph.D. degrees in music technology from İstanbul Technical University, Centre for Advanced Studies in Music (MİAM), İstanbul, Turkey in 2005 and 2012 respectively. Tamer has been a collaborator of the CompMusic research project funded by the European Research Council during 2014–15. He has been releasing music and performing live as an independent musician since 2006. Tamer continues to produce music and work as a freelance mastering engineer. His current research interests include mastering audio, auditory perception, psychoacoustics, audio signal processing, and sound synthesis & design.

Yeşim Ulusu is a member of the Advertising Department at Bahçeşehir University. She received her Ph.D. in Advertising and Promotion from Marmara University. She is currently teaching undergraduate courses on introduction to marketing, advertising campaign, and graduate courses on integrated marketing communication. Her research interests include creative industries, new trends in the marketing field. She participates in congresses and continues her researches at national and international levels.

Printed by
CPI books GmbH, Leck